WOODWORK TECHNOLOGY

for Schools and Colleges

John Strefford
Guy McMurdo

Illustrated by Barry Davies

SCHOFIELD & SIMS LTD. HUDDERSFIELD

0 7217 4008 1

First printed 1978

Also available: METALWORK TECHNOLOGY for Schools and Colleges (0 7217 4007 3) by John Strefford and Guy McMurdo

Printed in England by Bemrose and Sons Limited

PREFACE

This book has been prepared for students studying for G.C.E., C.S.E. and S.C.E. examinations in Woodwork.
The subject matter has been used very successfully for this purpose and has been treated in a simple, straightforward manner which will be readily understood by the student.

ACKNOWLEDGEMENTS

The authors and publishers wish to thank the following organisations for their co-operation in the preparation of this book.
Record Ridgeway Tools Ltd. (permission to illustrate tools).
Educational Publications Ltd. (sketch of wood-boring insects. Wall Chart No. 12 currently available to schools).
Messrs. Cuprinol Ltd. (information on insects and fungi).

J. STREFFORD
G. McMURDO

CONTENTS

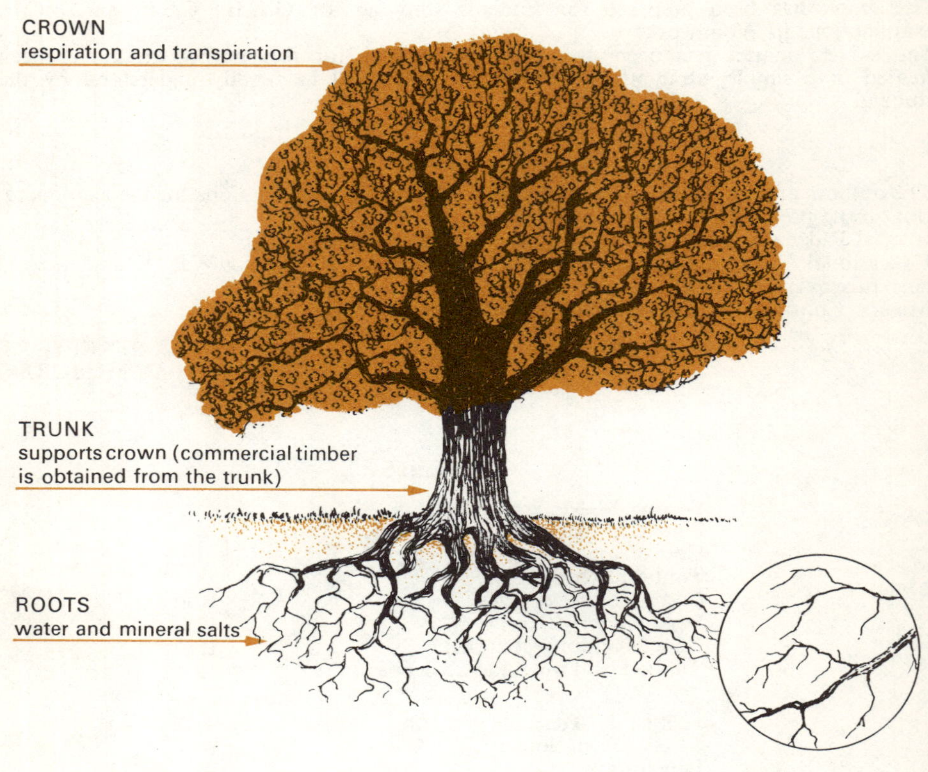

Timber is a natural product which displays many variations in quality and characteristics. The study of timber starts with the living tree and examines the stages of felling, conversion and seasoning which prepare the timber for use by the craftsman. A tree grows by obtaining food from the air and the soil. Small hair roots, which grow out from the larger roots of the tree, absorb the dissolved mineral salts in the soil. The mineral salts are contained in the water taken in by the roots.

Whilst the roots are absorbing this fluid nutriment, the leaves are taking in atmospheric air through thousands of tiny mouths called *stomata*. The leaf cells contain a green-coloured matter called *chlorophyll*. With the aid of the sun (by means of a process called *photosynthesis*) the chlorophyll retains the carbon dioxide from the air and the oxygen is released.

The fluid absorbed by the hair roots travels by osmosis up cells in the sapwood into the branches and thence to the leaves of the tree. It is there changed chemically, by the carbon dioxide absorbed through the leaves, into a more refined sap. This refined sap, containing sugars and starches, descends from the leaves and branches to the cambium layer of the tree, where it forms new wood. Excess moisture is given out through the leaves. This process of giving out excess moisture by the leaves is known as *transpiration*.

A tree breathes by taking in carbon dioxide and giving out oxygen. The reverse process happens during darkness.

TREE STRUCTURE

Pith (Medulla) The pith is at the centre of the tree trunk and the branches. Originally it was the young sapling from which the tree grew. It is a pulpy composition of dead cells, quite useless as timber.

Heartwood (Duramen) This is the part of the tree which is mostly used in timber constructions. Sap does not flow in heartwood as the cells have hardened. The heartwood gives support to the tree. As the cells have hardened and no longer carry sap, this part of the tree is less liable to attack by insect pests and decay. The heartwood of a tree is usually darker in colour and more pleasing in appearance than the sapwood.

Sapwood (Alburnum) This is the part of the tree which surrounds the heartwood. The sapwood cells convey water and mineral salts up to the branches and hence to the leaves of the tree, to be changed into food for the tree. Sapwood has little value as timber because of the starches contained in the cells. The presence of these starches makes it susceptible to attack by insects.

Cambium Layer This is a layer of cells surrounding the sapwood. The function of the cambium layer is to make new wood (sapwood), which is added to the previous year's growth, and to make new bark to replace dead bark.

Bast (Phloem) This is immediately under the bark of the tree, outside the cambium layer, and its function is to transfer the food made in the leaves to all the other parts of the tree.

Bark (Cortex) This is the protection for the growing tree. It prevents transpiration from the cambium layer and the sapwood. Bark is composed of fibrous cells and is fed from the bast. As the tree grows outwards the bark splits and it is replaced by more bark from the bast. Eventually, as new bark is formed, the old dead bark falls from the tree.

Rays (These were formerly known as *medullary rays*. The word *medullary* is no longer in use as all the rays do not extend from the medulla or pith to the cambium layer.) The function of the rays is to convey food from the bast to the inner parts of the tree. Rays vary in size in different trees and in some trees, such as oak, they form a pleasing pattern in the cut timber.

Growth Rings (Annual rings) These are the distinct patterns of each year's growth. Spring wood, or early wood, is formed in spring and summer when growth is rapid and vigorous. Autumn wood, or late wood, is formed in the autumn and winter when growth is slower and less vigorous, with the cells more densely packed than the cells in spring wood. This difference in the density of the cells in one year's growth shows quite distinctly in some trees. Trees which grow in the tropics have an even growth all year round, therefore the annual rings are less distinct.

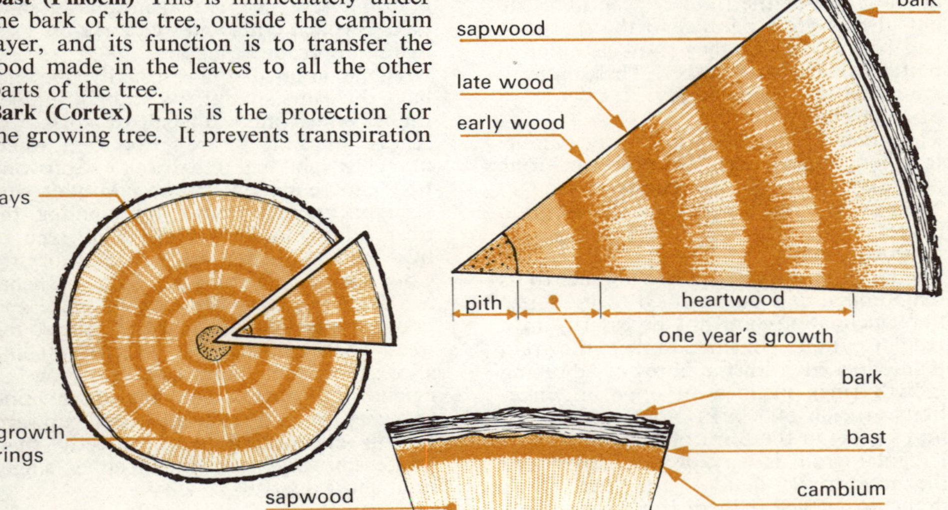

SOFTWOODS AND HARDWOODS

Softwoods belong to the group of trees known as *conifers (gymnosperms)* and have needle-shaped leaves with the seeds contained in cones. Conifers are usually evergreen.

Hardwoods belong to the group of trees known as *broad-leaved trees (angiosperms)*, and have broad leaves, with the seeds contained in a seed case, e.g. acorn and chestnut. They can be deciduous or evergreen.

By calling timbers softwoods or hardwoods, we are simply distinguishing between two main groups of trees. Some softwoods, like yew and pitch-pine, are harder than some hardwoods. Balsa and obeche, though hardwoods, are softer than some softwoods.

Conifers are simpler in structure than broad-leaved trees. Basically, the conifer has one type of cell called *tracheid*. This is an elongated cell, its length being much greater than its width. Tracheid cells perform the functions of strengthening the tree and conducting the sap to the branches and leaves. The cells are either thin-walled or thick-walled. The thin-walled cells are formed during spring and summer growth and carry sap. The thick-walled cells are formed during autumn and winter growth and they strengthen the tree. It is this difference in the formation of the cells in one year's growth that shows as growth rings or annual rings.

Broad-leaved trees, or hardwoods, have two distinct types of cell. One of these cells is fibrous and is similar to the tracheid cell. The fibrous cell is much more sharply pointed than the tracheid cell, and not so uniform in shape. The function of the fibrous cell is to give strength to the growing tree. The other type of cell found in hardwoods is known as a *vessel*, or *pore*, *cell*. There is no type of cell in softwoods resembling the vessel cell, so its presence in or absence from a wood establishes which of the two main types the wood belongs to. The vessel cells are long tubes running the length of the tree trunk. They carry sap up to the branches and leaves.

There is a third type of cell, called *parenchyma*. This is not often found in softwoods, but is quite common in hardwoods. The parenchyma cell is used to store food for the tree.

GRAIN

The direction of growth of a tree's fibres in relation to its longitudinal axis is known as the *grain* of the timber. The fibres do not always grow parallel to the tree axis, and because of this they show as different patterns on the sawn timber. These patterns are called the *grain figure*.

Straight grain

The fibres of the tree are mostly parallel to its longitudinal axis. The timber is strong and easy to work. Timber with straight grain usually has a poor ornamental grain figure.

Irregular grain

The fibres of the tree are not parallel to its longitudinal axis but inclined to it. These fibre inclinations are not necessarily in a regular pattern. In some timbers the grain is interlocked, with the fibres of adjoining growth rings inclined in opposite directions to each other. In other timbers the fibres grow in the form of a spiral.

Irregular grain is very pronounced where the tree trunk divides into two large branches, or where there is a swollen butt growing on the tree.

Trees with any type of irregular grain can, if converted properly, produce attractive grain figures, such as that in quarter sawn oak. Swollen butts and tree forks are used mainly to produce veneers.

Irregular grained timber usually does not have the same strength as straight grained timber and is more difficult to work.

Knots in timber are produced where branches join the tree trunk. Softwood trees can be made to produce knotless and straight grained timber by planting the trees fairly close together. This type of tree cultivation can be seen in Forestry Commission plantations. Side branches are discouraged by the lack of space and poor penetration of sunlight. As the young trees grow in stature, selective felling allows the remaining trees to grow in height and girth. The growth of side branches is still restricted and upward growth encouraged more directly than where softwoods are grown either singly or at short intervals.

CONVERSION OF TIMBER

When a log arrives at the sawmill it is cut into boards, planks, battens, etc., by circular saws or band-saws. This process of cutting up a log is known as *timber conversion*.

The way in which a log is cut is important. Valuable timber can be wasted if the cutting is carelessly done.

There are two methods of converting a log:

1. through and through cutting (or slash sawing);

2. quarter sawing.

1. Through and through cutting is the simplest method of conversion, as the boards are cut to the desired thickness, parallel to each other on the longitudinal axis of the log. When a log is sawn in this manner, the boards tend to "cup" and attractive grain patterns can be lost. The grain figure shown by slash sawn timber is known as slash grain.

2. When a log is quarter sawn most of the boards are cut on the radius of the log. When cut in this manner radial shrinkage is much less than when the log is slash sawn. The tendency for the boards to cup is also much reduced in quarter sawn timber. The attractive grain figure of some woods, such as oak, is shown to advantage in quarter sawn timbers.

When a tree is slash sawn, the timber is cut tangentially to the growth rings. The face of the board or plank which is furthest away from the pith will shrink more than the face which is nearest the pith, giving rise to the deformation of the timber known as *cupping*.

When a tree is quarter sawn (radially) it is cut at right angles, or very nearly at right angles, to the growth rings. Shrinkage on both faces of the plank or board will tend to be equal, therefore the effect of cupping will be negligible. Most of the shrinkage will take place at the edges of the board, making the board or plank narrower.

In both tangentially and radially sawn timber, longitudinal shrinkage is usually very slight and can therefore be discounted.

If the grain of the timber is irregular, the ends of the board tend to spring towards each other causing the board to bow. In some timber, whether quarter sawn or slash sawn, more than one of these shrinkages can occur causing the board to twist or warp.

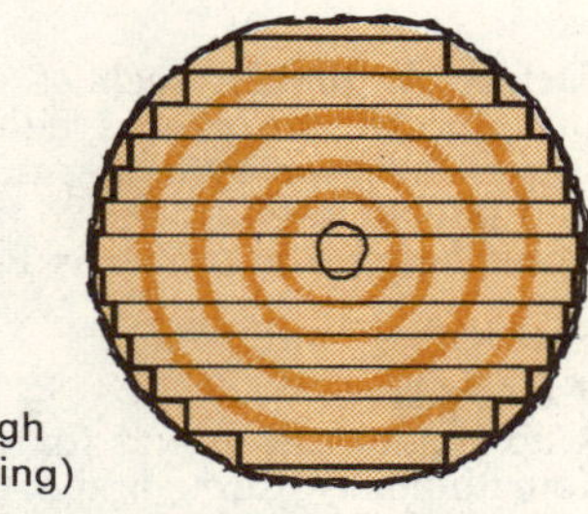

through and through cutting (slash sawing)

typical slash grain figure

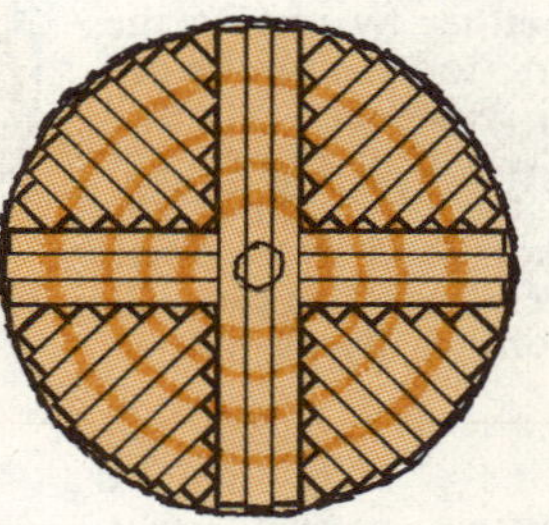

quarter sawn timber

quarter sawn oak figure

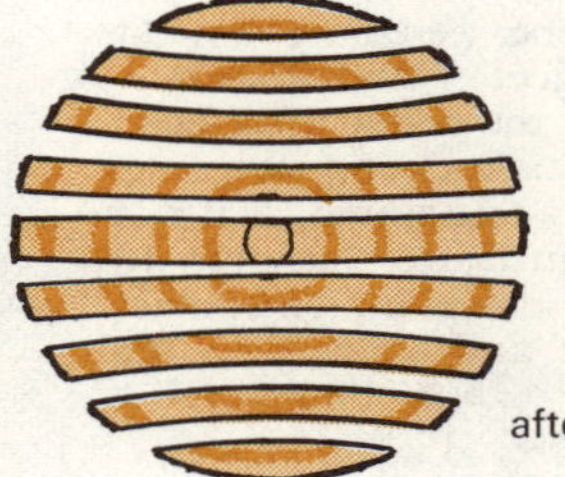

cupping caused by tangential shrinkage after log has been slash sawn

Defects in timber, such as shakes, splits and checks, are caused either when the tree is felled or by bad seasoning. Stains and discolourations, due to fungus attack, occur before the timber is fully seasoned.

A tree is best felled in the winter as the branches, having shed their leaves, are lighter than in summer, and damage to the tree as it strikes the ground is much less likely.

SHAKES

Cup shakes

Cup shakes can extend for some distance longitudinally through the timber. They are probably caused by strong winds straining the tree while it is growing or by the shock sustained by the tree when it is felled. The fibres of adjoining growth rings, where the cell density varies, are torn apart. During conversion much of the log can be wasted because of cup shakes.

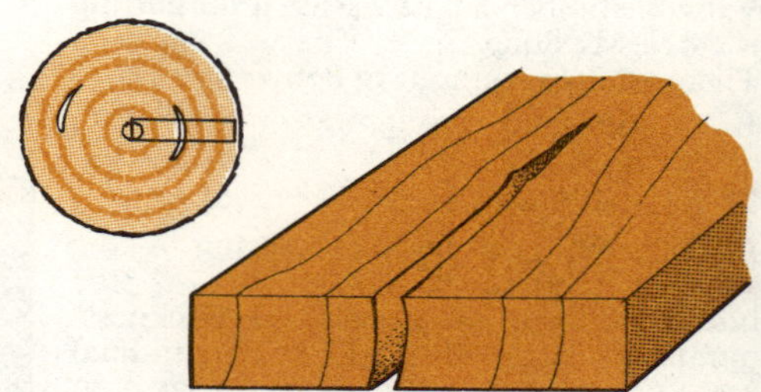

Heart shakes

Heart shakes occur along the path of the rays, and are caused either by leaving the timber in log form too long before conversion or by bad seasoning. The cell walls of the rays are very thin and do not have the strength of the fibre cells. The cells in the rays contain food in the form of moisture, and uneven shrinkage can take place when this moisture is drying out.

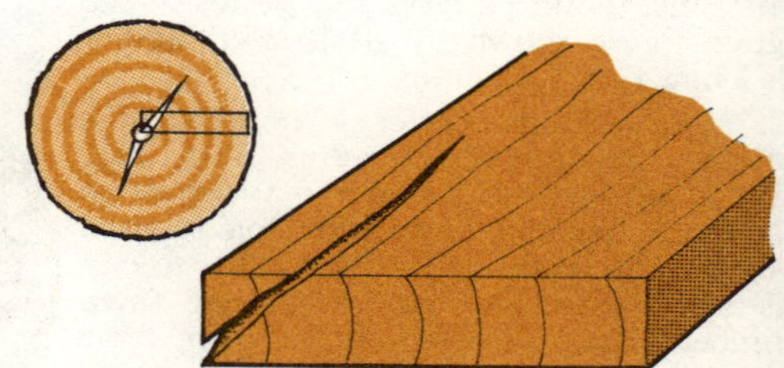

Star shakes

Star shakes occur when several heart shakes start from the same part of the pith. The causes of star shakes are the same as those which result in heart shakes. The appearance of star shakes in a log is a sure sign that it has been left too long before conversion.

Thunder shakes

Thunder shakes in timber were once thought to be caused by the effect of electric storms, but they are actually the result of a felled tree striking an obstruction, such as another felled tree or a tree stump, as it hits the ground. This can cause the grain to become impacted at the point of contact with the obstruction and so weaken the grain structure.

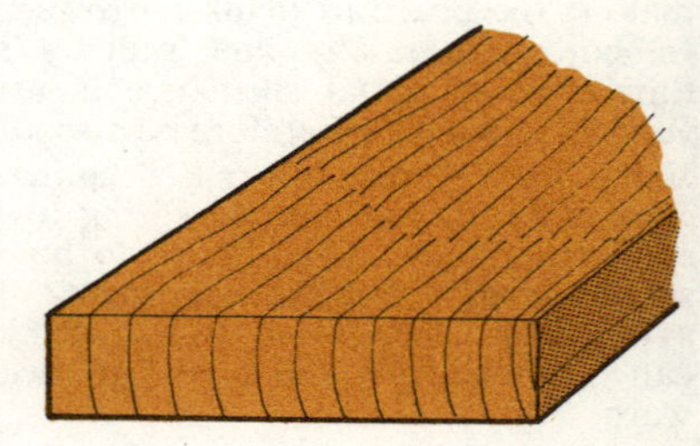

SPLITS AND CHECKS

Surface splits

Surface splits are caused by the surface of the board drying out more quickly than the inside of the board. The surface of the board shrinks while the inside of the board remains in its normal state. The fibres are forced apart by this uneven surface tension.

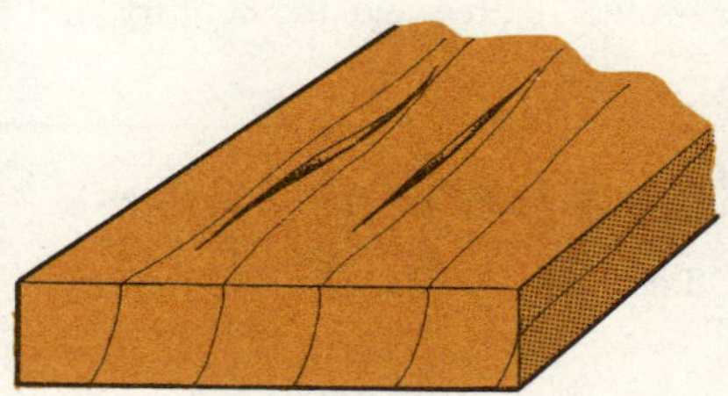

Honeycomb checks

Interior splits (honeycomb checks) are the result of poor seasoning. Occasionally a board will set (dry out) with the surface still at, or near, its original width. Later, when the inside dries out, it shrinks, and splits can occur in the interior of the board.

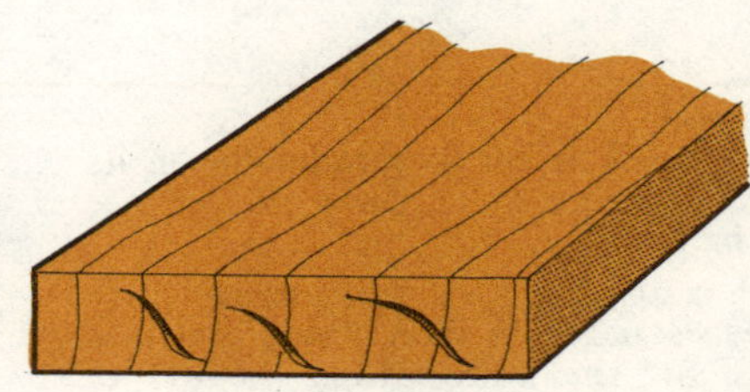

End splits

End splits occur for the same reason as surface splits. The evaporation of moisture is greater at the ends of boards than elsewhere, thus end splits are very common in natural seasoned timber. The ends of boards should be protected in some way.

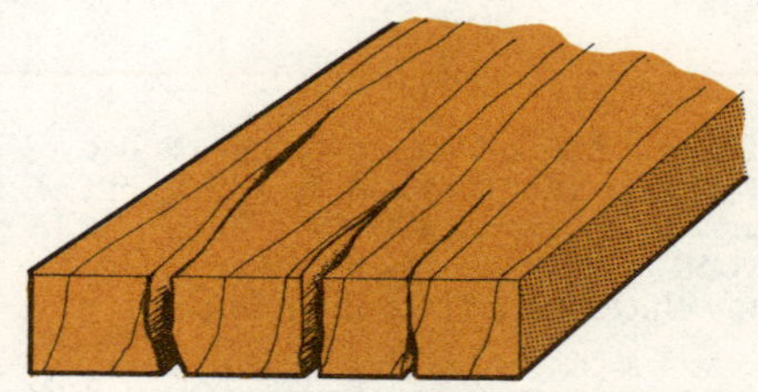

STAINS AND DISCOLOURATIONS

Once a tree has been felled, it is liable to attack by fungus or insects. The species of fungus responsible for staining and discolouring timber does not harm the structure of the timber; it lives on the contents of the sapwood cells and not on the cell walls themselves. To prevent discolouration, logs should be converted as soon as possible after felling and the seasoning process begun immediately.

Fungus can only attack timber with a moisture content of 20% or more. Therefore the percentage moisture content should be reduced as quickly as possible to less than 20%; this is difficult using natural seasoning methods, and in natural seasoned softwoods it is quite common for the timber to show a blue stain caused by this fungus.

HARDWOODS

These timbers are available in lengths of 1.8 metres and upwards. The widths and thicknesses of imported hardwoods depend on the species of tree and the country of origin.

SOFTWOODS

Softwoods are supplied in lengths from 1.8 metres increasing by lengths of 300 mm to 6.3 metres.

Baulk

A baulk is a piece of timber which is roughly squared before it is fully converted. Baulk dimensions are at least 115 mm by 100 mm.

Half timber

When a baulk is cut longitudinally on its axis, both pieces of timber produced are called half timber.

A **flitch** is any baulk or half timber which has been squared in such a way that it is suitable for the knife-cutting method of producing veneers.

Plank

A softwood plank is a piece of timber which is more than 275 mm in width and between 50 mm and 100 mm thick. A hardwood plank can be of any width and any thickness greater than 50 mm.

Deal

Deal is a term applied to softwoods 250 mm to 280 mm in width and from 50 mm to 100 mm thick.

Board

A softwood board is 100 mm or more in width and less than 50 mm thick. A hardwood board can be of any width but is always less than 50 mm thick.

Strip

A strip is a piece of timber which is less than 100 mm in width and less than 50 mm thick.

Batten

Battens are cut from softwoods only. Their widths range from 100 mm to 200 mm, and their thicknesses from 50 mm to 100 mm.

Square

As the name implies, this timber is cut square in section. The sizes range from 25 mm to 150 mm square.

Scantling

A scantling is a piece of timber 50 mm to 115 mm in width and from 50 mm to 100 mm thick.

Waney edge

A waney-edged board is one where the sawn section retains part of the bark. Waney-edged boards have little commercial value, but they make attractive and unusual fencing and garden furniture.

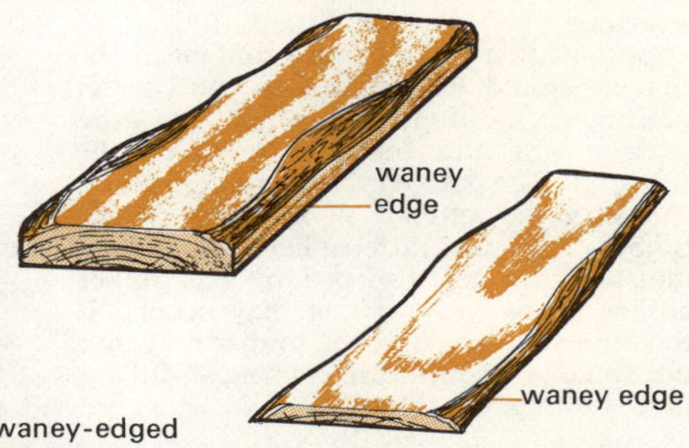

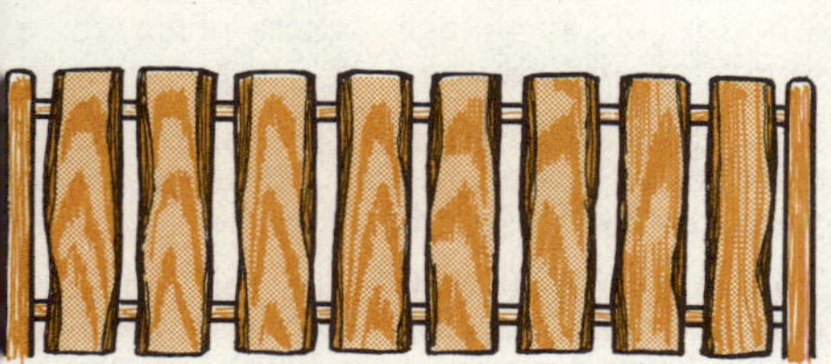

waney-edged fencing

REVISION EXERCISES

1. Why is the pith useless as commercial timber?
2. What is meant by "transpiration"?
3. What function do the rays perform?
4. What is a growth ring?
5. Give a reason why sapwood is undesirable as commercial timber.
6. Why is heartwood preferred for timber constructions?
7. Give two methods of log conversion.
8. What is the simplest method of converting a log into boards?
9. Sketch a typical slash grain figure.
10. What effect can slash sawing have on boards cut from a log?
11. What is the advantage of quarter sawing a log?
12. What is meant by the "grain" of a piece of timber?
13. Irregular grained timber can be difficult to work, but has it any desirable features?
14. What is the probable cause of shakes in timber?
15. With the aid of sketches, show the difference between cup shakes and heart shakes.
16. What defect occurs in a log if it is left too long before conversion?
17. What is the main cause of splits in timber?
18. What is meant by a "waney-edged board"? Give a use for boards with waney edges.

The seasoning of timber is extremely important and must be carried out efficiently. Bad seasoning can ruin any timber. The aims of seasoning are:

(1) to reduce the moisture content of the timber;

(2) to prevent attack on the timber by fungi and wood-boring insects;

(3) to increase the strength of the timber and make it easier to work.

When a tree is felled, the cell cavity and cell walls contain a large amount of water. In this condition the felled tree is known as "green" timber. To reduce the moisture content to the desired level the timber is seasoned, i.e. partially dried out. It is important that the moisture content of the timber should be reduced to the correct percentage, and this depends on the environment and the use to which the timber is to be put. Atmospheric conditions can vary the amount of moisture in the timber. If the atmosphere is damp, moisture can be absorbed by the timber and warping and swelling may occur. If the atmosphere is dry, the timber may give out some of its moisture causing shrinkage and splitting.

The correct percentage of moisture content in timber, for most uses, varies from 11% to 20%. If the moisture content is above 20%, the timber can be affected by dry rot. It is inadvisable to have floor boards, door panels, door-frames and furniture made of timber with a moisture content of more than 12% or 13% in a normally heated room, as shrinkage will occur. 10% or 11% is more appropriate for centrally heated buildings.

The moisture content of timber can be very quickly ascertained by an electrical measuring instrument. It can also be found by the following method. Take a sample of the timber and weigh it, then place it in an oven and dry it out completely. When the sample is thoroughly dry, i.e. the weight cannot be reduced any further, the moisture content can be calculated by a simple formula:

$$\frac{\text{wet weight} - \text{dry weight}}{\text{dry weight}} \times 100 = \text{moisture content.}$$

SHRINKAGE OF TIMBER DURING SEASONING

It is generally desirable that the moisture content of timber should be reduced to the correct percentage as quickly as possible, and that the timber should not be damaged during the process.

If care is not taken, damage to the timber may occur in the form of splitting, checking and warping. In certain conditions, staining and discolouration may also occur. Little or no shrinkage takes place in timber during the early stages of seasoning, but with the moisture content at about 30%, shrinkage becomes evident. The most severe shrinkage takes place in the direction of the growth rings, i.e. from the pith towards the bark. Shrinkage also occurs at right angles to the direction of the growth rings (radial shrinkage), but only about half that which occurs in the direction of the growth rings. A very small amount of shrinkage takes place in a longitudinal direction.

It is these differences in the amounts of directional shrinkage that cause timber to warp during seasoning.

The rate of evaporation of the moisture content must be carefully controlled. If the timber is dried out too quickly, excessive and uneven shrinkage occurs, causing such defects as splits, surface checks and internal checks (honeycomb checks).

Stains are caused in timber by certain types of fungi attacking the timber while the moisture content is sufficient to sustain life. The spores can enter the timber through splits, shakes and checks. When the moisture content has become too low to sustain life, the timber is immune to attack by fungi and insects.

METHODS OF SEASONING

The two most common methods of seasoning are natural, or air, seasoning and kiln seasoning. Quite often the two methods are combined, the timber having a preliminary air seasoning period followed by a short kiln seasoning.

Natural seasoning

Natural, or air, seasoning is relatively slow as it relies on air being heated by the sun and circulated around and between the boards by the action of the wind. It is an inexpensive method of seasoning.

The timber should be stacked on a well-drained site, preferably one covered with an ash and cinder mixture or concrete. Any growth of weeds and grass will prevent free circulation of air around the stack. If the stack is too wide the inside dries slowly and stains and decay can develop. The stack should be no more than two metres in width.

A solid foundation of brick piers, which allow free circulation of air, should be built to a height of about one third of a metre, with the piers one metre apart. Strong creosoted battens are laid on the brick piers and the timber to be seasoned is piled on the battens.

A space of about 12 mm should be left vertically between the boards. The boards are separated by clean, dry pieces of timber, called piling sticks, which are about 25 mm wide and 12 mm thick. The distance between piling sticks on the length of the board depends on the thickness of the boards being stacked and the nature of the timber. Softwoods and hardwoods which do not warp easily and are 50 mm or more in thickness can have the piling sticks placed at intervals of one metre. If the boards are less than 50 mm thick the distance between the piling sticks should be reduced to half a metre. Hardwoods such as beech, birch and elm, which do have a tendency to warp, should have piling sticks at intervals of half a metre on boards over 50 mm thick, and one third of a metre on boards less than 50 mm thick. Wherever possible, only timber of the same species and thickness should be stacked in the same pile.

The stack must be protected from rain and direct sunlight. A sloping weather-board roof, big enough to overhang the stack on all sides, should be erected over the stack. To prevent the ends of the boards drying too rapidly and splitting, the end grain can be painted. Wooden cleats can also be used, but they should be tacked only in the middle of the cleat, as cleats nailed along their whole length can cause splitting at the board ends as shrinkage takes place. In very hot weather, the ends of the boards can be shaded with sacking.

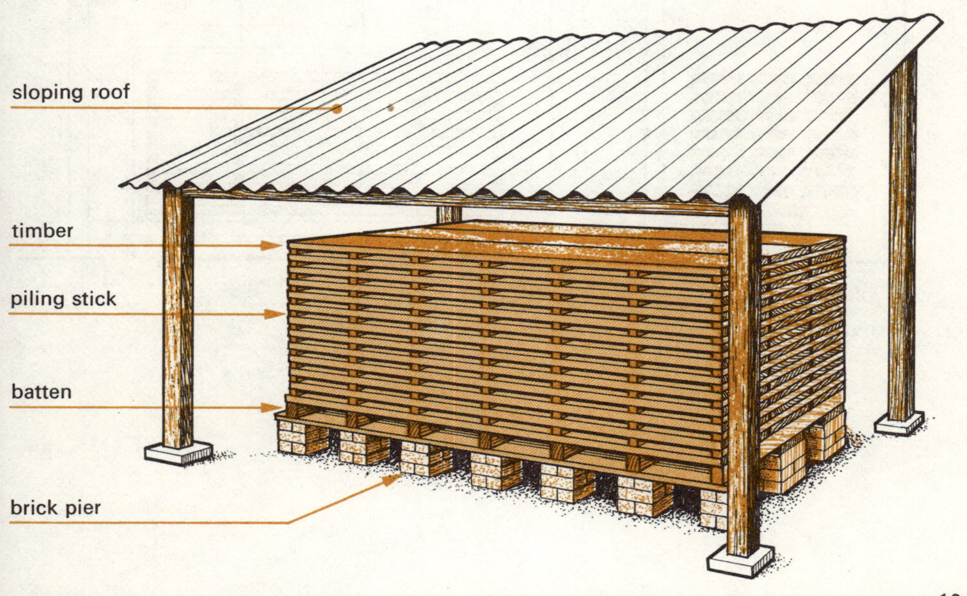

Different species of timber, and different thicknesses of timber, will require longer or shorter drying times for the moisture content to be reduced to about 18—20%. At this percentage of moisture content very little further drying can be accomplished by natural seasoning, and the timber is placed in the kiln to reduce the moisture content to that required for general interior use.

To reduce the moisture content of timber to 18–20% by natural seasoning: (a) softwood boards of 25 mm thickness, when stacked in the spring, take two to three months; (b) softwood boards of 50 mm thickness, stacked at the same time of the year, will take three to four months; (c) hardwood boards of 25 mm thickness take from nine to twelve months, and (d) hardwood boards of 50 mm thickness can take up to two years.

The advantages of natural seasoning are that it is cheap, it does not require expensive equipment, and once the stack is set it can be left without an operator.

The disadvantages of natural seasoning are that the rate of evaporation depends on weather conditions, it is a slow process, and for interior use the timber has to be further dried, either in a warm room or in a kiln, depending on the desired moisture content.

Kiln seasoning

Kiln drying of timber is quicker than air drying as higher temperatures can be reached and the air is circulated more effectively. A kiln is constructed of bricks and is heated by pipes containing hot water or steam. The heating pipes are laid at the bottom of the kiln so that hot air can rise through the stack. The humidity

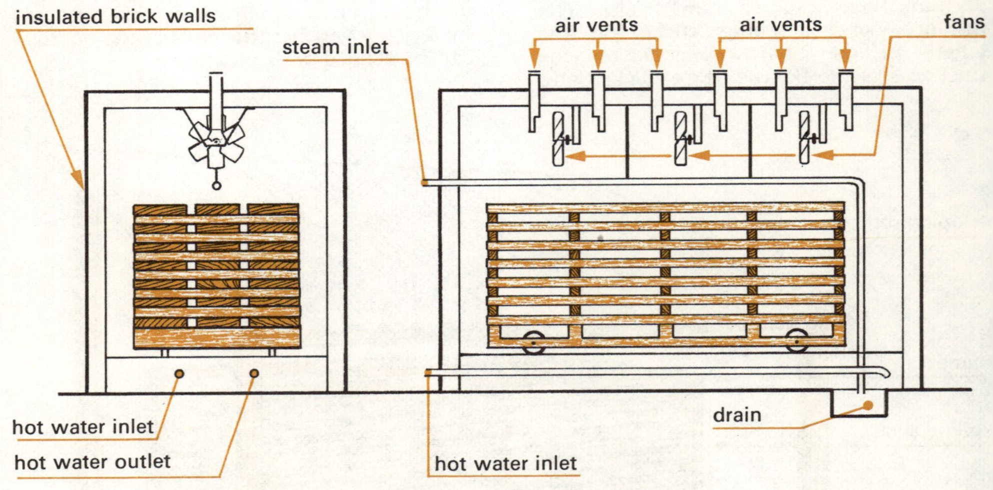

in the kiln is controlled by releasing jets of steam into the kiln. Some kilns rely on the tendency for hot air to rise and cool air to fall to circulate the air (natural draught kilns), while other kilns have fans installed to provide the necessary air circulation (forced draught kilns).

There are two main types of kiln:

(1) The compartment kiln, in which the timber is stacked on a trolley in the same manner as for natural seasoning. The trolley is then pushed into the kiln where it remains stationary throughout the drying process. The drying process is controlled by means of heated pipes and steam jets.

(2) The progressive kiln, in which the timber is stacked on a trolley as for natural drying and the trolley pushed into the kiln. In this kiln the trolley does not remain stationary but is moved slowly through the kiln. The air at the loading end of the kiln is cool and wet. As the trolley moves through the kiln the air temperature and humidity, controlled by heated pipes and steam jets, gradually change to warm and dry. The advantage over the compartment kiln is that as successive stacks of timber are fed into the kiln, dry timber is continuously available at the unloading end.

Kiln seasoning is much quicker than natural drying. Softwoods 50 mm thick, that have already been dried to 20% moisture content by natural seasoning, can be dried in the kiln to 11% moisture content in a period of from one to four weeks. Hardwoods in a green condition can be dried in the kiln to 11% moisture content in a period of from three to twelve weeks.

The advantages of kiln drying are that the amount of heat and humidity can be controlled; the circulation of air is uniform; the timber is seasoned quickly (in progressive kilns the operation is almost automatic); and the timber can be dried to any required moisture content.

The disadvantages of kiln drying are that it is expensive and that natural draught kilns require a skilled operator.

FUNGAL DECAY IN TIMBER

Fungi which attack timber are plants which feed on the cell contents and, in some instances, on the cell tissue itself.

The fungi which are responsible for sap stains in timber do not harm the fibres of the timber, but the fungi which feed on the cell tissue seriously weaken the strength of the timber and in a great many instances render it useless for constructional purposes.

All species of fungi live on the starches and sugars in the timber. The sapwood contains more of these foods than the heartwood, with the result that sapwood is more readily attacked by fungus. But if conditions favourable to fungus growth are present, heartwood can also be attacked.

Fungus can attack timber only if it contains a supply of food (sugar and starch) and has a certain percentage of moisture content (above 20%). A supply of oxygen must also be present. Timber used in the construction of pier supports is not attacked by fungus under the water-line, due to the absence of air. That part of a fence post under ground is not attacked by fungus for the same reason.

Even properly seasoned timber, if used in damp conditions, can absorb moisture from the atmosphere and create the moisture content essential to the growth of fungi. A suitable wood preservative should be applied to the timber to discourage fungal attack. There are many different types of fungi: those that attack growing timber; those that attack freshly cut timber before conversion; and those that attack timber already in commercial use. Of these three types of fungi, the last is of most concern to the consumer, and can be classified as dry rot, cellar fungus or mine fungus.

Dry rot is the most damaging of these fungi. It has the ability to penetrate brick and plaster walls to reach fresh timber. Once established, it can attack dry timber by first moistening it with water carried in its strands. The fungus is white in colour, with grey strands spreading outwards from the parent plant. The rotted timber is brown in colour, with cracks running with the grain and across the grain. This type of timber decay is known as "cubical rot", due to the pattern left on the timber by the rot. The decayed timber is dry and powdery.

Cellar fungus (wet rot) attacks only wet timber. As its name implies, it is found mostly in damp, poorly ventilated cellars. It is not as persistent as dry rot. The fungus is yellowish in colour, with no strands. The rotted timber is dark brown and brittle, with long cracks running with the grain.

Mine fungus is also a cubical rot, but it requires a considerable amount of moisture. Conditions in coal-mines are most favourable to the growth of this fungus, and pit-props are frequently attacked by it. It is similar to dry rot, but it does not have water-carrying strands. The fungus is spread by spores. The appearance of the rotted wood is similar to that of wood attacked by dry rot.

Once fungus has attacked timber, it is difficult to eradicate it. All affected timber must be removed and destroyed by burning. The surrounding walls, ceiling, etc., must be treated with a fungicidal agent. Unaffected timber must be treated with a preservative, and new timber must be protected before installation. If possible, the conditions which encourage the growth of fungus should be avoided.

INSECT ATTACK

Damage done to timber by insects can be considerable. Timber-destroying insects are flying beetles which infest the timber by laying eggs in cracks or crevices. The eggs hatch and the grubs or worms (larvae) bore into the wood, leaving tunnels behind them. The larvae live in the timber for at least one year, and in some cases for several years, depending on the amount of starch available for food. When the larvae are fully grown they bore their way almost to the surface of the timber and pupate for a few weeks until the beetle is formed. The beetle bores its way out of the timber, leaving exit holes in the wood. It is at this stage that the presence of "woodworm" is recognised.

Wood-boring beetles

The most common wood-boring beetle is the furniture beetle (*Anobium punctatum*) which usually attacks old furniture, wall panelling, etc. The beetles emerge from the timber between June and August and fly to any suitable timber where they lay their eggs. Timber unprotected by polish or preservative, such as the undersides of drawers and table tops, is very vulnerable to attack.

The death-watch beetle (*Xestobium rufovillosum*) belongs to the same family as the furniture beetle. It attacks old timbers, the oak beams of churches being particularly susceptible. The beetles emerge from the timber between April and June and lay their eggs in cracks, splits and old exit holes in the wood. During the mating season the beetles rap on the wood with their heads, causing a ticking sound. This sound gives rise to their common name of death-watch beetle.

Powder post beetles (*Lyctus brunneus*) are particularly dangerous in timber yards. They lay their eggs in the sapwood vessels of hardwoods from April to August. All softwoods, and birch trees, are immune from attack by this beetle as its eggs are too large to enter the pores of the timber. Only sapwood is attacked, as the larvae need starch for food and starch is normally absent from heartwood.

Longhorn beetles (*Hylotrupes bajulus*) do not cause extensive damage in Britain. They confine their activities to sickly trees, and timber lying on the forest floor. The larvae live in the bark and sapwood and make large, oval-shaped tunnels in the wood.

Pin-hole borers (*ambrosia beetles*) only attack freshly felled timber and die off when the timber is seasoned. The presence of these beetles can be recognised by the tunnels made by the larvae. The tunnels are dark in colour and usually run across the grain of the wood.

Marine borers
Marine borers attack timber which is used in salt water. These are not insects but molluscs and crustaceans. Piles for docks and piers and timbers used in the construction of boats are liable to be attacked by these borers. The best known marine borers are the *Teredo navalis* (shipworm) which is a mollusc, and the *Limnoria lignorum* (gribble) which is a crustacean.

The teredo is the more dangerous as it is capable of destroying timber in a very short time.

Some timbers, particularly ekki and greenheart, are resistant to attack from marine borers. These timbers, sprayed with a suitable preservative, are generally used for constructions in brackish or sea water.

Common furniture beetle (*Anobium punctatum*)
This beetle is dark brown to almost black in colour and is about 2 mm to 5 mm in length. The larvae are fleshy white in colour and are small and curved. The bore dust or *frass* feels gritty when rubbed between the fingers.

Powder post beetle (*Lyctus brunneus*)
This beetle is reddish-brown to black in colour and about 2 mm in length. The body of the beetle is in two separate parts with two antennae, one on either side of the head. These antennae end in two enlarged joints. The larva is small and whitish in colour, with two brown spots on the rear part of the body. The bore dust is like flour to the touch.

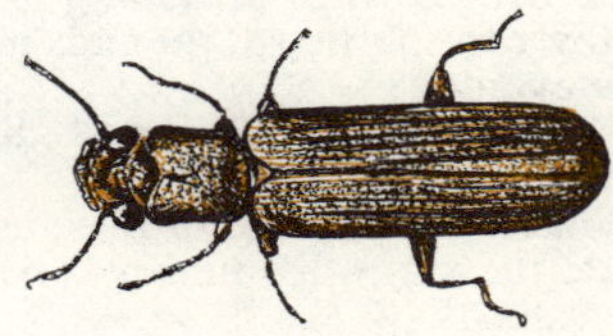

Death-watch beetle (*Xestobium rufovillosum*)
This beetle is about 6 mm to 8 mm in length, and is mottled brown in colour. The head of the beetle is broad and flat. The larvae are similar to the larvae of the furniture beetle. The exit holes made by this beetle are larger than those of other beetles. The bore dust is easily recognised as it contains pellets which can be seen quite easily.

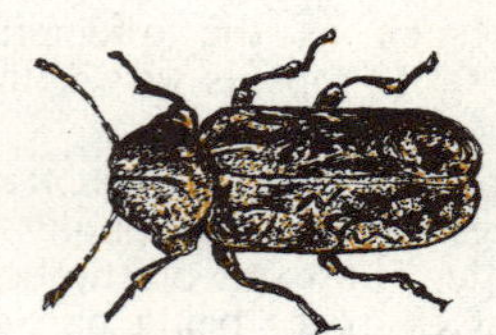

Longhorn beetle (*Hylotrupes bajulus*)
This beetle can vary from 6 mm to 20 mm in length. It is quite distinctive in appearance, with two shiny spots on top of the head and white hairs on the wing covers. The bore dust consists of coarse fragments and small pellets of wood.

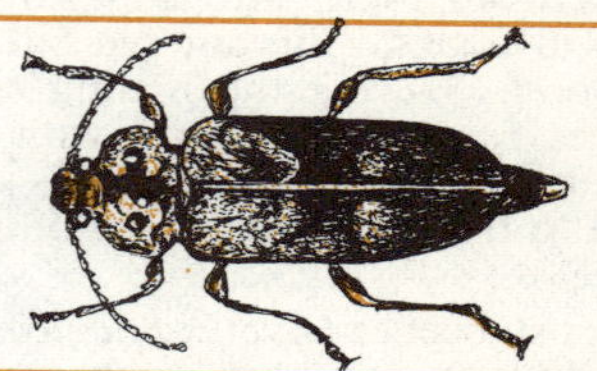

Pin-hole borers (*ambrosia beetles*)
These beetles belong to the families *Scolytidae* and *Platypodidae*. The beetles are 4 mm to 8 mm in length. The larvae live only in unseasoned timber. The beetles carry a fungus which leaves a dark stain on the tunnels as they bore through the wood.
Only a few species of this insect are found in Britain, although many more are found in other parts of the world, especially the tropics. Attack by these beetles ceases when the timber is seasoned.

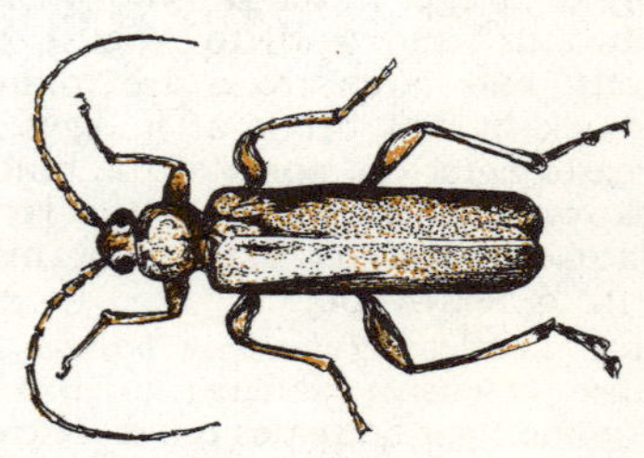

1. What determines the moisture content of timber?
2. Give reasons why timber must be seasoned before use.
3. What are the two main methods of seasoning timber?
4. Why must the rate at which moisture evaporates from timber be controlled?
5. During natural seasoning, timber should be stacked on a well-drained site. Why?
6. Why is a space of 12 mm left between the boards when seasoning?
7. How can splitting at the ends of boards be avoided?
8. List some advantages and disadvantages of natural seasoning.
9. What is the purpose of injecting steam into the kiln when timber is being kiln seasoned?
10. What is the basic difference between natural draught kilns and forced draught kilns?
11. What are the advantages of kiln drying?
12. Below what percentage of moisture content is timber immune to fungal attack?
13. What three conditions encourage fungal attack of timber?
14. Why is dry rot classified as cubical rot?
15. How can fungus which has attacked timber be eradicated?
16. How do timber-destroying insects attack timber?
17. Which is the most common of the timber-destroying beetles?
18. How can attack by the furniture beetle be avoided?
19. Where, in particular, would you find the death-watch beetle?
20. Write down what you know about marine borers.

SOFTWOODS

Cedar (Asia, Central America, North America and Europe)
This is a reddish-pink, durable timber well suited to outdoor constructions. It is widely used in the building industry for roofs, exterior walls and panelling, and for garages and garden huts.

Cypress (Asia and Canada)
This is a very durable timber, yellowish-brown in colour, which is unaffected by heat and moisture. It is used for the construction of water barrels and tanks, and is ideal for use as framing in green-houses.

Douglas fir (North America)
This timber is also known as Oregon pine. It is a strong, hard-wearing timber, reddish-brown in colour. Douglas fir is used for many purposes, including the construction of ladders, railway sleepers, pit-props, fencing, oars and plywood veneers.

Larch (North America and Northern Europe)
A very durable timber, this is similar to Douglas fir in appearance. It is used mainly for fencing, gateposts and pit-props.

Parana pine (South America)
This timber is characterised by its lack of durability. It is yellowish in colour, having reddish streaks, mostly in the heartwood. It works well, but tends to split easily when nailed. It is used by coach-builders, and by the building industry for interior framing.

Pitch-pine (North America and Northern Europe)
This is a durable timber with a high resinous content. It is a yellowish-brown colour, with prominent dark growth rings. A strong timber, it is used for railway sleepers and heavy gateposts, and by the building industry for use as decorative panels and stairways.

Yellow pine (North America and Europe)
This is not a durable timber. It is light-coloured, but yellows with age. Yellow pine works easily and does not warp or twist readily. It is used mainly by engineer's pattern makers.

Redwood (Northern Europe)
Known also as Scots pine and red deal, this is a durable timber of a reddish-brown colour. It is used in the building industry for flooring, rafters, etc.

Sitka spruce (North America and Northern Europe)
Reasonably durable, this timber is a pale straw colour. It is used in the aircraft industry, for making ships' masts and for interior building.

Canadian spruce (North America)
This timber is fairly durable and it is pale straw or pale yellow in colour. It is used for making packing-cases, ladders and trestles, and for framing.

European spruce (Northern Europe)
A fairly durable timber, this is often called white deal. It is white in colour and is used in the building industry, by coach-builders and for making packing-cases. The North American whitewood, also called white deal, is almost identical to European spruce.

Yew (English)
This is an expensive timber with limited availability. It is golden in colour and the grain varies in appearance. It is a durable timber and is used for exterior joinery—windows, door-frames, window-sills and cladding; interior joinery—skirting, staircases, doors and door-frames; and interior fittings—traditional furniture, shop fittings and radio and TV cabinets.

HARDWOODS

Afrormosia (Africa)
This is a very durable timber, dark brown in colour and often used as a substitute for teak. It is widely used in shipbuilding and in the manufacture of high quality furniture and high quality veneers.

Ash (North America and Northern Europe)
This is a tough, durable timber, cream to pale brown in colour. It has good bending qualities and is used to make hammer shafts, hockey sticks and good quality furniture.

Balsa (Central America)
This hardwood is very soft and light in weight. It is softer than any of the softwoods. It is cream-coloured and is used largely for model making, as an insulating material, and for lifebelts and life rafts.

Beech (Europe)
Beech is prone to attack by fungus. It is pale pink in colour and has good bending qualities. Beech is used to make mallet shafts, rolling-pins and furniture. Because of its close grain it is popular for wood turnery.

Box (Northern Europe)
This is a very durable timber, yellowish-white in colour. It is used extensively for some types of scientific instruments (metre sticks, etc.), chisel handles and decorative inlays.

Elm (Britain and North America)
Pale brown in colour, this is a tough, durable timber. It is much used for coffins, boat-building, coach-building and some types of furniture.

Ekki (Africa)
A very tough, durable timber, this has a natural ability to resist attack by marine borers. It is red to dark brown in colour, and is used largely for pier piles and dock gates and for bridge building.

Greenheart (Central and South America)
This timber has the same characteristics as ekki. It is a very hard, tough, durable timber which also resists attack by marine borers. It is used for pier piles and dock gates and in the construction of wooden bridges.

Hickory (Northern Europe and North America)
A tough, elastic, durable timber. It is used extensively in the manufacture of sports goods (tennis-racket handles, skis, etc.).

Mahogany (African)
The most common of the mahoganies, it is reasonably durable and varies from light red to deep red in colour. It is used for making furniture, wall panels and veneers.

Mahogany (Spanish)
This is superior to African mahogany. It is a red-brownish colour, and lends itself particularly to wood carving because of its excellent working qualities. It is used extensively for the making of good quality furniture, shipbuilding, wood turning and high quality veneers.

Mahogany (Honduras)
A timber with properties similar to Spanish mahogany, it is light reddish, toning to a dark red in colour. It is used for furniture making and shipbuilding, by engineer's pattern makers and to produce high quality veneers.

Oak (English)
This is a strong, durable timber, golden brown in colour with a highly figured grain. When the timber is quarter sawn, the surface shows a silver flash. This timber is widely used for making furniture, parquet and block flooring, and for boat-building, wine casks and veneers.

Oak (Japanese)
Softer than English oak, this timber also has a less prominent figure. It is easier to work than English oak and is used for making furniture and flooring, for boat-building and to produce veneers.

Silky oak (Australia)
This oak is also softer than English oak, coloured brown with a reddish tinge. It is easily worked and it is used for furniture making and wall panelling. It also produces a high quality veneer.

Obeche (West Africa)
This is a creamy white to pale yellow timber. It is very easy to work and is soft for a hardwood. It is used for interior joinery work, cores for blockboards, some types of furniture and model making.

Rosewood (India)
A dark brown timber with prominent growth rings, it is used mainly for high quality utensil handles (kitchen knives, etc.), good quality furniture and veneers.

Teak (India and Burma)

This strong, durable timber, dark brown in colour, is an oily timber and because of this it polishes to a matt finish. The oily content makes it resistant to attack by insects. It is moisture and fire resistant and is widely used in shipbuilding. Teak is also used to make high quality furniture, laboratory work-benches and parquet flooring.

Sycamore (Northern Europe)

A strong, creamy-white timber, it is used a great deal in wood turnery, as its close grain gives a smooth finish. It is also used as wall panelling and parquet flooring. It produces a highly figured veneer.

Sapele (Africa)

This is a mahogany also from Africa, but it is of a finer quality than the common African mahogany. It is dark red in colour, and the grain shows a distinct band of darker colour. It is used to make high quality furniture, wall panelling and veneers.

Walnut (West Africa)

This is a fairly strong, durable timber of a golden brown colour, marked by black streaks. It is fairly easy to work, but care must be taken to avoid splitting when nailing. It is used for furniture making, inlaying, gun-stocks and wall panelling. It produces good quality veneers.

PLYWOOD

Plywood consists of thin layers of timber called *veneers* glued together. The layers, or plies, are glued with the grain directions at 90° to each other. Because of this cross-bonding, plywood shrinkage is minimal, as movement across the grain of each ply is restricted by the adhesive and the adjoining cross-ply. Plywood is made up from an odd number of veneers, the most commonly used being three-ply. Plywoods of more than three veneers are known as multi-plywoods.

The logs selected to produce veneers should be of large diameter, and as cylindrical and straight as possible. The log is cleaned of its bark and steamed, or cooked in boiling water, to soften the wood fibres. This softening process is necessary to avoid excessive tearing when the log is being cut.

The two most common methods of cutting veneers are rotary-cutting and knife-cutting.

Rotary-cutting

In the rotary-cutting process the log is fixed in a large lathe by means of "dogs". A knife, the full length of the log, is fed up to the revolving log. The knife is advanced by a system of gears so that a uniform thickness of veneer is cut. These gears can also be set to provide veneers of different thicknesses.

By this process a continuous sheet of veneer is cut. The veneer can be cut to any desired length as it comes off the log, or rolled like linoleum onto a spindle. The width of the veneer will be the same as the length of the log.

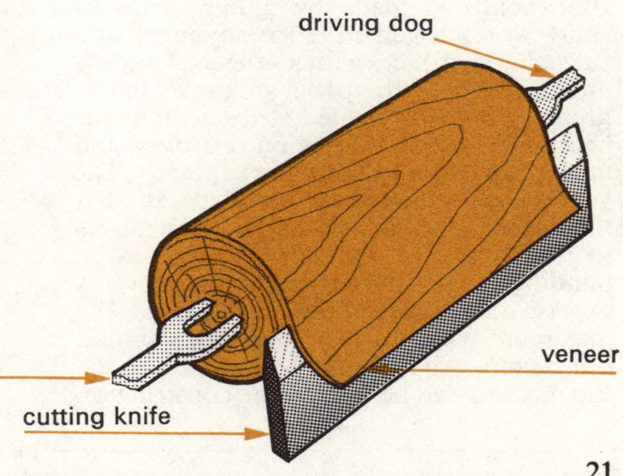

Knife-cutting

Knife-cutting is used to obtain the more valuable veneers. The knife is fixed vertically, with its cutting edge uppermost. The log, or segment of log, called the flitch, is drawn diagonally across the knife-edge. After each stroke the flitch is moved forwards to provide the required thickness of veneer.

Knife-cutting can also be done horizontally. The flitch is bolted to a strong frame, and the knife slides forwards and across the flitch by means of a carriage, as each successive veneer is cut. The veneer is not cut in a continuous roll as in rotary-cutting. The width of the veneers varies from 150 mm to 500 mm, and their length is the length of the log.

Plywood used for general purposes is made from veneers cut by rotary-cutting. For decorative purposes, plywood can have one outside surface faced with knife-cut veneer.

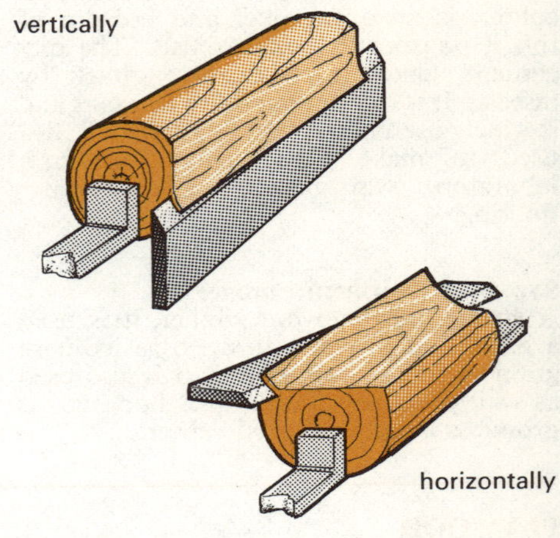

Uses for plywood

Plywood is an ideal material for use as interior wall lining. It is obtainable in large sheets, therefore large areas can be covered quickly. It is easily fixed to wall battens without danger of splitting. It does not shrink or warp, and it has good sound-deadening and heat-insulating properties.

Plywood can be used as flooring. Worn and uneven floor boards can be covered quickly. Its heat-insulating properties are useful when it is used as an underlay for linoleum, carpet felt, etc. Its resistance to warping maintains a level surface.

Special plywoods can be used for exterior work. For fixing to brick or stone structures, or directly on to framing for garages and huts, an exterior grade, known as W B P (weather and boil proof) plywood, is used. A special marine plywood can be used for dinghies and canoes.

Advantages of plywood

Plywood does not expand, shrink, warp or twist in the same way as solid timber of the same thickness, because of the cross-bonding of its veneers. Plywood can be nailed and screwed without danger of splitting. Thinner plywoods can be used to form curved surfaces.

Blockboard

Blockboard is made by gluing strips of solid wood together, edge to edge, and surfacing both sides with a veneer. Twisting and warping of the panel are prevented by gluing the solid wooden strips so that the heart side is facing down on one piece and facing up on the adjoining piece. The veneers are glued to these strips so that the veneer grain is running at right angles to the grain of the strips. The cross-bonding of the veneers and strips prevents excessive shrinkage of the blockboard. The maximum width of the glued strips should not be more than 25 mm.

Blockboard can be used in the construction

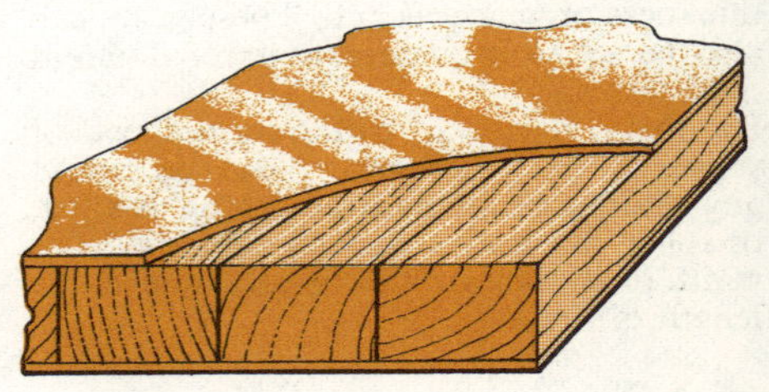

of doors, wall panelling, room partitions and flooring.

Lamin board

Lamin board is constructed in the same way as blockboard. The glued strips should not exceed 7 mm in width. The construction of this board makes it heavier than blockboard, and it is more expensive to manufacture.

The uses for lamin board are the same as for blockboard.

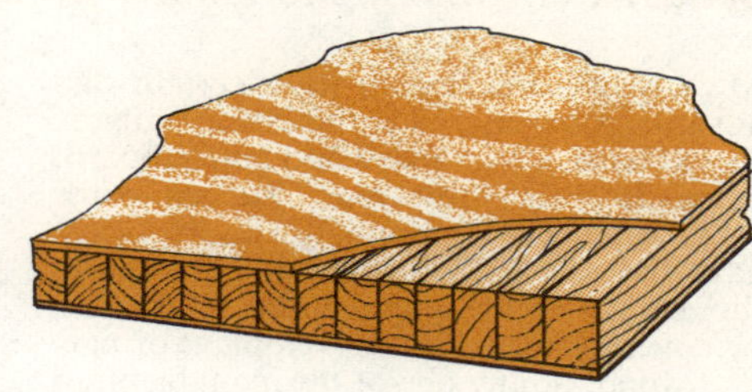

Batten board

This is a variation of blockboard. The glued strips are up to 75 mm in width. Its uses are similar to those of blockboard.

Chipboard

This board makes use of machine chippings. Very strong, it has many advantages over solid timber because of its resistance to shrinkage and warping. It can be made in large sheets.

The core consists of wood chippings glued and then compressed. To each face of this core smaller chippings are then glued and also compressed to make the finished surface.

This board is used for flooring, wall panelling and kitchen furniture tops.

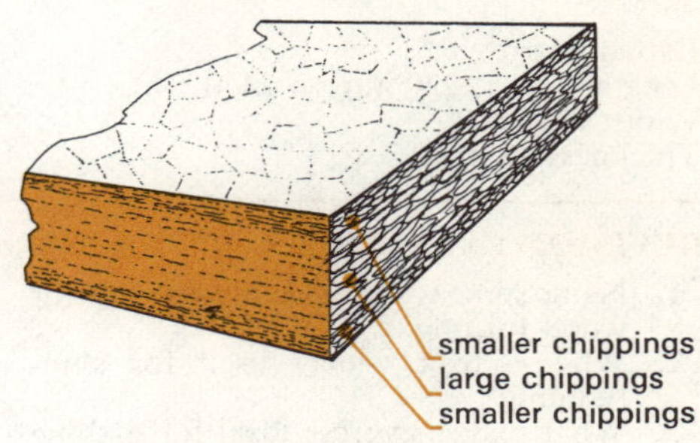

Hardboard

Hardboard is made by mixing wood-pulp with water. The water is removed and the moist pulp is then pressed at a temperature of 200°C. To aid the bonding of the wood fibres, about 5% bitumen is added to the pulp. Hardboard can be surfaced with decorative laminates, or printed with a wood grain pattern.

Hardboard is inexpensive and it is used as door panels, partitions and backing for cabinets. It can also be used for curved surfaces.

Insulating board

Insulating board is similar to hardboard. The wet pulp is partially dried and rolled to the required thickness, then completely dried by circulating hot air. To give the board a low density, it is not compressed.

Perforated hardboard

This hardboard is often called peg-board. The most common is perforated with 5 mm holes spaced 8 mm apart. This type of board is used for ventilation panels, display racks and, with suitable brackets, for workshop and garage tool racks.

DISADVANTAGES OF MAN-MADE BOARDS

Most man-made boards have certain disadvantages compared with natural timbers. Blockboard, lamin board and batten board, when used for table tops, kitchen work tops, cabinet or cupboard doors, must have the edges of the board, particularly those edges showing end grain, concealed by covering the edges with lippings of natural wood, or any one of the manufactured facing strips.

Because of their density, hardboards have the ability to hold fast when screwed into position, but they can fracture easily at the screw or nail head if struck by a sharp blow, or if sustained pressure is applied to the board.

Chipboard has poor screw-holding ability. It also has the disadvantage of not cutting cleanly with a plane or chisel. It is not practicable to attempt jointing hardboards or chipboards, because of their fibrous nature.

COMMON SHEET SIZES

Plywood
Lengths from 1220 mm to 1830 mm.
Widths from 915 mm to 1370 mm.
Thickness from 3 mm to 25 mm.

Lamin board
Lengths from 1220 mm to 2440 mm.
Width 1220 mm.
Thickness from 12 mm to 25 mm.

Batten board
Lengths from 1220 mm to 2440 mm.
Width 1220 mm.
Thickness 20 mm.

Blockboard
Lengths from 1220 mm to 2440 mm.
Width 1220 mm.
Thickness from 15 mm to 25 mm.

Chipboard
Lengths from 1220 mm to 2440 mm.
Widths from 1220 mm to 1525 mm.
Thickness from 10 mm to 25 mm.
For special purposes the thickness can be up to 35 mm.

Hardboard and perforated hardboard
Lengths from 1220 mm to 2745 mm.
Widths from 760 mm to 1700 mm.
Thickness from 3 mm to 25 mm.

REVISION EXERCISES

1. Name some woods that are popular for wood turning.
2. Why is teak widely used for ship-building?
3. What makes cypress ideal for making greenhouse frames?
4. List five hardwoods that produce high quality veneers.
5. Name suitable timbers for making each of the following:
   (a) hockey stick   (b) gun-stock
   (c) rolling-pin   (d) metre stick
   (e) skis   (f) wine cask
   (g) water barrel   (h) garden hut
   (i) utensil handles.
6. Which softwood is used to make plywood veneers?
7. What are the two methods of cutting veneers?
8. Describe briefly the process of rotary-cutting.
9. Why is it necessary to soften the wood fibres before cutting veneers?
10. How are the wood fibres softened?
11. How are the more valuable veneers obtained?
12. What are the respective grain directions of the veneers of plywood?
13. List some of the uses of plywood.
14. List some of the advantages of plywood.
15. How is twisting and warping prevented on a blockboard panel?
16. Describe the difference between blockboard and lamin board.
17. How is chipboard made?
18. How does insulating board differ from hardboard?

SAFETY PRECAUTIONS

(1) There must be adequate space between work-benches and machines to avoid overcrowding.
(2) The workshop lighting should be of adequate standard.
(3) Benches and machines should be kept clean and always brushed down after use.
(4) Any spillage on the floor, such as polish, oil or water, must be wiped up.
(5) Extra care should be taken when handling long pieces of timber in the workshop.
(6) All work which is in cramps should be stored in a safe place.
(7) Never leave small cuttings or pieces of waste wood on the floor. They should be deposited in the scrap box.
(8) Every student should know the position of the emergency stop button.
(9) All loose clothing, such as ties, scarves, etc., should be removed or tucked away.
(10) Only one person should operate a machine at a time.
(11) Never carry cutting tools in pockets.
(12) Make sure the handles of all hand tools are secure.
(13) Make sure that all vice handles are left slack.
(14) Always check that mallet and hammer-heads are securely fixed to the shaft.
(15) Always walk, never run.

HANDSAWS

When handsaw blades are manufactured they are hammered in the centre of the blade, causing the metal to spread slightly, thereby putting the blade into a state of tension. This eliminates any tendency of the blade to buckle when in use. The blade is also tapered in thickness, the thickest part being its cutting edge at the handle end. This is known as "double taper ground" and helps to reduce the amount of set required by the blade.

The blades are made from high carbon steel alloyed with vanadium or molybdenum to give increased toughness and so maintain the efficiency of the cutting edges for long periods of working without recourse to constant sharpening. The number of teeth per 25 mm is stamped on the blade near the handle. Handsaws are grouped as follows:

(1) saws with teeth designed for sawing with the grain of the wood;

(2) saws with teeth designed for sawing across the grain of the wood;

(3) saws with teeth designed for special purposes.

The teeth of all saws are bent slightly to right and left alternately. This makes the saw cut wider than the body of the saw-blade, and so prevents the saw from jamming as it passes through the wood. This alternate bending of the teeth is known as the "set" of the teeth. The channel left in the wood by the set of the teeth is called the "kerf".

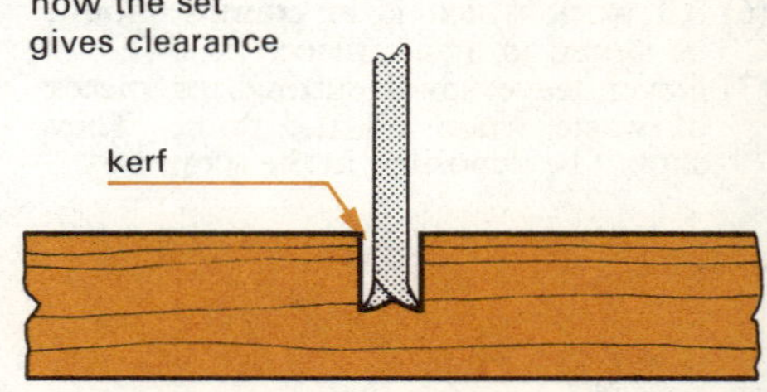

Rip-saw

The rip-saw is used for cutting in the direction of the grain of the timber and has $3\frac{1}{2}$ to 4 points per 25 mm. The blade lengths range from 500 mm to 750 mm, the length of blade selected depending on the height of the workman. The cutting action is similar to a row of chisels placed directly one behind the other, each tooth removing a shaving the full width of its cutting edge.

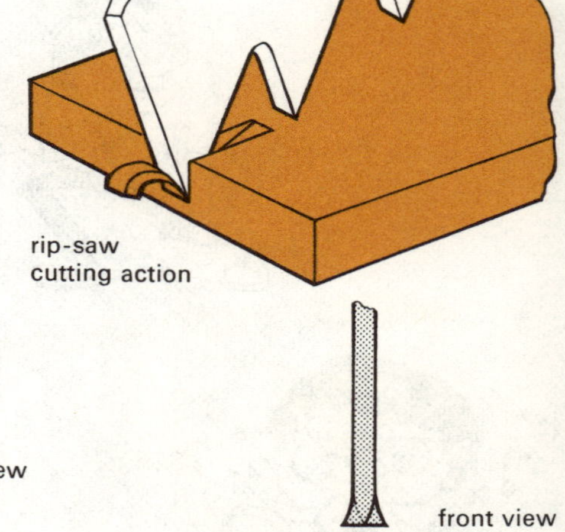

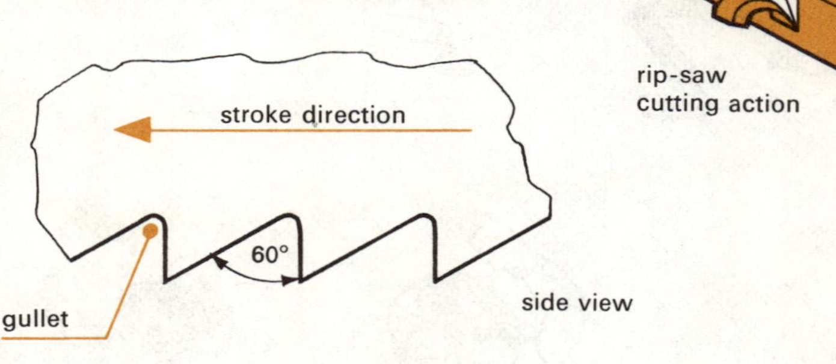

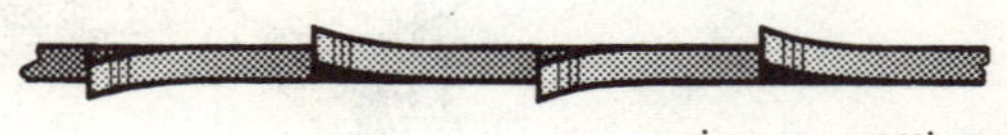

Ripping in the vice

This is the method adopted when ripping short boards. The board is placed in the vice at a convenient height and held by the left hand to prevent vibration. The saw is positioned on the waste side of the line, and guided by the thumb of the left hand bearing on the side of the blade. The saw is started by drawing it backwards a few times, making a groove into which the saw runs and so preventing it from jumping out of the desired position. The sawing stroke is commenced, keeping the saw, forearm and eye in a straight line, and continued until the saw is half-way down the board. The board is then removed from the vice and turned over so that the uncut end is uppermost. The saw is again positioned on the waste side of the line and the sawing operation recommenced. The second saw cut should meet the original cut in the middle of the board.

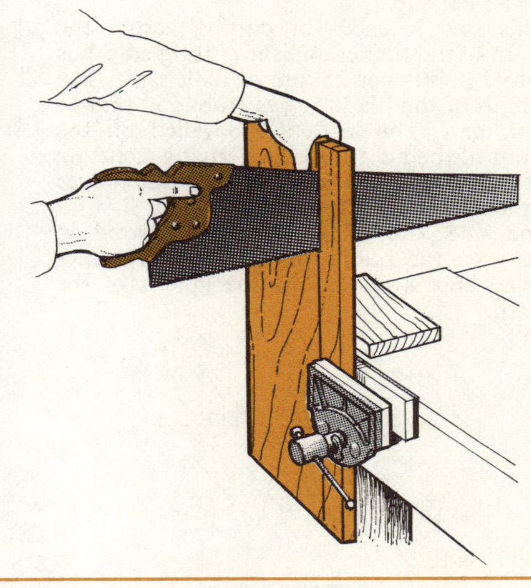

Ripping on trestles

This is the method adopted when ripping long boards. The board is placed on trestles of a convenient height. The saw is placed on the waste side of the line, and the thumb of the left hand placed on the side of the saw-blade to guide it until sawing has started. The board is held in position by placing the right knee on top of it. Sawing continues until the first trestle is reached. The trestle is removed and placed behind the saw. This procedure is repeated when the second trestle is reached, and in this way allows the board to be completely sawn over its full length.

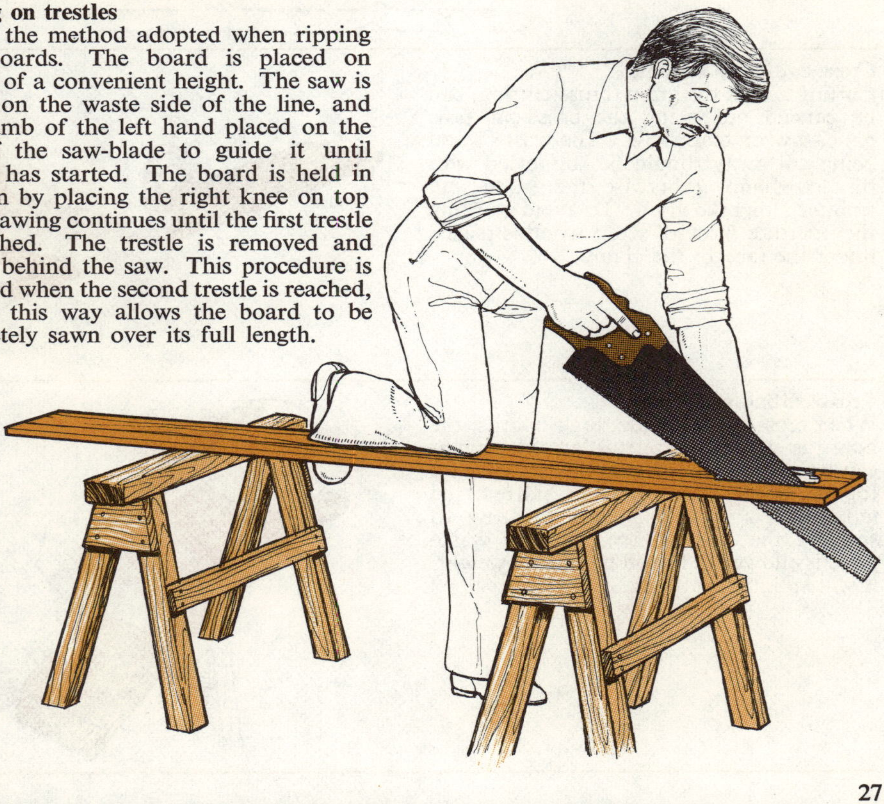

Cross-cut saw

This saw is used for cutting across the grain of the timber and the cutting edge has 5 to 7 points per 25 mm of its length. The length of the blade varies from 550 mm to 700 mm. The teeth are bevelled on the front of their cutting edges, giving a cutting action similar to a series of knife-edges which sever the fibres of the wood, first on one side, then the other. The wood in between the points of the teeth crumbles away and is ejected by the gullets of the teeth.

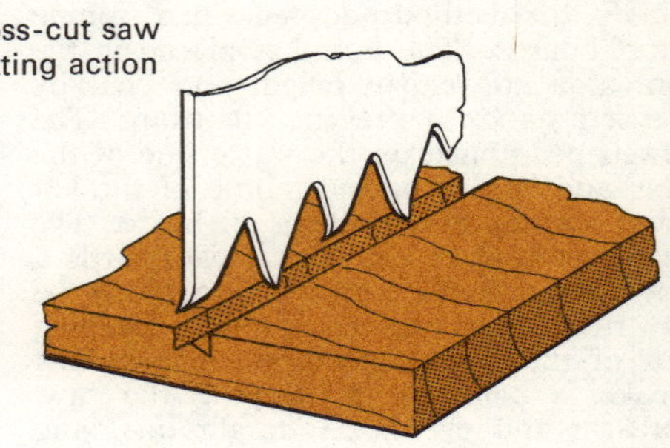

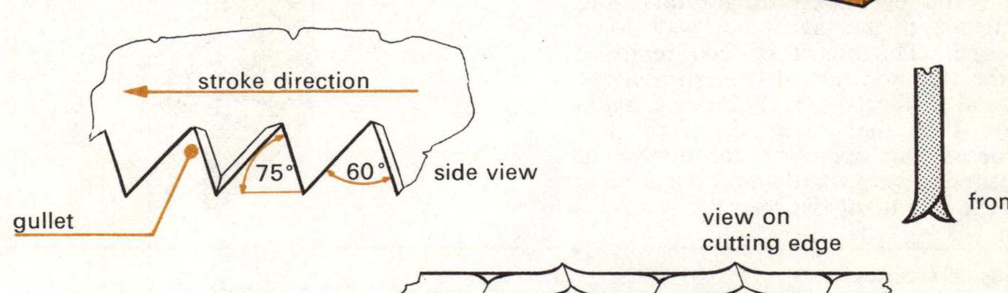

Cross-cutting in a clamp

Cutting across the grain (cross-cutting) can be carried out using the cross-cut saw, panel-saw or tenon-saw. The waste wood being cut away should be supported with the left hand, otherwise the wood will splinter along the grain. To avoid marking the board, a piece of scrap wood is placed under the face of the clamp.

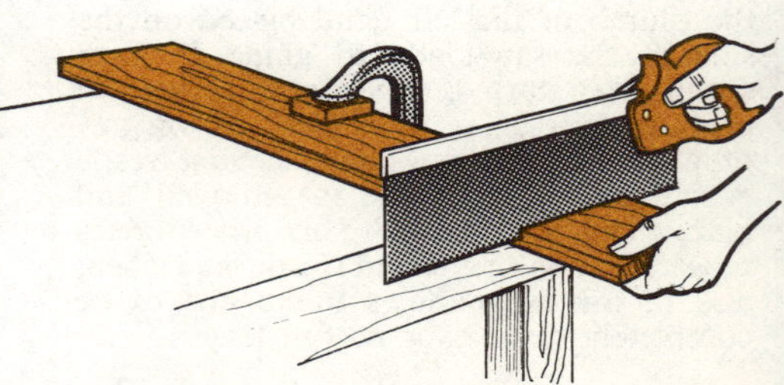

Cross-cutting on trestles

When cross-cutting wide, long boards, the board is supported on trestles. The board can be steadied by placing the left knee on top of it. When sawing has started, the left hand is placed outside the saw to support the waste piece. If this waste piece is allowed to fall off by its own weight, it will splinter the board.

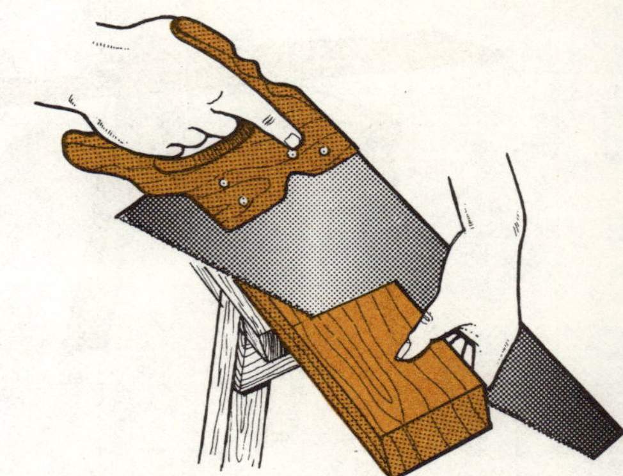

Panel-saw

The formation of the teeth and the cutting action of the panel-saw are similar to those of the cross-cut saw. The blade has 8 to 10 teeth per 25 mm of its length, and the length of the blade ranges from 450 mm to 600 mm. The saw is used for cutting thin boards or panels up to a thickness of 20 mm.

Tenon-saw

This is also known as the back saw because of the steel or brass back fitted to the blade which keeps the blade in tension and provides sufficient weight to feed the saw through the wood. The number of points or teeth per 25 mm of its length is 12 to 14. The tenon-saw is used mainly for cutting tenons or other work of similar size. The blade varies in length from 250 mm to 350 mm.

Dovetail saw

This is a smaller type of tenon-saw and it can have either a closed or an open handle. The blade is 150 mm long and has 18 to 22 points per 25 mm of its length. This saw is used mainly for cutting dovetails when making cabinet drawers and when cutting any other fine work.

Sawing at the bench

Tenon-saws and dovetail saws are used for sawing at the bench. To mark cutting lines on the wood, the marking gauge is used to mark lines with the grain, and the marking knife and try-square to draw lines across the grain.

When the wood is marked to the required size, it is held in the vice or on the sawing board (bench hook). On the sawing board the wood is held firmly with the left hand, with the thumb guiding the saw-blade. The saw is always placed on the waste side of the line and the saw, forearm and eye should all be in the same straight line to prevent the saw from straying off the cutting line. It can be an advantage, after marking with the marking knife, to remove a wedge of timber on the waste side of the line. This creates a shoulder on the cutting line against which the saw-blade can be accurately positioned.

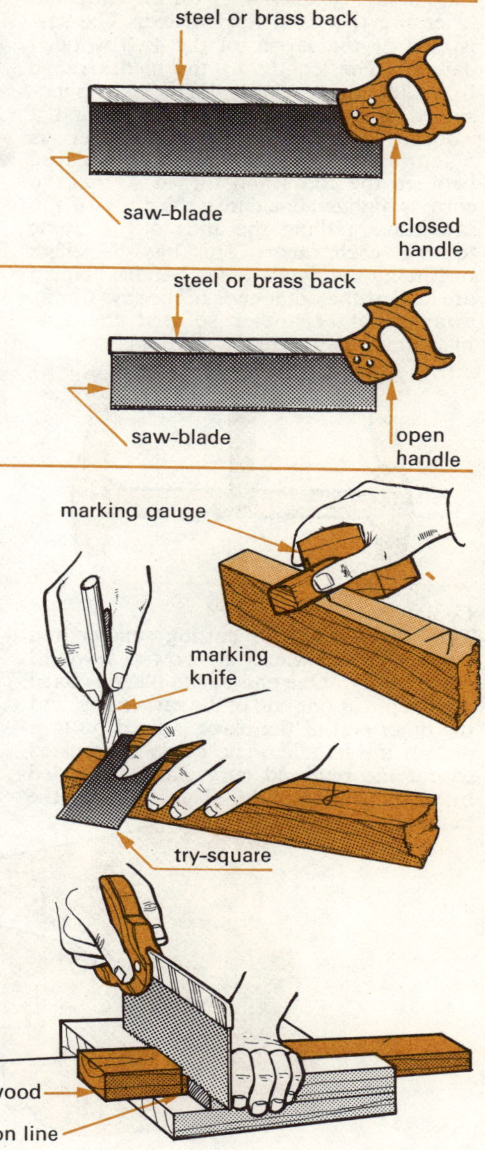

Bow-saw

This saw is designed for cutting curves on shaped work. It has a deep beechwood frame and a narrow blade which can be rotated in any direction by means of the wooden handles. The saw-teeth face the larger handle to enable the blade to cut in tension. Care should be taken when turning the blade to ensure that it is not twisted. The saw is held by the larger of the two wooden handles. The lengths of the blades range from 200 mm to 450 mm. The blade is tensioned by means of a double cord and a wooden strip, in the same manner as a tourniquet. The wooden strip is placed between the cords and turned so that the cord is tightened against the ends of the saw-frame, pulling the ends of the frame towards each other. This has the effect of forcing the two wooden handles, which are held at the other ends of the saw-frame, away from each other so that the saw-blade can be correctly tensioned.

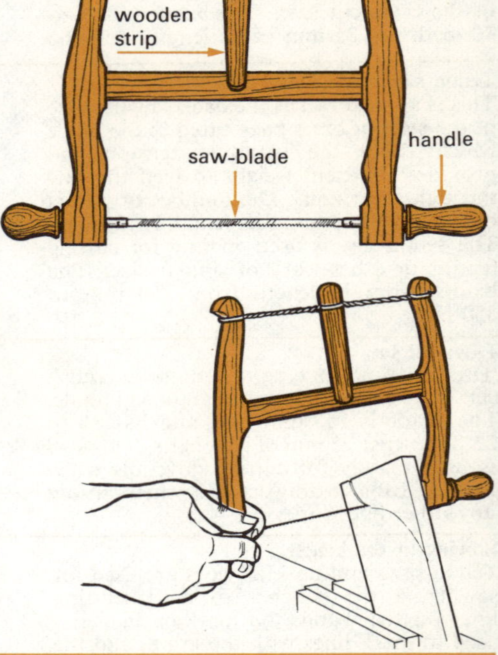

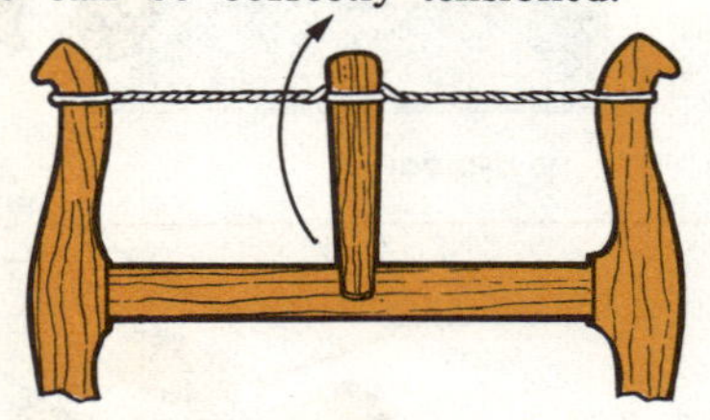

Coping saw

This saw is used for cutting smaller and sharper curves where the bow-saw would be unwieldy. One end of the blade is fixed on to a pin at one end of the saw-frame, and the other end of the blade is fixed on to a pin on the handle. The blade is adjusted to cut the required curve, and tensioned by turning the handle. The length of the blade is 150 mm.

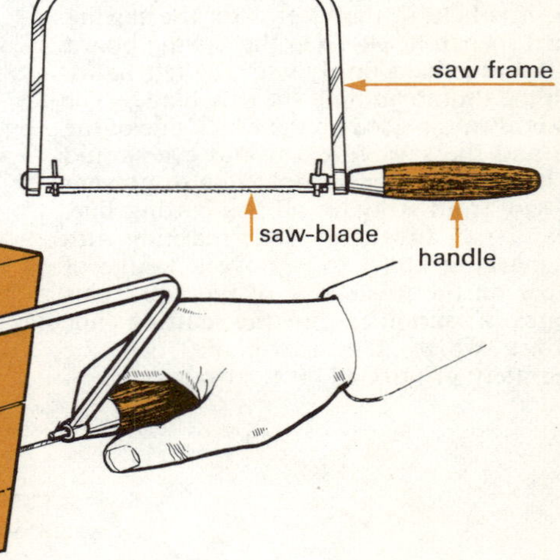

Compass-saw

This saw is used to cut curves where the frame of the bow-saw or coping saw would be an obstruction. The compass-saw is supplied with three interchangeable blades, known as a "nest of saws", and their lengths range from 300 mm to 450 mm.

The three blades have the same set and tooth form as the teeth of the cross-cut or handsaw. They differ in their lengths and in the distance between the cutting edge and the back of the blade. The narrowest blade cuts small curves, and the broadest blade cuts larger curves.

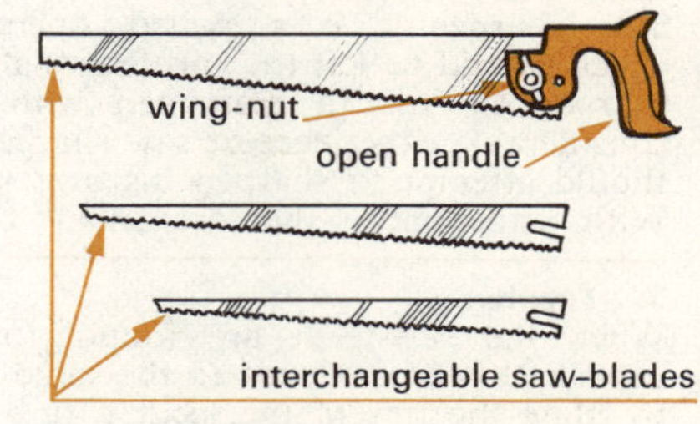

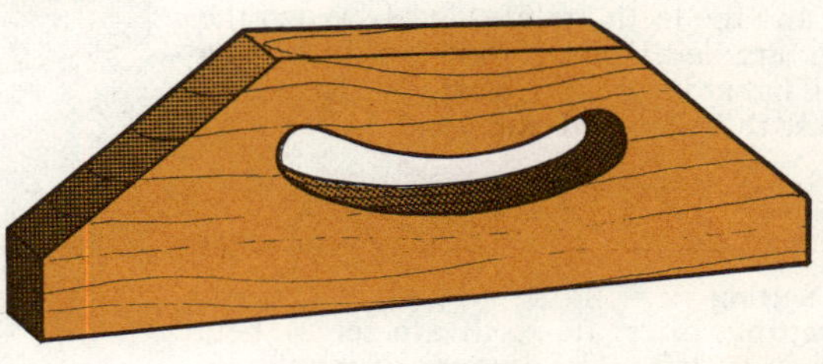

Pad-saw

The pad-saw is also known as the keyhole saw. The blade is much narrower than the smallest blade of the compass-saw. This enables the pad-saw to cut quick inside curves (curves of small radii) and shapes where it would be impracticable to use other saws. The pad-saw blade lengths range from 250 mm to 350 mm. Because of the small sections and curves to be cut, the blade of the pad-saw is left softer than other saw-blades, thus lessening any tendency for the saw-blade to snap. The blade may be kept short as it can pass through the handle. Use as short a length as possible to lessen the tendency of the blade to flex. If the blade is bent in use it can easily be straightened by finger pressure.

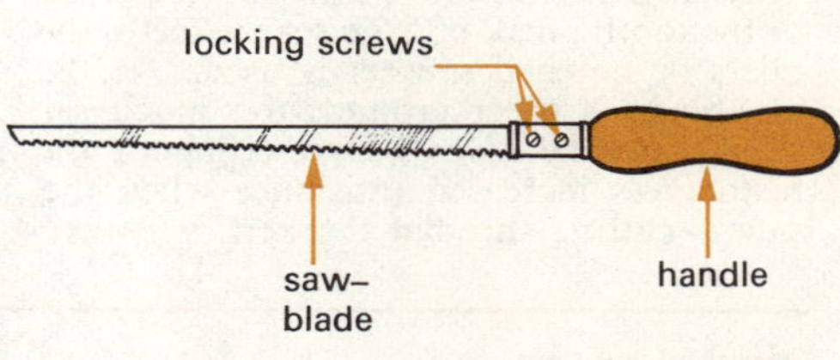

Saw sharpening is a skilled operation which should be left to a professional saw sharpener. Only a craftsman who has considerable experience at saw sharpening should attempt to sharpen his own saws. With experience, the craftsman could attempt to sharpen his saws every alternate time, with the expert sharpening the saws on the other occasions.

To recondition a saw, four procedures are necessary: topping, setting, sharpening and side filing.

1. Topping

When the saw-teeth are found to be uneven, they are reduced to the same level by filing the tips of the teeth with a fine file. The saw is held in the sharpening vice and the teeth are filed level. When the teeth are level, each tooth will show a small flat at its point. A straight-edge is used to test that the teeth are level.

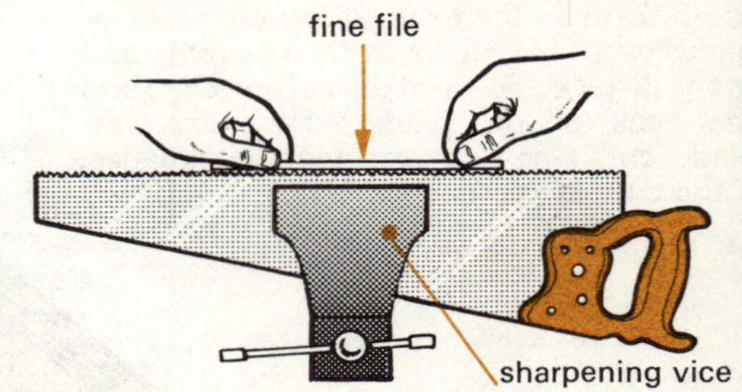

2. Setting

In setting, alternate teeth are set or bent to right or left. The amount of set should not exceed half the depth of the tooth. This ensures that the metal will not crack or the tooth break off. To set the teeth, the pliers or notched saw-set is used. As the saw-blade is taper ground, too much set should not be given. Oversetting of the teeth gives increased resistance when the saw is cutting through the kerf.

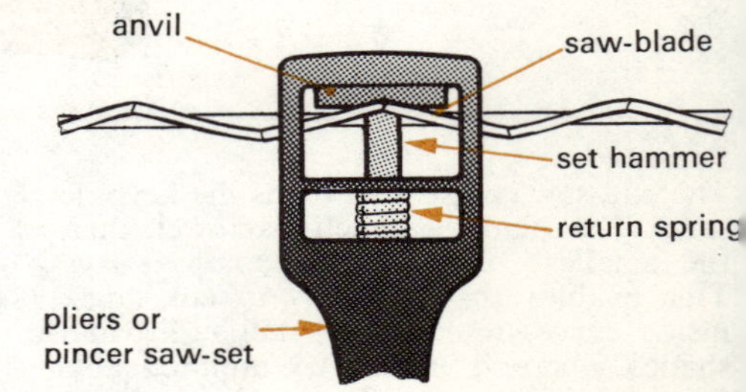

Notched saw-set

The notched saw-set is a difficult tool to use. The slots in the set are of different sizes to suit small or large saws. The set is positioned over the tooth on the saw-blade, and the handle of the set is moved downwards slowly and carefully until the tooth is at the correct set.

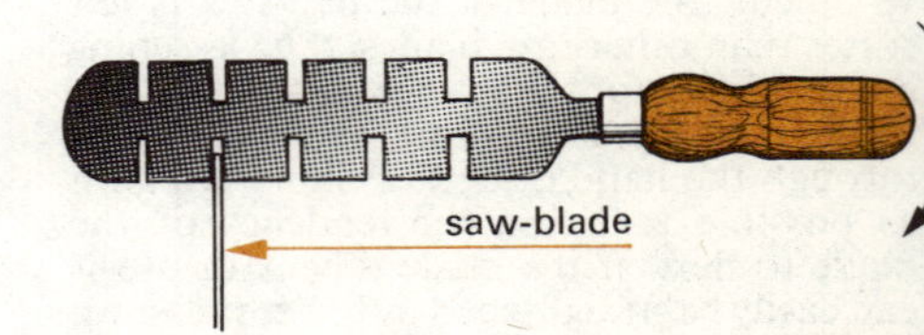

Pliers or pincer saw-set

The pliers or pincer saw-set has an anvil cut with a vee slot and a hammer. The saw-tooth is located against the vee slot and the hammer is pushed against the tooth by depressing the movable arm. The hammer is returned to its open position by the return spring.

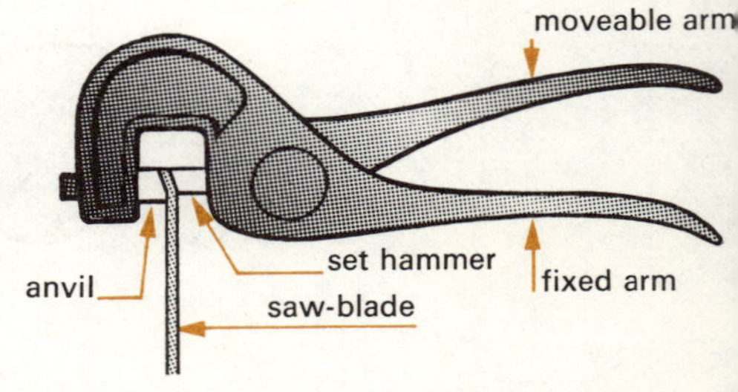

3. Sharpening

When the saw is being sharpened it is held in a vice and each alternate tooth is filed to the correct angle, measured from the side of the blade. The sharpening angle on cross-cut saws used for general purposes is 45°, but saws that are used mainly to cut hardwoods should have a sharpening angle of 60° to give the tooth greater strength. Rip-saw teeth are best sharpened at 90° to the edge of the saw-blade. The direction of work is from the handle of the saw to the front of the saw. When every alternate tooth has been sharpened the saw is reversed in the vice and the remaining teeth sharpened in the same manner as before.

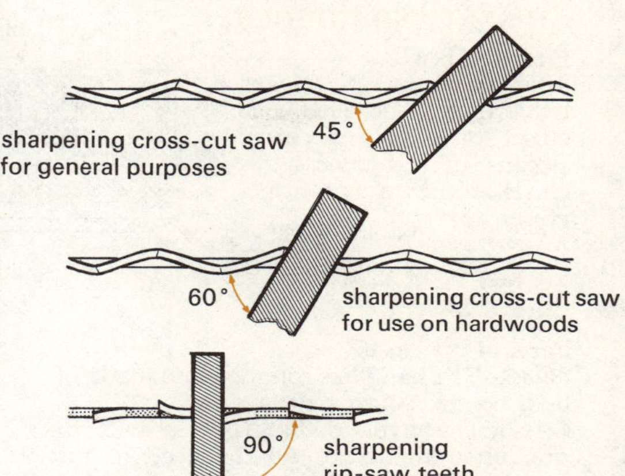

4. Side dressing

This process levels off any slight irregularities that may have been produced when the teeth were being set and sharpened. The saw is laid on its side on a flat surface and an oilstone is run along the edge of the teeth for the entire length of the blade. The saw is turned on to its other side and the oilstone again run down the edge of the teeth. Any burrs or ragging, caused by the action of the file, are smoothed by the oilstone.

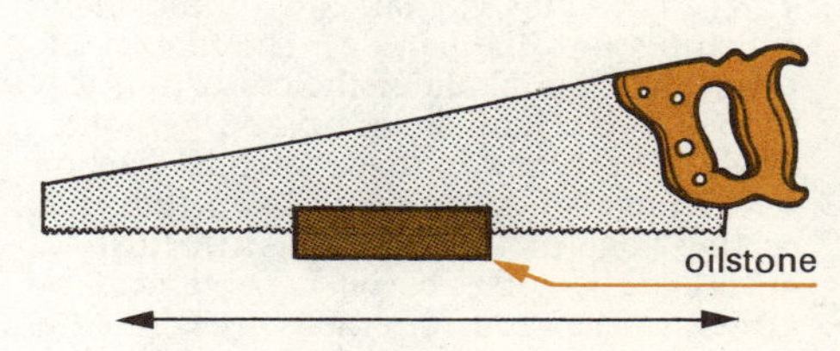

REVISION EXERCISES

1. What is meant by the "set" of a saw?
2. What is meant by "double taper ground"?
3. Sketch the tooth form of a rip-saw and state the gullet angle.
4. Describe the cutting action of a hand-saw or cross-cut saw.
5. What purpose is served by the brass or steel back on a tenon-saw?
6. Sketch and name a saw suitable for cutting curves.
7. Why is the blade of a pad-saw left softer than other saw-blades?
8. How is the waste wood carried away from a saw cut when using a cross-cut saw?
9. Sketch the blade tensioning arrangement of a bow-saw.
10. What is meant by the "kerf" when sawing wood?
11. What could be the cause of the saw jamming in the wood?
12. What precaution should be taken when cross-cutting to prevent the wood from splintering as the waste wood is cut away?
13. Describe the cutting action of a rip-saw.
14. When rip-sawing in the vice, why should the wood be held by the left hand?
15. What is the panel-saw used for?
16. When using a saw, what procedure should be followed to prevent the saw-blade from straying off the cutting line?
17. When would a coping saw be used in preference to a bow-saw?
18. What tooth form has the blade of a compass-saw?
19. What is the name given to the set of blades supplied for a compass-saw?
20. What other name is given to the pad-saw? Can you give a reason for this name?

CHISELS AND GOUGES

Firmer chisel

This chisel has a thicker blade than a bevelled-edge chisel or a paring chisel. Because of its thickness, this chisel is known as a firmer chisel.

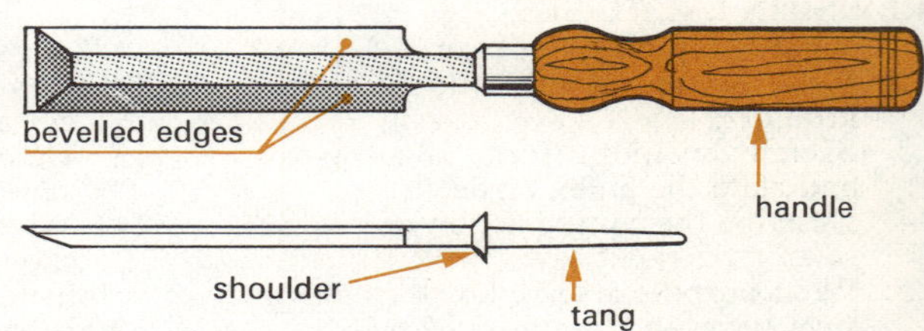

Parts of the chisel

Handle The handle is rounded and made of box, beech, ash or plastic.

Ferrule The ferrule is a brass or steel collar or ring fitted tightly round the neck of the handle. This prevents the handle from splitting when the tang of the chisel is fitted into the handle.

Tang The tang is that end of the blade which fits into the handle. The tang is left softer than the blade of the chisel and it is shaped like a long square-based pyramid.

Blade The blade is made of high carbon steel which is hardened and tempered. The cutting edge of the chisel has two distinct bevels. The first bevel is obtained by grinding the end of the chisel on the grindstone to an angle of 20° to 25°. The second bevel is obtained when the ground chisel edge is sharpened or honed on the oilstone to an angle of about 30°.

Shoulder The shoulder is that part of the chisel immediately behind the tang. Its function is to prevent the tang from being driven too far into the handle.

Size of chisel The size of a chisel is given by its width. The width of a chisel can range from 3 mm to 50 mm.

Uses of a firmer chisel The firmer chisel is used for all general chiselling purposes, e.g. removing the waste wood of various joints, etc. The blade of the firmer chisel is strong and this enables the chisel to accept light blows from a mallet.

Bevelled-edge chisel

The bevelled-edge chisel is lighter than the firmer chisel. The blade is bevelled along its length on both sides.

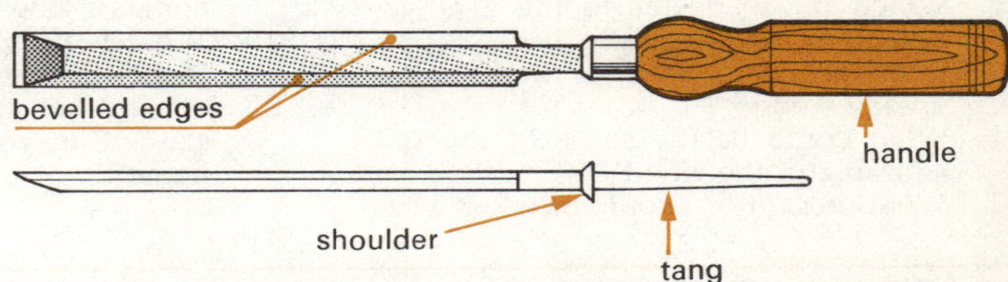

Parts of the chisel

The parts of the bevelled-edge chisel are the same as the parts of the firmer chisel.

Size of chisel The size of this chisel is given by its width. The width of a bevelled-edge chisel can range from 3 mm to 50 mm.

Uses of a bevelled-edge chisel The bevelled-edge chisel is used for light work, particularly the cutting of dovetail joints where the bevelled blade is able to fit between the dovetails.

Paring chisel

The paring chisel has a thinner blade than the firmer or bevelled-edge chisel and is much longer. It is usually bevel-edged.

Parts of the chisel
The parts of the paring chisel are the same as the parts of the firmer and bevelled-edge chisel.

Size of chisel The size of the chisel is given by its width. The widths of paring chisels range from 3 mm to 50 mm.

Uses of a paring chisel This chisel is used for removing the waste wood from long grooves. The paring chisel is a specialist chisel used mainly by engineer's pattern makers. The depths of cuts, and the accuracy required to make the involved shapes necessary for pattern making, make the use of a paring chisel essential.

Mortise chisel
The blade of the mortise chisel is very much thicker and stronger than those of other chisels to prevent twisting in the mortise, and also to enable it to withstand mallet blows and the pressure put on the blade when it is used as a lever to remove the waste wood from mortises.

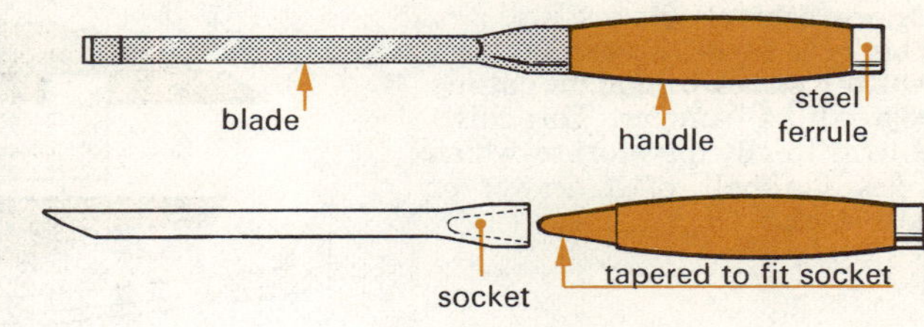

Smaller mortise chisels can have a tang which fits into the handle. A thick leather washer is placed over the tang, between the shoulder of the chisel and the ferrule on the handle, to absorb the shock of the mallet blows. The cone-shaped socket on larger mortise chisels makes for greater strength. Heavier mallet blows can be absorbed by the handle, which has not been weakened by having a hole bored in it to receive the tang of the chisel.

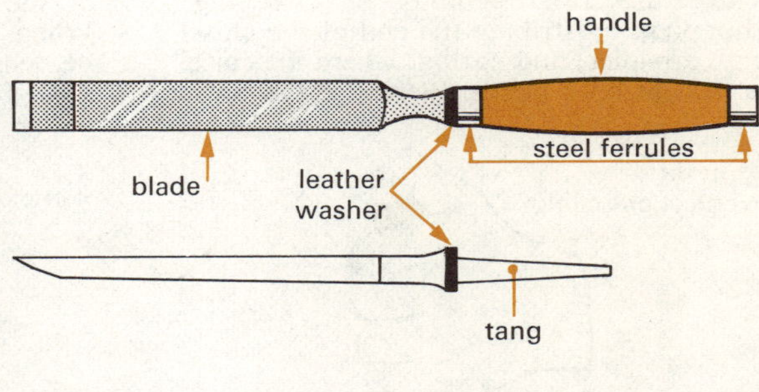

A steel ferrule is fitted to the end of the handle to prevent the handle splitting under the impact of the mallet blows.

Registered chisel
This is a general purpose chisel. It is not as thick as a mortise chisel but it is stronger than the firmer or bevelled-edge chisels. It is intended for use on heavy work, but it is often used to remove mortises. This chisel, like the mortise chisel, is fitted with a steel ferrule on both ends of the handle.

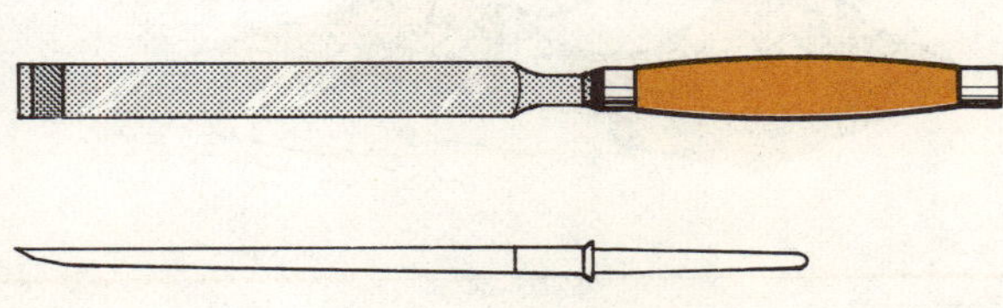

Swan-neck or mortise lock chisel

This chisel is similar in size and thickness to a mortise chisel, but it is forged in such a way that the cutting end is spoon-shaped and curved upwards towards the cutting edge. The swan-neck chisel is used to cut and clean out the deep mortises necessary to hold door locks.

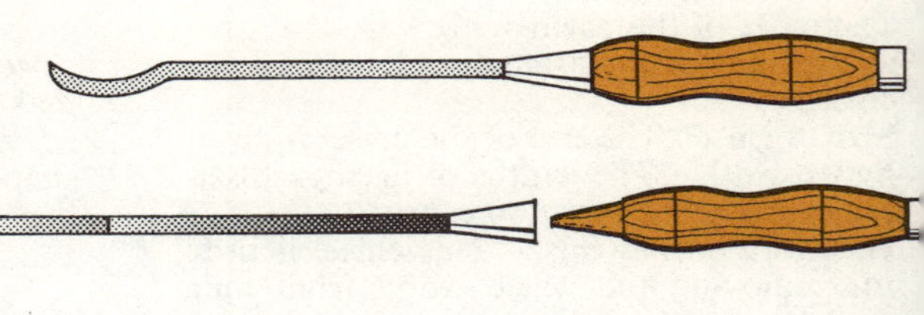

Drawer lock chisel

This is a small, all-metal chisel which is struck behind the cutting edge with a hammer. This chisel is used to cut the mortise which takes the bolt of a drawer or desk lock.

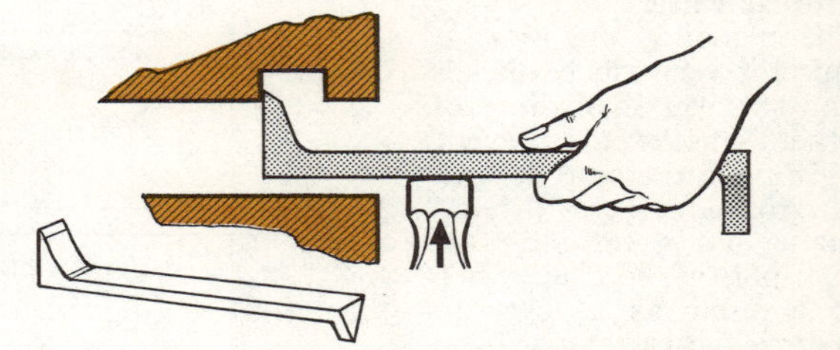

Paring with the chisel

There are two methods of chiselling: chopping, by striking the end of the chisel with a mallet; and paring, where the chisel is held in both hands. Paring is the cause of most accidents when using a chisel. When paring, both hands should always be behind the cutting edge of the chisel.

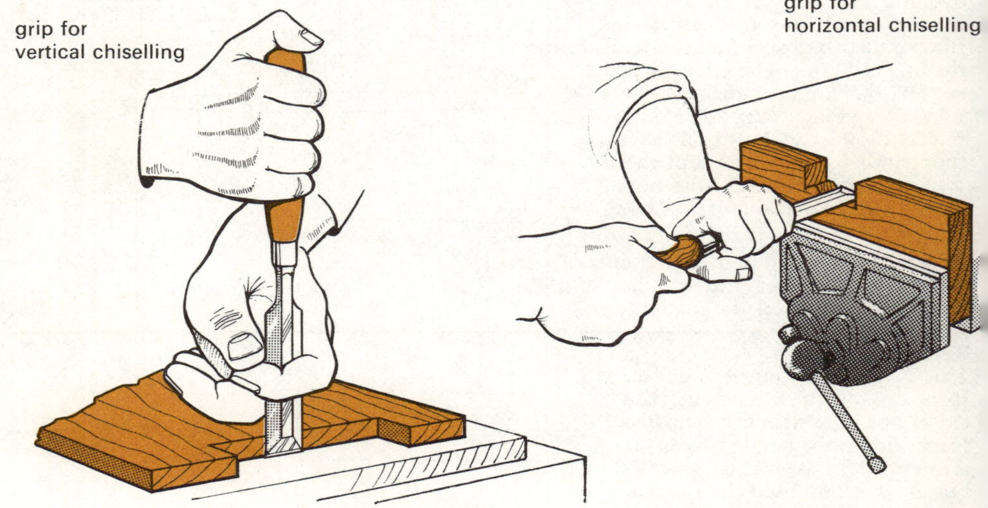

Gouges

Gouges are used for grooving, fluting and cutting out diameters, hollows and depressions in wood.

These gouges are: firmer, scribing, crank and spoon. They are measured by the diameter of the curve cut by the gouge. The gouge diameter ranges from 6 mm to 300 mm.

Firmer gouge

The firmer gouge is ground and sharpened on the outside of its diameter. It is used to cut shallow depressions in wood. Small diameter firmer gouges can be used to countersink holes bored in the wood.

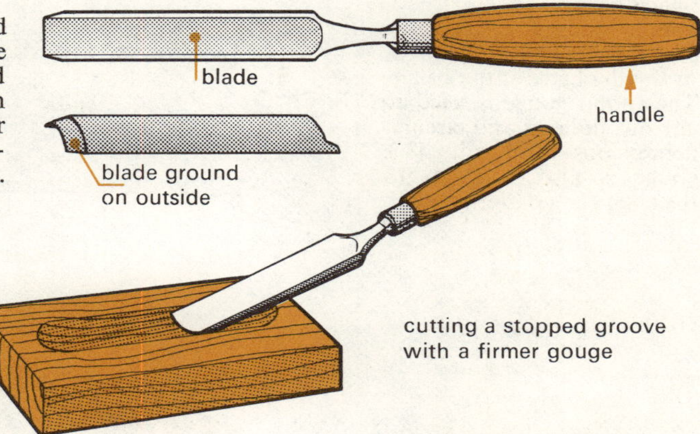

Scribing gouge

The scribing gouge is ground and sharpened on the inside of its diameter. It is used mainly to cut through circular grooves, but it can be used to cut fluted decorations.

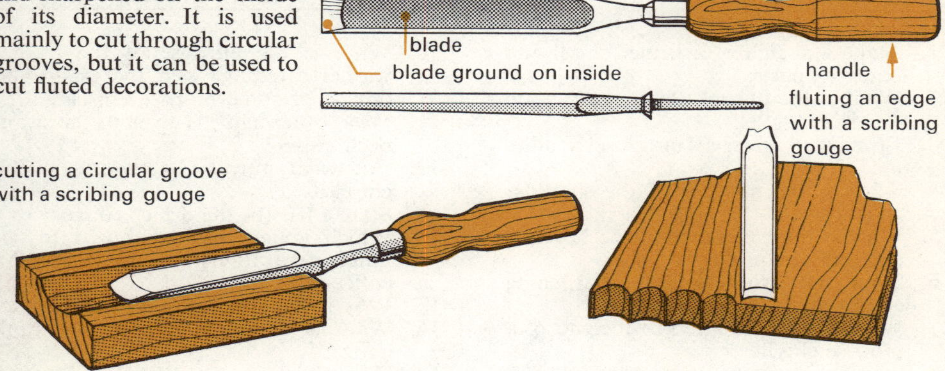

Crank gouge

The crank gouge is ground and sharpened on the inside of its diameter. Because of its bent, or cranked, tang, which lifts the handle clear of the surface of the wood, this gouge can be used to cut long circular grooves. Crank gouges are an essential tool in the engineer's pattern maker's tool kit.

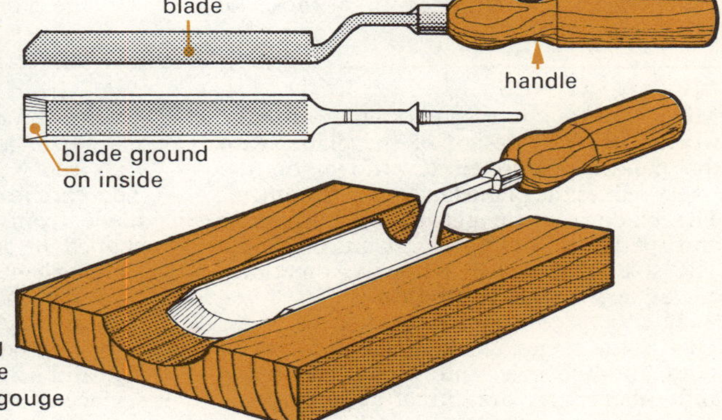

Spoon gouge

Spoon gouges are ground and sharpened on the inside of the diameter of the gouge. The spoon gouge is used to cut out hollows and circular depressions in wood. This gouge is also essential to the engineer's pattern maker.

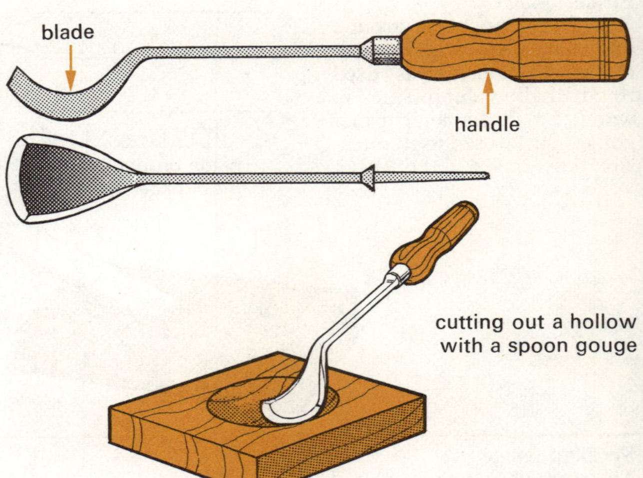

cutting out a hollow with a spoon gouge

REVISION EXERCISES

1. Make a sketch of a firmer chisel and name its parts.
2. What is the purpose of the ferrule on a chisel handle?
3. From what materials are chisel handles made?
4. What is the purpose of the shoulder on a chisel?
5. What is the advantage of the bevelled edges on a chisel?
6. State the grinding and sharpening angles on a chisel.
7. Why is a ferrule fitted to the end of a mortise chisel?
8. State the safety rule when paring with a chisel.
9. Why is the blade of the mortise chisel thicker and stronger than those of other chisels?
10. What is the purpose of the leather washer fitted between the blade and ferrule of some mortise chisels?
11. What other name is given to the swan-neck chisel?
12. For what purpose is the swan-neck chisel used?
13. State a use for the firmer gouge.
14. Which gouge would be used to cut fluted decorations on the edges of a coffee-table?
15. Why is the crank gouge so called?
16. What is the main use of the crank gouge?
17. What is the main use of the spoon gouge?
18. Why is a hammer never used to strike the handle of a chisel or gouge?

METAL PLANES

Metal planes now predominate in the workshop. The design of the plane, with the handle positioned low down on the body, makes the plane fairly easy to control. The blade adjustments are easy to make and the body does not twist out of shape. The sole of the steel plane is sometimes corrugated to reduce friction.

Body

This is the metal block, machined on the sides and the sole, into which the blade and other parts are fitted. The body is made from high quality cast iron, which gives evenness of wear and provides high resistance to twisting.

Cap iron

The cap iron is necessary to prevent the blade from vibrating or chattering. It is shaped in such a way that it diverts the shavings into the body escapement. This prevents the mouth of the plane from choking. A properly fitted cap iron prevents the fibres of the wood from tearing, and so ensures a smooth finish on the surface of the timber.

Blade

The blade is made from tool steel, hardened and tempered. It is held in position on the cap iron by means of a large cheese-head screw. The blade and cap iron must be adjusted correctly for good results. The correct position for the blade in relation to the cap iron varies according to the wood, but the cutting edge of the blade is never more than 2 mm in advance of the edge of the cap iron.

Lever cap

The lever cap retains the blade and cap iron in position in the plane. To release and remove the blade and cap iron, the cam on the lever cap is released by bringing the lever forward.

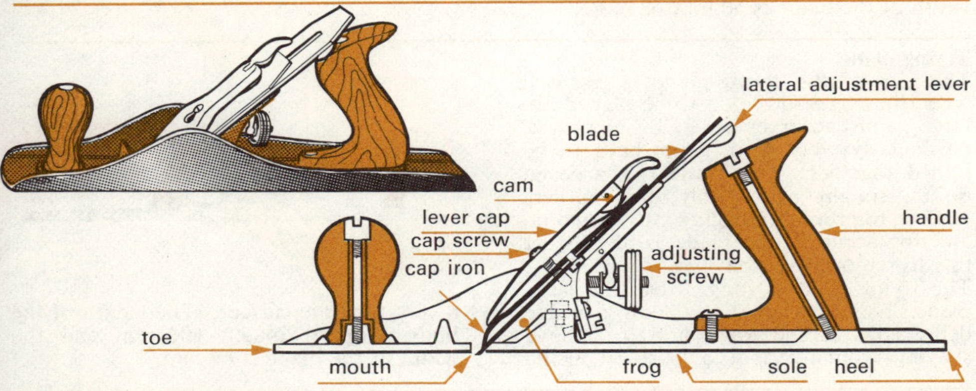

Lateral adjustment lever

This lever permits the blade to be adjusted from side to side (laterally). If one corner of the blade is projecting further out of the mouth of the plane than the other corner, and the blade is not parallel with the sole of the plane, this is corrected by moving the adjustment lever to the same side of the plane. To make sure that the blade is straight in the plane you must look along the sole.

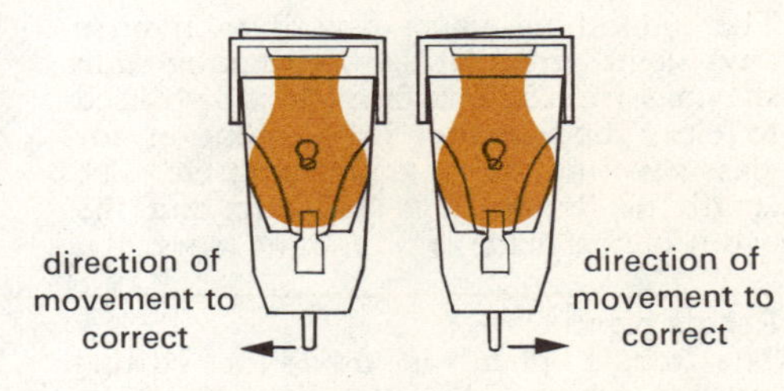

Adjusting screw

The adjusting screw controls the length of blade that protrudes from the sole of the plane, thereby controlling the thickness of the shaving removed from the wood.

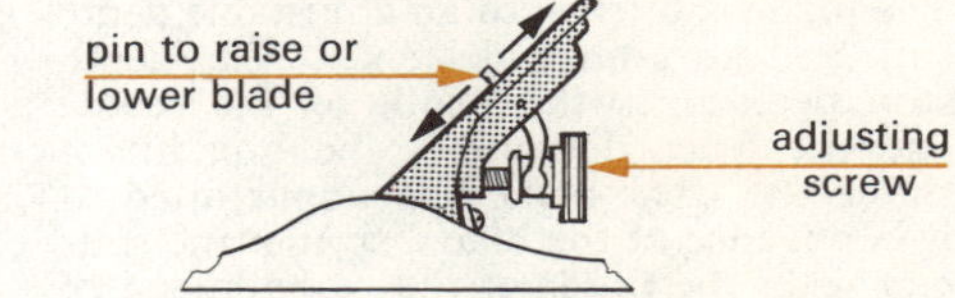

Frog screws

The width from front to back of the mouth of the plane is controlled by the adjustment of the frog screws. The adjustments are made as follows.
(1) Slacken screws B.
(2) Rotate screw A clockwise or anti-clockwise as desired.
(3) Tighten screws B to lock the mouth of the plane in the desired position.

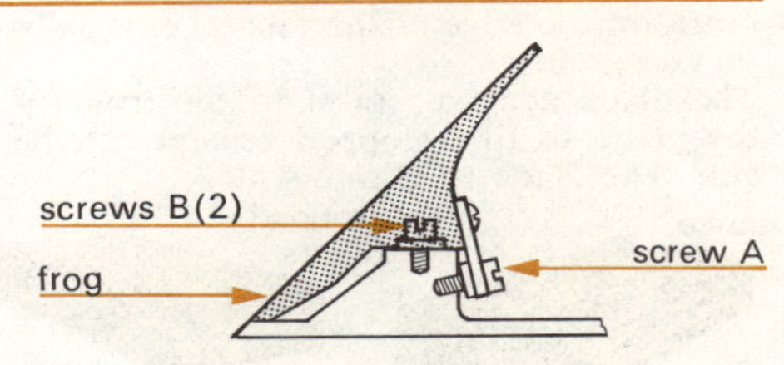

Jack-plane

The name "jack-plane" is derived from the fact that this plane is used for a wide variety of work. It is used to remove marks left on the timber by the saw, to bring timber down to size, to make the surfaces of the timber flat and square and for all other planing operations. The length of the body is approximately 400 mm and the width of the blade is 50 mm or more.

Trying-plane

The use of the trying-plane is essential when the pieces of wood to be planed are large and accuracy is all important, particularly when long edges have to be joined together. The blade is sharpened quite straight with only the corners relieved to prevent it digging into the wood, and for accuracy the blade is always set fine to remove thin shavings.

The trying-plane is longer than the jack-plane. This extra length enables it to bridge depressions in the wood and to remove shavings from high spots only, so producing a very accurate surface. The length of the body is approximately 600 mm and the width of the blade is 60 mm.

Smoothing-plane

The smoothing-plane is used to remove any slight irregularities by taking thin shavings from the surface. It is also used to clean up surfaces in preparation for glass-papering, staining, polishing, etc. The length of the body is 230 mm and the width of the blade is 50 mm or more.

Rebate plane

The rebate plane is used for cutting recesses (rebates) along the edges of timber. The plane is fitted with an adjustable depth stop and an adjustable fence. The depth stop determines the depth of the rebate and the fence determines the breadth of the rebate. The plane has a spur fitted to it in advance of the blade, so that the spur can sever the fibres of the wood ahead of the blade. This provides a clean-cut finish on the edge of the rebate, especially on end grain.

The blade can be moved to the front of the plane so that stopped rebates can be cut. The blade is 25 mm wide.

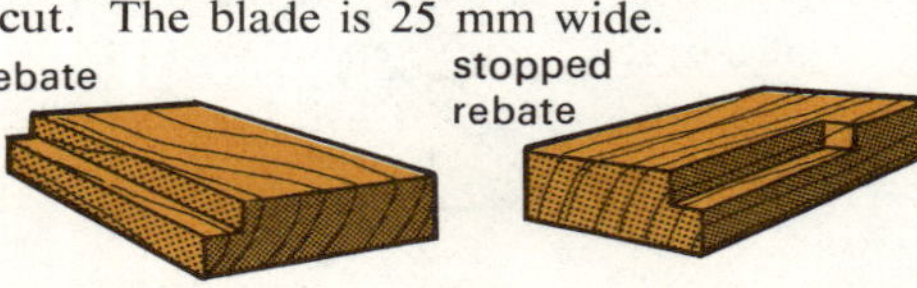

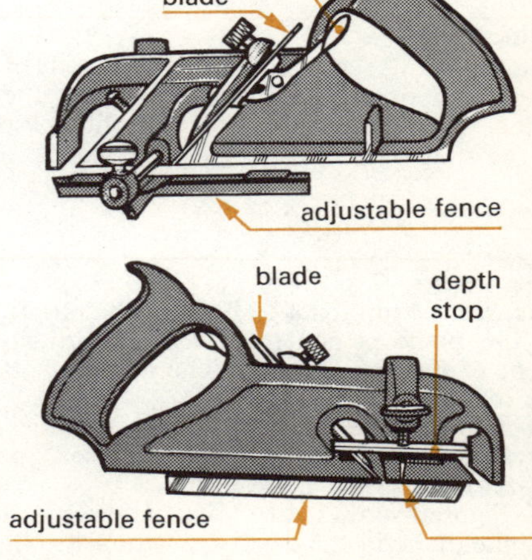

Plough plane

The plough plane is used for cutting grooves. It is supplied with blades of varying widths ranging from 3 mm to 15 mm. The position and depth of the groove to be cut are determined by the settings of the adjustable fence and the depth stop respectively.

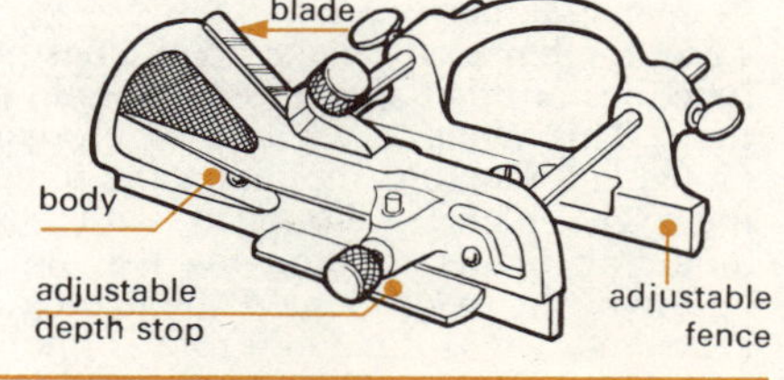

Shoulder plane

This small plane is used mainly to trim the shoulders of tenon joints where a good fit is required. The blade is set at a very low angle with the ground bevel facing uppermost.

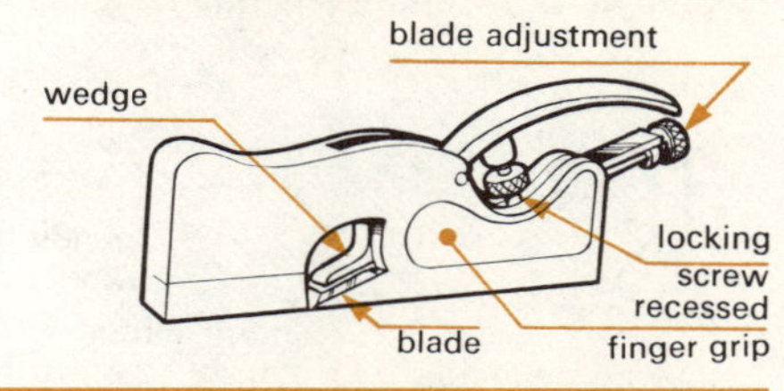

Block plane

The block plane is used for small, fine pieces of work calling for a high degree of accuracy. It is especially suitable for fitting mitres. As with the shoulder plane, the blade of the block plane is set with the ground bevel uppermost and at a low angle, making this plane most useful on end grain.

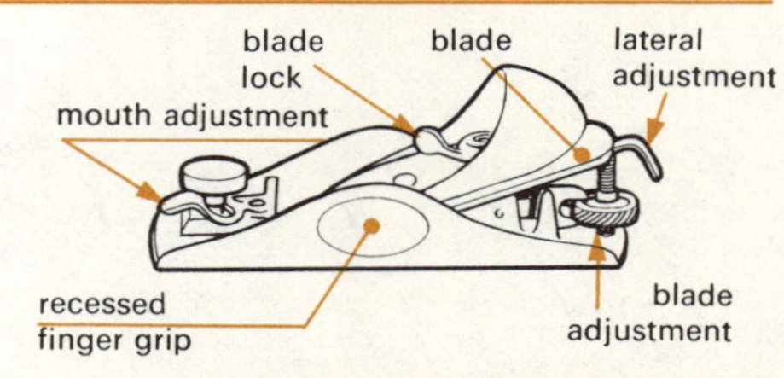

Router plane

The router plane is used to clean out and level off the bottom of trenches. It is supplied with a set of blades of various widths, ranging from 5 mm to 12 mm. The wooden counterpart of the router plane, known as the "old woman's tooth", is still widely used.

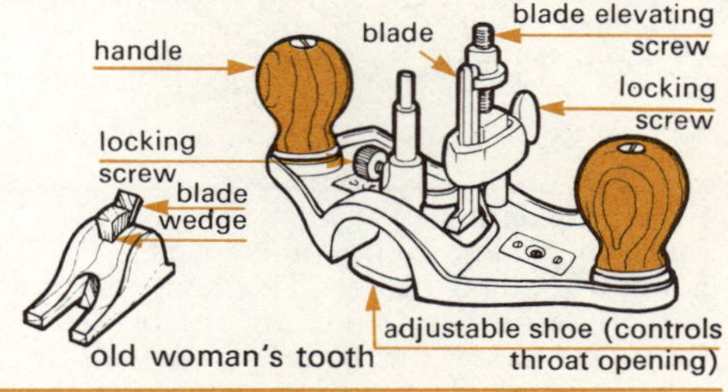

Bull-nosed plane

This is a small plane, 75 mm to 100 mm in length, with the blade fixed close to the toe of the plane. This permits the plane to be used close up to the ends of chamfers and stopped rebates.

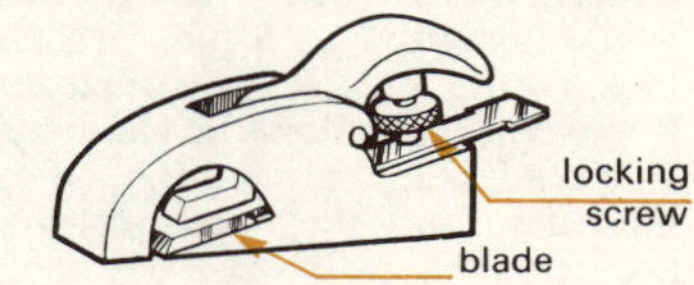

Compass plane

The sole of the compass plane is a thin, flexible metal plate and its curve can be adjusted by means of a screw. This enables the sole of the plane to be adjusted to accommodate different curves of sweeps.

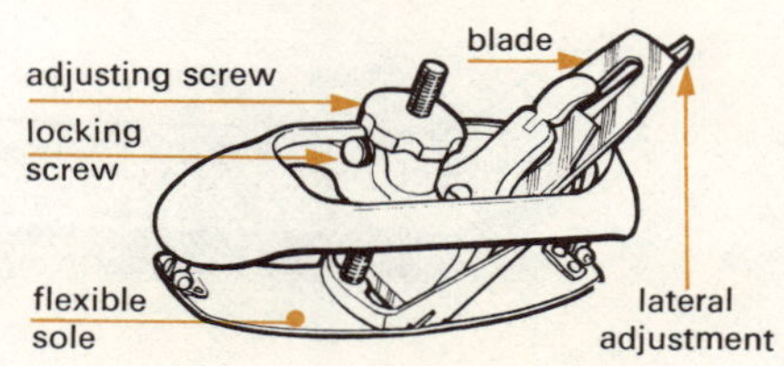

Combination plane
The combination plane combines the functions of other specialised planes in one tool. This plane is capable of grooving, ploughing, rebating, moulding and tongueing. The plane is supplied with seven moulding blades ranging from 3 mm to 12 mm in width, nine ploughing or grooving blades ranging from 3 mm to 20 mm in width, and three tongueing blades.

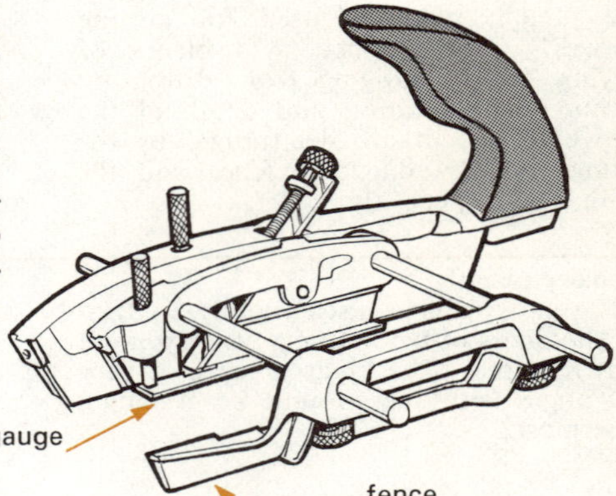

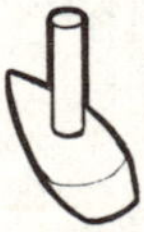

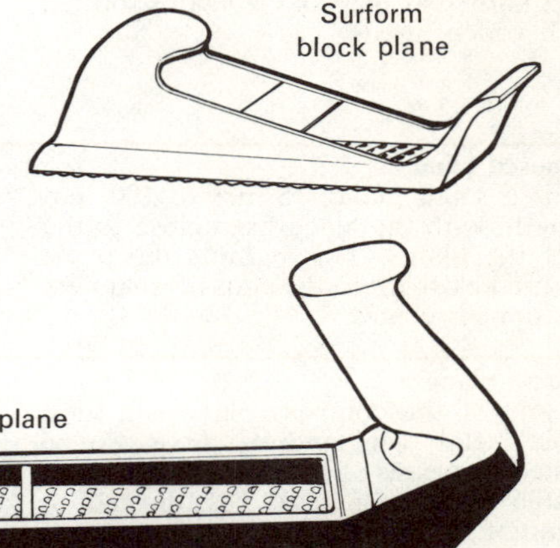

shaving deflector for use with tongueing cutter

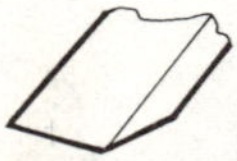

plough cutter (3 mm to 12 mm)

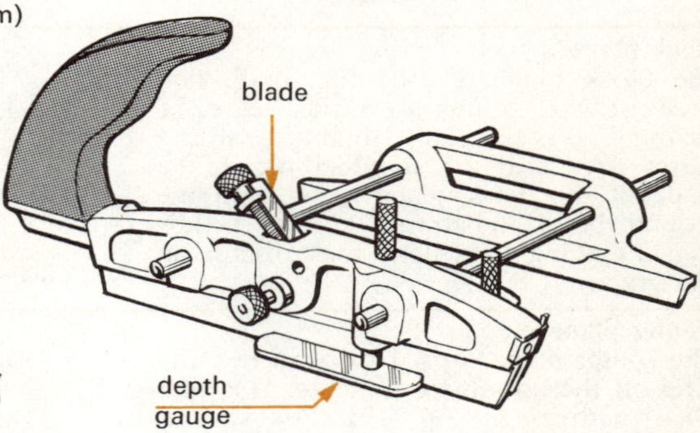

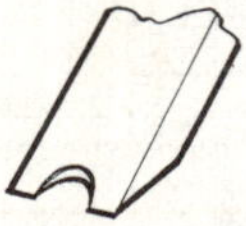

beading cutter (3 mm to 12 mm)

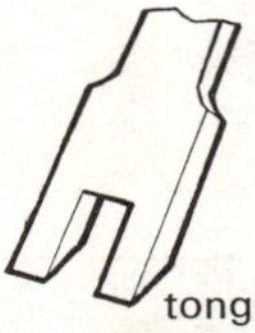

tongueing cutter (3 mm, 4 mm, 6 mm)

Surform planes
Surform planes, unlike other planes, have a multi-toothed blade. The body of the plane is a hollow frame and the blade of the plane takes the place of the sole in other planes. The cutting surface of the blade is similar to a file with many chisel-like teeth, but it is constructed like a honeycomb to allow the shavings to escape. The blades can cut wood, plastic, metal and masonry, and they are not sharpened, as are other plane blades, but replaced when necessary.

Surform block plane

standard Surform plane

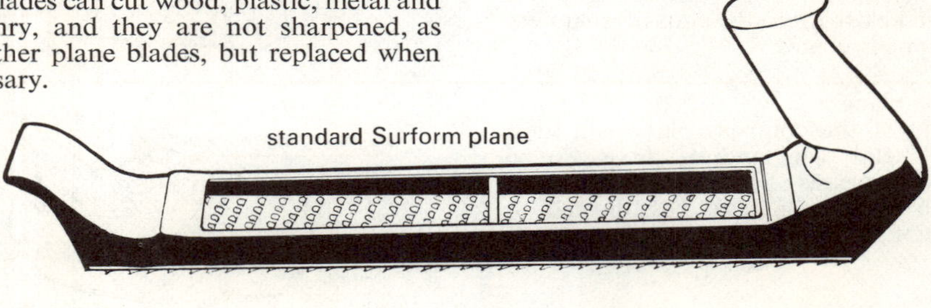

Planing procedure

To plane straight and flat, the forces on the plane must be such that the blade of the plane is not allowed to cut upwards at the beginning of the stroke or downwards at the end of the stroke.

At the start of the stroke, the nose of the plane is firmly held down with the left hand and the right hand pushes the plane along the surface of the wood.

At the end of the stroke, the left hand relaxes the downward force and when the plane blade passes the end of the wood the left hand lifts the front of the plane.

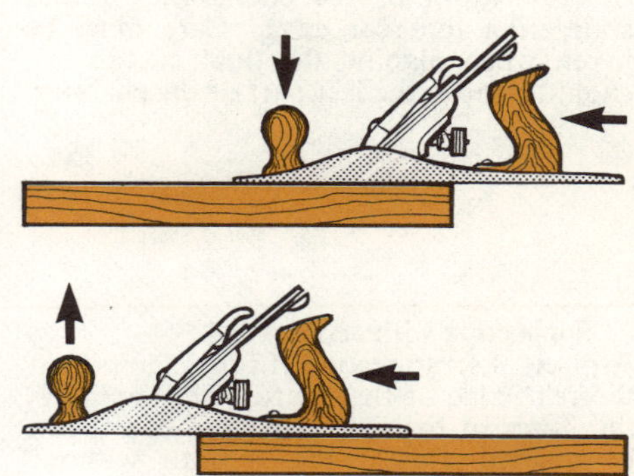

Common faults

The wood starts to taper at the beginning of the stroke because the nose of the plane is not being held down.

The wood starts to taper at the end of the stroke because the nose of the plane is not being lifted.

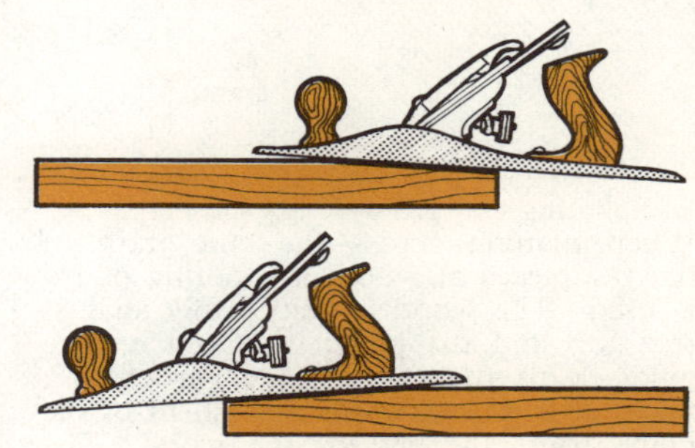

Planing end grain

Due to the structure of timber it is impracticable to plane end grain from one edge to the other in one continuous stroke. When end grain is planed across its full width the rear edge will splinter. This can be avoided in one of several ways.

1. Planing from either edge

The board is planed part way across and then reversed and planed part way from the other edge. The high spot in the centre of the board end can then be planed down without splitting either edge.

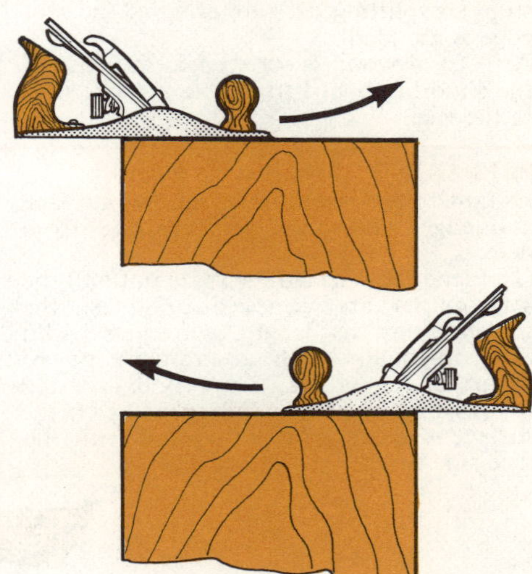

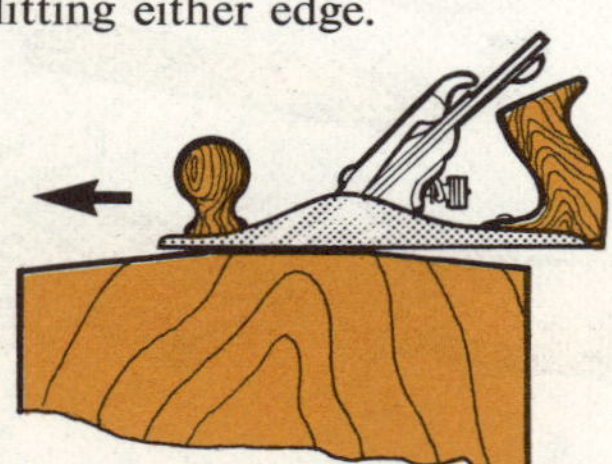

2. Cutting a chamfer

A chamfer is cut on the rear edge of the board. This enables the plane to cut across the full width of the end grain without splintering the rear edge. Care must be taken when planing the final cut as this should remove the last part of the chamfer.

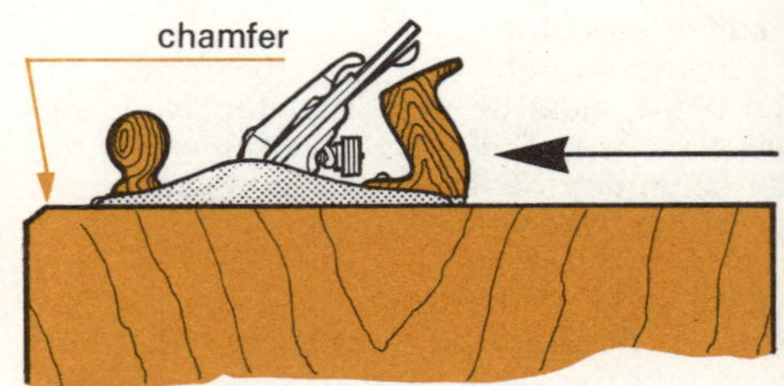

3. Supporting with scrap wood

A piece of scrap wood is firmly clamped to the rear edge of the board. This supports the fibres of the wood and the board can be planed for its full width without splintering on the rear edge.

4. Shooting end grain

When planing across the end grain of narrow pieces of wood, a shooting board is used. The wood is held firmly against the stop and the plane is placed on the guide, with the plane blade vertical. A backwards and forwards movement of the plane trims the end of the wood. The fibres of the wood are supported by the stop, so splitting or splintering at the rear edge is avoided.

A piece of wood is screwed to the base of the shooting board to enable it to be held in the vice.

PREPARING TIMBER TO SIZE

Examine the timber and select the best face and edge, i.e. those that are free from defects.

(1) Plane the selected face side until all the saw marks are removed and test the timber along its length, across its width and diagonally with a straight-edge to ensure that it is flat. The wood is tested for twisting by using winding sticks. If the surface is accurate, it is marked with the face side mark.

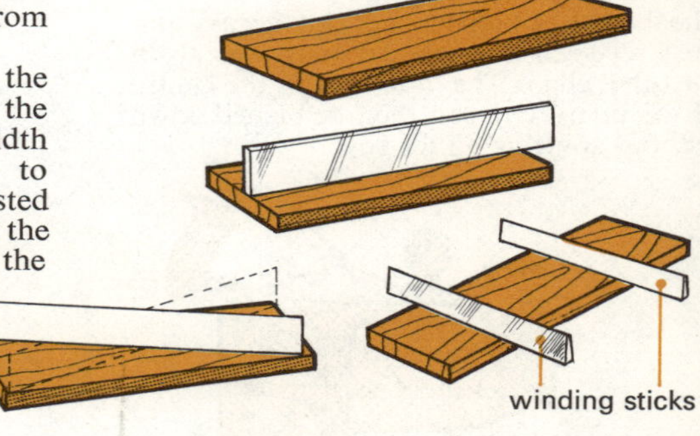

(2) Plane the face edge and test for straightness lengthwise with a straight-edge, and for squareness to the face side with a try-square. If the edge is accurate, mark it with the face edge mark.

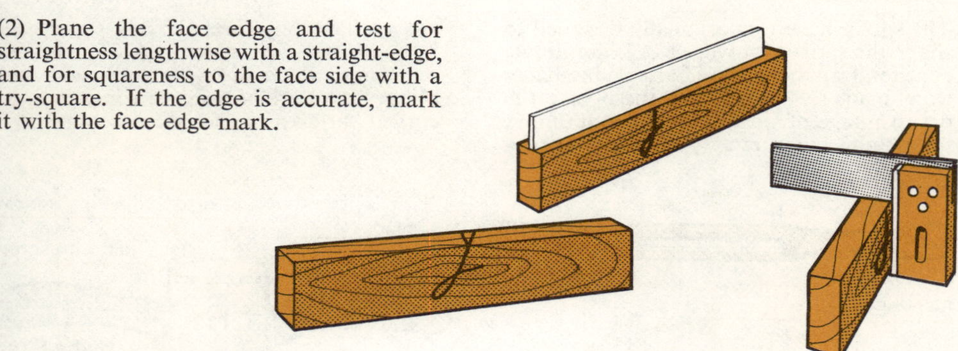

(3) Set the marking gauge to the required width and, holding the stock firmly against the face edge, mark the width on both sides of the wood. Plane off the excess timber down to the gauge line and test for straightness lengthwise with the straight-edge and for squareness with the try-square from the face side.

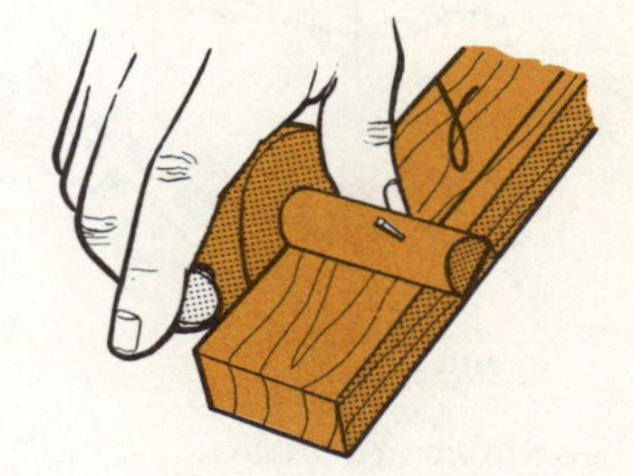

(4) Set the marking gauge to the required thickness and, holding the stock firmly against the face side, mark the thickness on both edges of the wood. Plane off the excess timber down to the gauge line, and test for straightness with the straight-edge and for squareness with the try-square from the face edge.

(5) Plane one end of the wood using a trying-plane and a shooting board. From this planed end mark off the required length, squaring the line round on all four surfaces. Saw off the waste wood and plane the end down to the line using the trying-plane and shooting board.

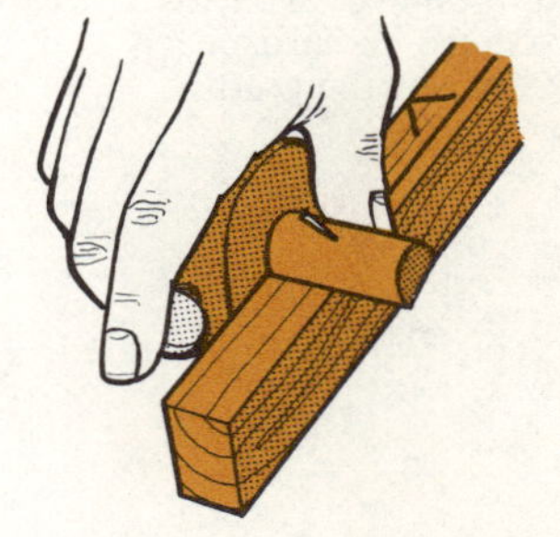

SPOKESHAVES

The spokeshave was originally designed to shape the spokes for wheels of horse-drawn coaches, farm carts, etc. Early spokeshaves were made of wood, but these had the disadvantage of wearing at the mouth and becoming inaccurate. Wooden spoke-shaves have now been largely superseded by the metal type which has a fine adjustment and which does not wear with use. Spokeshaves are now used mainly to finish curved surfaces to the desired contour.

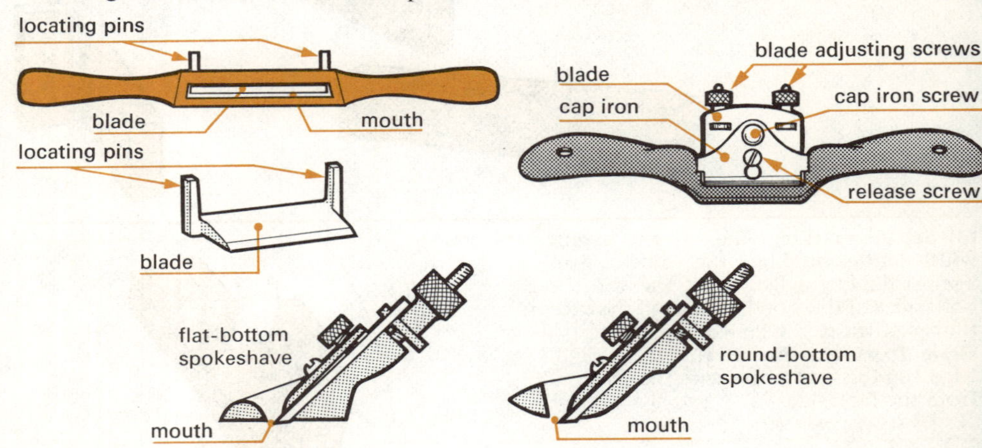

Using a flat-bottom spokeshave
Cutting an outside (convex) curve using a flat-bottom spokeshave. The workpiece is cut from its centre towards each end to avoid cutting against the grain.

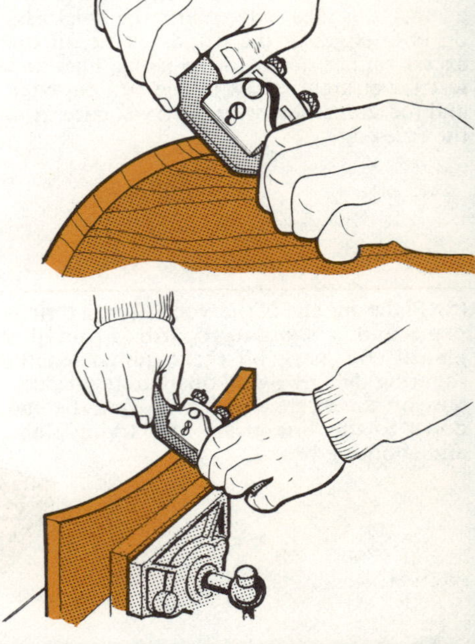

Using a round-bottom spokeshave
Cutting an inside (concave) curve using a round-bottom spokeshave. The workpiece is cut from each end towards its centre to avoid cutting against the grain.

Scrapers produce a very good finish and are indispensable for working on wood which has an irregular grain structure.

Hand scraper

The hand scraper is simply a flat piece of high carbon steel, hardened and tempered. The width of the scraper is 75 mm and the cutting edges are 125 mm long. The scraper is held in both hands and is pushed or pulled over the surface of the wood, removing very fine shavings.

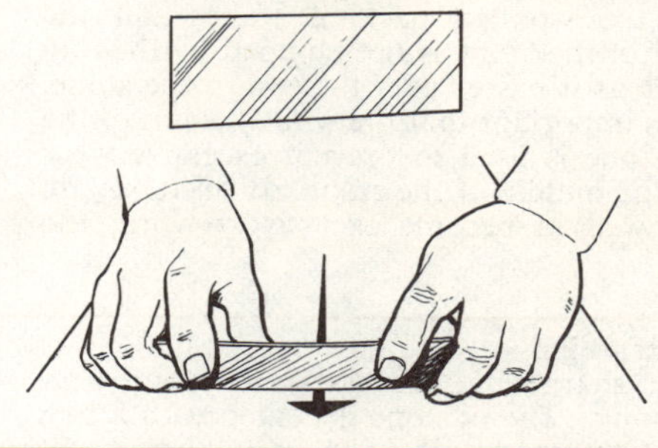

Cabinet scraper

The scraper blade is fitted into a two-handled metal stock. The blade adjusting screw permits a limited amount of curvature to the blade which makes the tool much easier to control. Its uses are the same as those of the hand scraper.

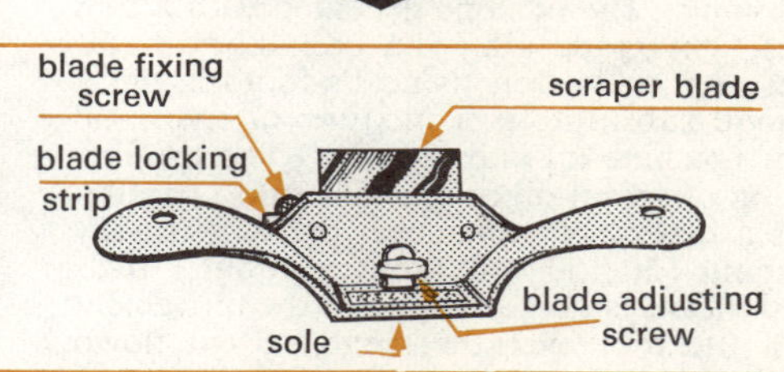

OILSTONES

Oilstones are used to cut a keen edge on cutting tools after they have been ground on the grindstone. There are two kinds of oilstone; artificial stones and natural stones.

Artificial oilstones are made from abrasive grits bonded together under pressure and high temperature and shaped to suit a specific purpose. Bench oilstones are rectangular in shape. Slipstones have various sections for sharpening gouges, carving tools, and grooving, tongueing and beading cutters. The most common of the artificial oilstones are India and carborundum, and these are obtained in coarse, medium or fine grades. Some artificial oilstones are double-sided, with one side of the oilstone coarse, or medium, grade and the other side fine grade. These are called combination oilstones.

Natural oilstones, such as Turkey, Arkansas and Washita, are named after the locality where they are obtained. Natural oilstones are expensive, and as they are not man-made they can vary in quality.

Oilstones are a vital part of a woodworker's tool kit. To obtain first-class service from an oilstone it must be protected from misuse or careless handling. It should be housed in a wooden box with

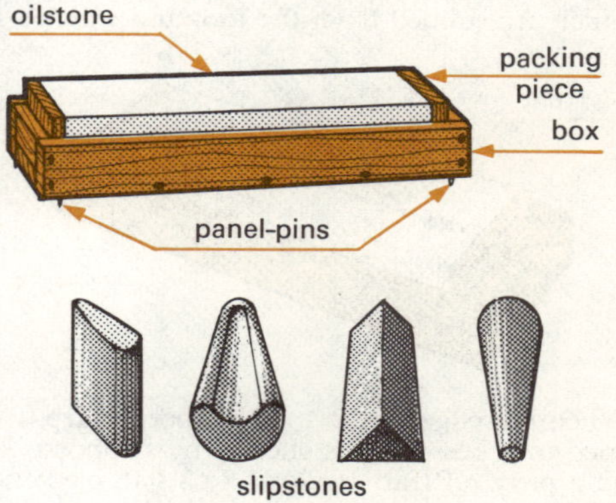

a lid to prevent damage to the stone and to keep it dust-free. The oilstone box should have panel-pins protruding from the bottom of the box at each corner. These panel-pins grip the surface of the work-bench and keep the oilstone steady while it is being used. So that the whole length of the oilstone can be used without damage to the stone or the tool being sharpened, pieces of hardwood are fixed at both ends of the stone, end grain level with the surface of the stone. When the tool, e.g. a chisel or plane blade, reaches the end of the stone, the tool edge is not damaged by the wooden packing piece, and the end of the stone is not chipped by the tool edge as it passes over the end of the stone. It is important that the whole length of the oilstone is used to prevent excessive wear in the middle of the stone. If oilstones are allowed to become excessively worn, the cutting edges of tools cannot be sharpened properly as the tool cannot be placed flat on the hollowed stone. Oilstones which are worn hollow can be flattened by rubbing the stone on a sheet of coarse emery cloth placed on a flat surface, or by rubbing the stone on a flat paving slab, using water and sand as the grinding medium.

Sharpening

The sharpening process is also known as honing. The oilstone is coated with a film of light grade oil. The best lubricant to use on an oilstone is neat's-foot oil, but a good substitute is a mixture of sperm-oil or machine oil and paraffin. The proportion of sperm-oil or machine oil to paraffin is a matter of preference, but it is usually about 50 : 50 oil and paraffin. This lubricant is necessary to aid the movement of the tool over the stone, to cut down friction and so reduce wear on the stone, and to wash away the particles of steel which are rubbed from the tool and which would clog the stone and give it a glazed and shiny surface, destroying its abrasive quality.

When sharpening, the tool is held on the oilstone at the sharpening angle of 30°, and rubbed over the stone from end to end. As the edge of the tool is rubbed, particles of steel appear on the edge in the shape of a wire. This wire edge must be removed. The tool is turned over and the flat side of the tool is placed flat on the oilstone and rubbed. It is important that the full length of the stone is used to remove the wire edge.

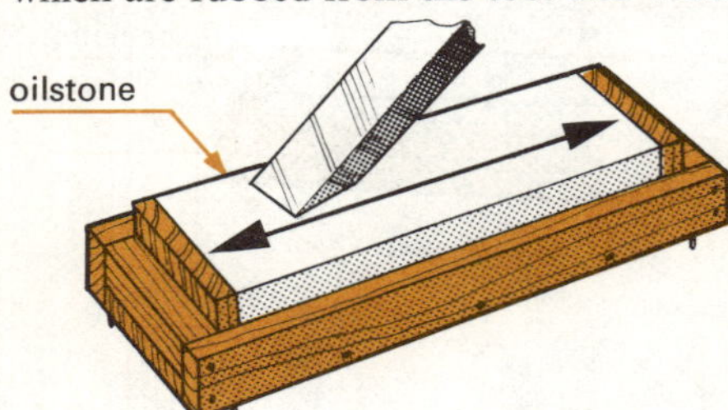

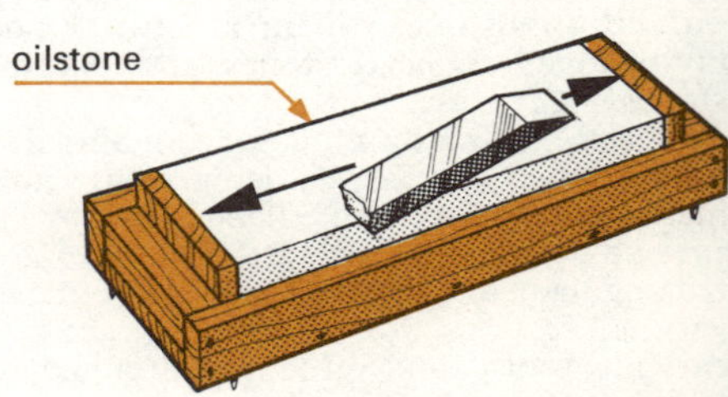

When the edge of the tool has been sharpened to a keen edge it should be stropped on a piece of leather glued to a flat piece of wood. This stropping removes any particles of the wire edge that may remain after honing.

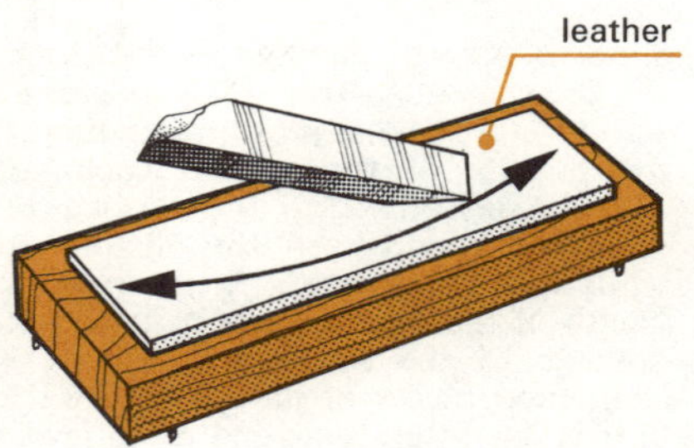

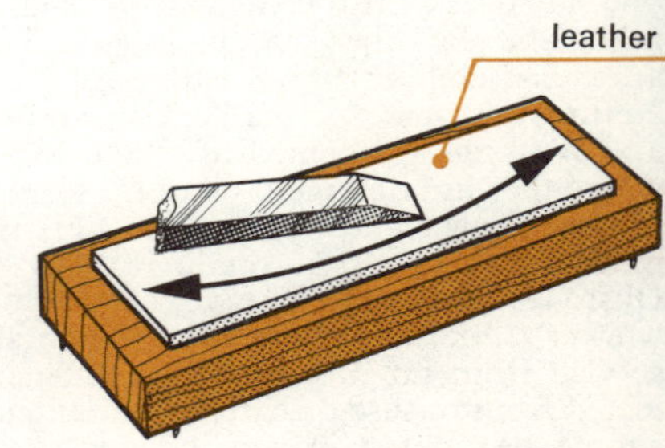

1. Give a possible reason for the mouth of a plane becoming choked.
2. What is the ideal distance from the cap iron edge to the blade cutting edge?
3. On an all-metal plane, what is the lever cap?
4. Which plane would you use to true a long edge or surface?
5. What is the purpose of the lateral adjustment lever?
6. In an all-metal plane, how can the thickness of the shavings be controlled?
7. What are frog screws used for?
8. Describe the uses of the smoothing-plane, bull-nose plane and jack-plane.
9. What is the function of the spur on a rebate plane?
10. Which plane is used to level off the bottom of a trench? Name its wooden counterpart.
11. What is the basic difference between Surform planes and standard planes?
12. When planing a piece of wood, what would cause the wood to taper at the start of the planing stroke?
13. How can tapering at the end of the stroke be avoided?
14. What is the danger in planing end grain across the full width of the board?
15. Describe briefly a method of planing end grain so as not to damage the wood.
16. State the stages of work when planing a piece of wood to size.
17. Sketch a metal spokeshave and name its parts.
18. What is the main disadvantage of the wooden spokeshave?
19. What tool is used to obtain a good finish on wood which has a difficult grain structure?

BORING TOOLS

Crank brace

The crank brace is used to hold and turn the various boring bits. At one end of the crank the head of the brace rotates on a ball-bearing washer in order to reduce friction. The other end of the crank accommodates the chuck which contains the two jaws which hold the bit. The chuck is attached to the brace by means of a threaded core on the end of the crank. The sweep of the crank for different braces can vary, but the most common size is 250 mm. The best type of brace is fitted with a ratchet. This enables the brace to be used in a confined space where it would be impossible to make a complete revolution of the crank.

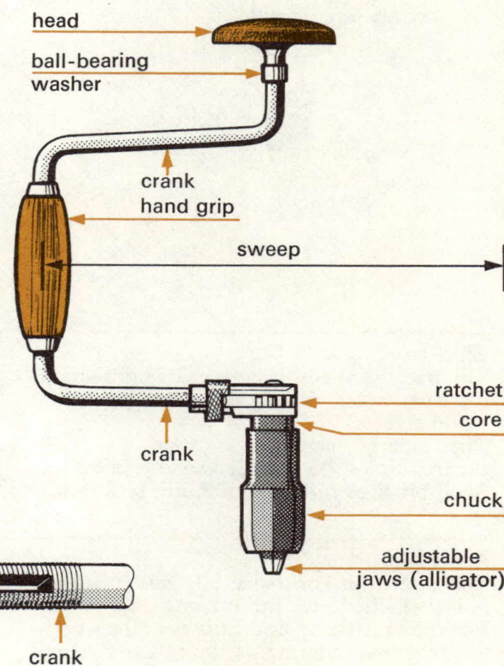

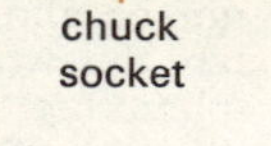

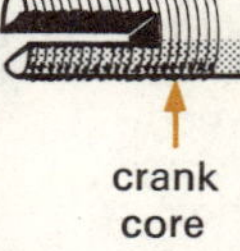

Wheel brace and breast-drill

Both the wheel brace and the breast-drill are used with parallel shank drills (engineer's type). The capacity of the wheel brace is up to 6 mm, and the capacity of the breast-drill is up to 12 mm.

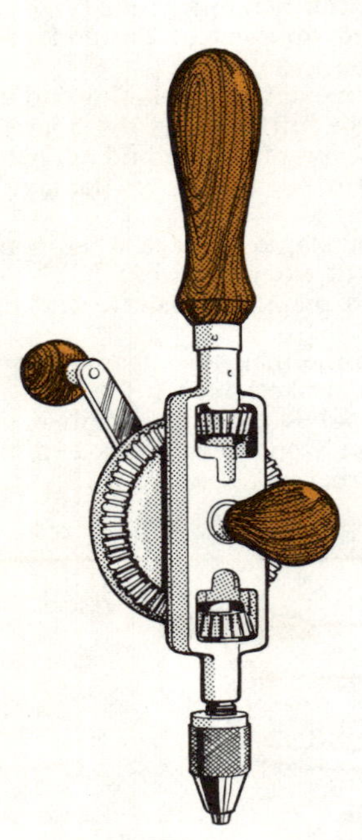

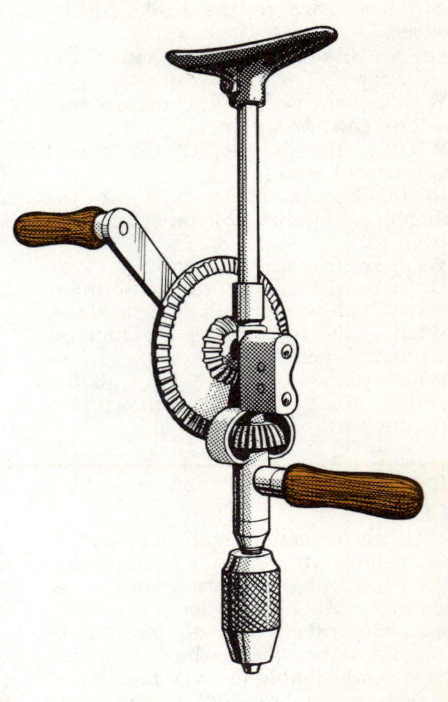

Shell-bits

The parallel shell-bit is used to bore small diameter holes, mainly clearance holes for wood-screws.

The tapered shell-bit is used to bore tapered holes, or enlarge existing holes.

Shell-bit sizes range from 3 mm to 8 mm.

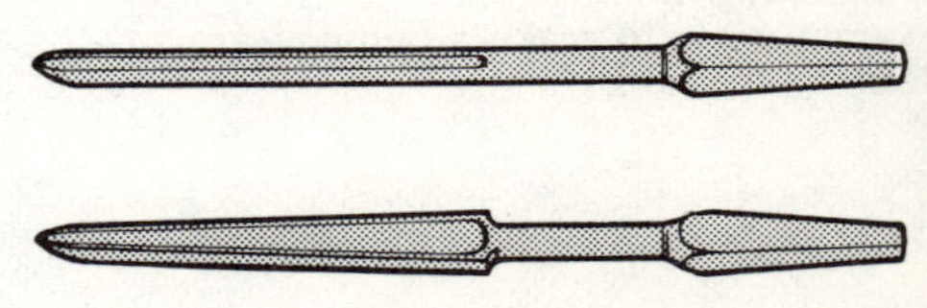

Auger bits

The auger bit, or twist bit, has a spiral point which draws the bit into the wood.

The spur cutters sever the fibres of the wood to prevent splintering as the router cutters remove the waste wood from the hole. This bit is used to bore deep holes, and it is especially useful when boring in end grain as the parallel sides of the bit prevent the point from straying off centre.

When boring right through a piece of timber, the bit should not be allowed to break completely through the wood, as this will cause severe splintering. When the spiral point appears through the wood the workpiece should be reversed and the point of the bit located in the position where the spiral point first appeared

through the timber. The remainder of the hole can then be bored out.
Auger bit sizes range from 3 mm to 30 mm.

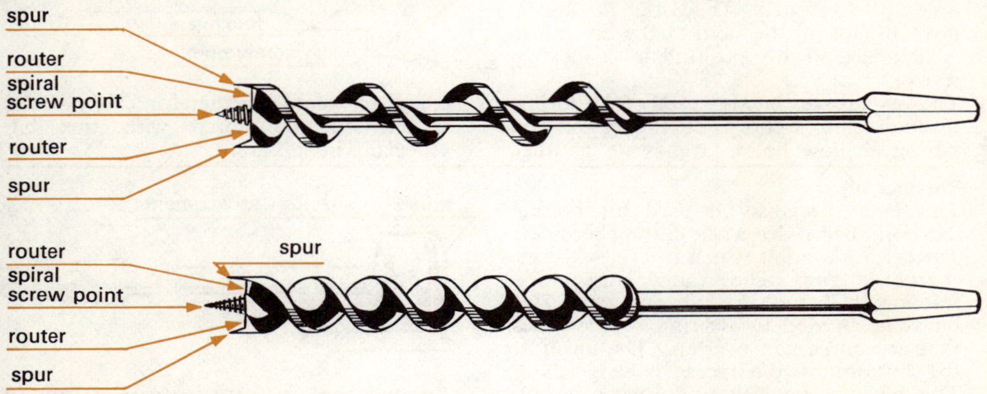

Solid nose auger bit

This is a specialist bit, used for heavy boring. It is excellent for boring at an angle, as the design of the nose allows the screw point to get a good start at the beginning of the boring operation. This bit does not have spurs to sever the fibres, therefore the hole being bored is not as cleanly cut as one bored with a bit that has spurs. This lack of clean cutting is more pronounced when boring across the grain. Solid nose auger bit sizes range from 3 mm to 30 mm.

Centre-bits

The centre-bit has a centre upon which the bit revolves, a spur to sever the fibres and a router to remove the waste wood.

The centre can be triangular in shape or it can be a screw point. The triangular point cuts its way into the wood and the screw point screws its way into the wood.

The centre-bit is used chiefly to bore through thin sections of timber, or when boring shallow holes. Deep holes should not be bored with a centre-bit as the bit tends to wander off centre, especially in end grain. This is because the bit does not have parallel sides to guide it.

When drilling a through hole, the procedure is the same as when using an auger bit. When the point appears through the wood, the workpiece is reversed and the hole bored out from the reverse side.

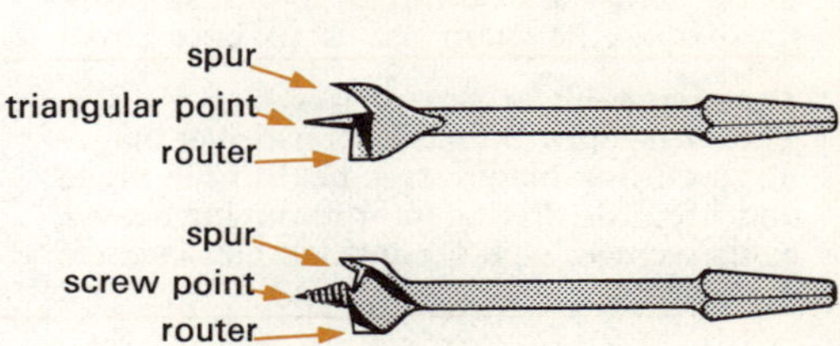

An alternative method, when boring a through hole, is to place a piece of scrap wood directly behind the workpiece where the hole has to be bored. The bit can bore through the workpiece directly into the scrap wood and, if care is exercised, the bit will leave a clean, unsplintered edge where it leaves the workpiece.

Centre-bit sizes range from 6 mm to 50 mm.

Expansive bit

The cutting action of the expansive bit is similar to that of the centre-bit. This bit is supplied with a set of adjustable cutters which can be set to cut any diameter of hole up to 150 mm. The cutter fits into a dovetail slot on the stem of the bit and it is tightened in any position by a locking screw.

The expansive bit is used for boring through thin sections of timber or for boring shallow holes. It has no parallel edges to guide it, therefore deep holes should not be bored with this bit, especially in end grain.

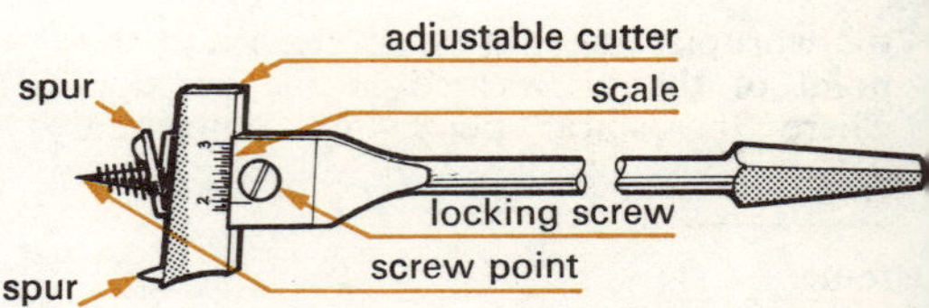

Forstner bit

This is a specialist bit used for boring flat-bottomed holes when cutting recesses. The bit has a point which is level with the sharpened rim. The router cutters are fractionally below the rim and pin. The bit is positioned by its rim, so the holes that are bored can overlap. The finish at the bottom of the recess is very good. This bit is particularly useful when boring holes at an angle.

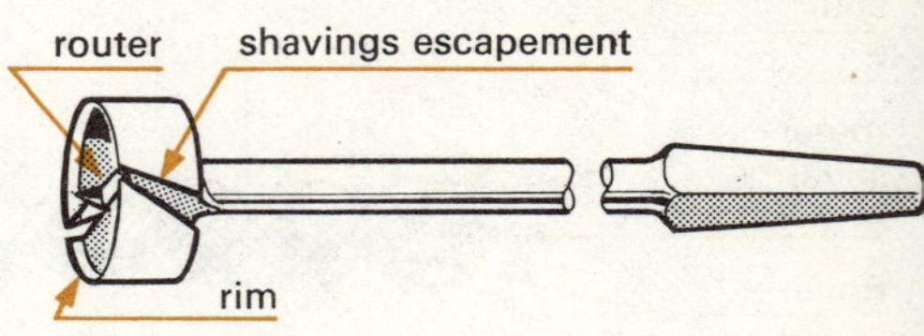

Forstner bit sizes range from 8 mm to 50 mm.

Gimlet

The gimlet is not much used in woodwork. In practice, its main use is to bore holes for screws. It can be used to bore holes in a confined space where it would be difficult to use a brace and bit. The cutting action of the gimlet is similar to that of the auger bit.

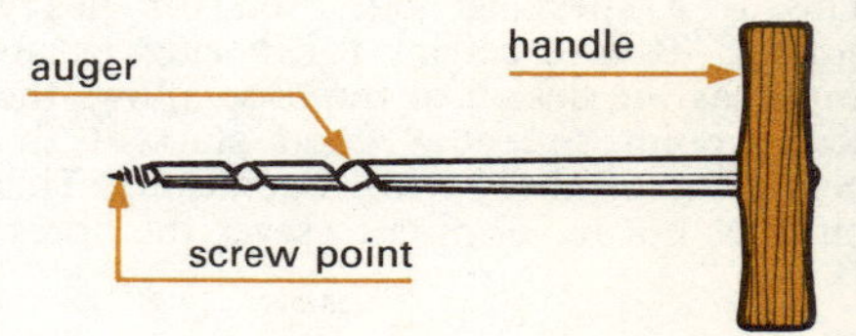

Bradawl

The bradawl boring tool is hand-held. It is rotated and pushed through the wood. Care must be taken to start it with the blade across the grain to avoid splitting the wood. Its main use is to bore small holes for nails, and pilot holes for small screws.

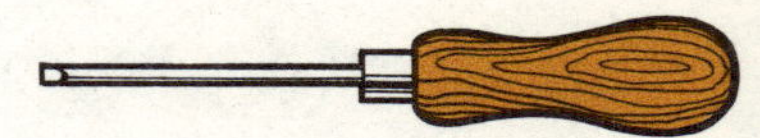

Turn-screw bit or screwdriver bit

The turn-screw bit has a screwdriver blade, not a cutting blade. It is held in the brace and used for driving in or removing heavy-gauge screws where considerable leverage is needed.

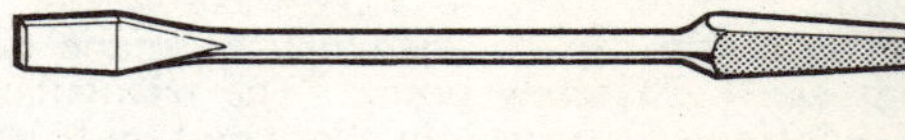

Countersink bits

These bits are used to countersink holes to accept the heads of countersunk screws. The choice of bit head is one of personal preference as all three are equally efficient.

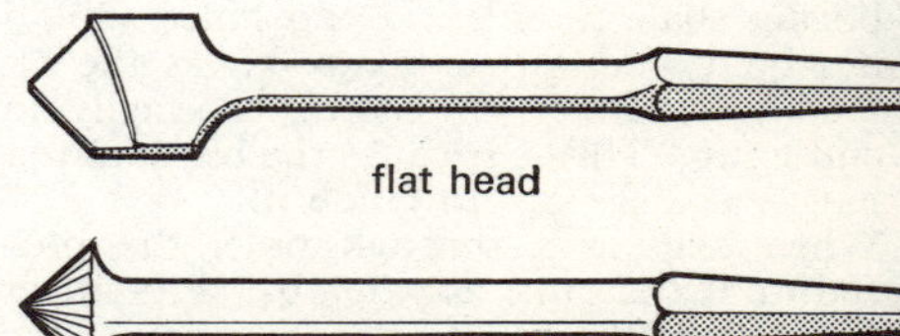

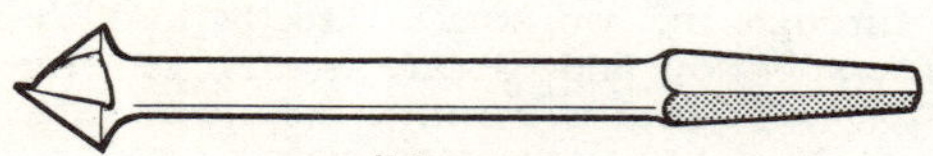

Dowel sharpener

This is used to sharpen dowel ends to aid their entry into bored holes.

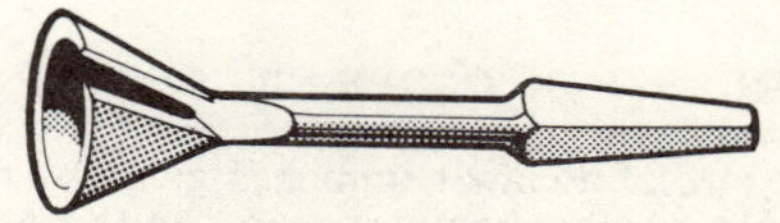

REVISION EXERCISES

1. Why does the head of the brace rotate on a ball race?
2. What purpose does the ratchet serve on a brace?
3. Name the components that make up the chuck of a brace.
4. Why is the centre-bit unsuitable for boring deep holes?
5. What is the purpose of the spurs on an auger or twist bit?
6. When would a parallel shell-bit be used?
7. Why is an auger bit used to bore deep holes?
8. What is the purpose of the spiral point on an auger bit?
9. Describe one method of boring a hole using a centre-bit.
10. When would a tapered shell-bit be used?
11. For what purpose would you use a Forstner bit?
12. Name two tools that are used for boring holes without the aid of a brace.
13. How is the cutter of the expansive bit held in position?
14. What precaution must be observed when using a bradawl?
15. What is the main use of the gimlet?
16. What tool would you use to bore pilot holes for nails?
17. How could a heavy-gauge screw be removed more easily from a piece of wood?
18. When would a countersink bit be used?
19. Name two different types of countersink bits.
20. Sketch the head of the snail horn countersink bit.

SCREWDRIVERS

The two most common types of screwdriver in use are the cabinet pattern and the London pattern. The cabinet pattern is forged from a circular blade, while the blade of the London pattern screwdriver is flat.

The blade lengths of both screwdrivers range from 75 mm to 300 mm.

cabinet pattern

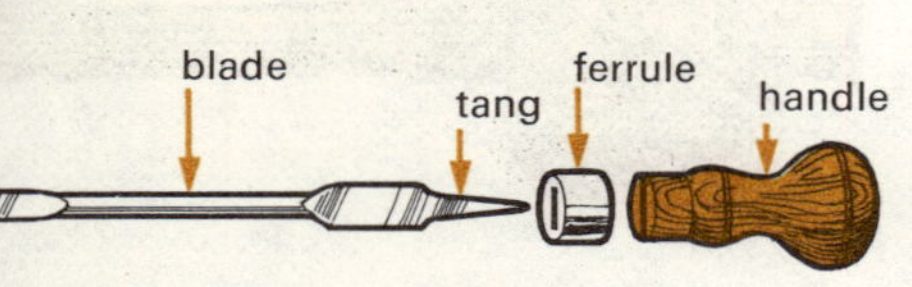

London pattern

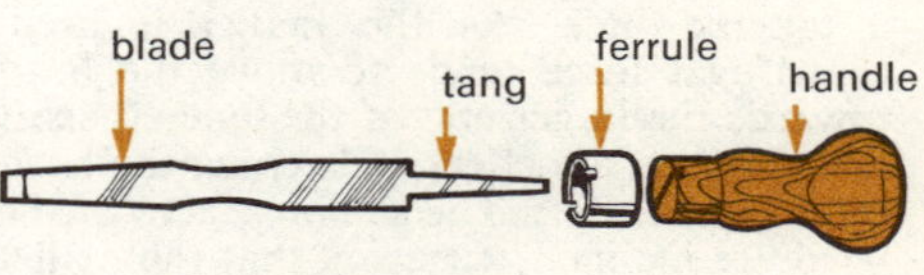

Phillips screwdriver

The Phillips screwdriver is designed for use with self-centring screws. The blade is circular and its end is shaped to fit the star-shaped recess in the screw head. The handle of the screwdriver is usually made of plastic moulded to the blade and keyed in position by two or more raised ridges on the blade.

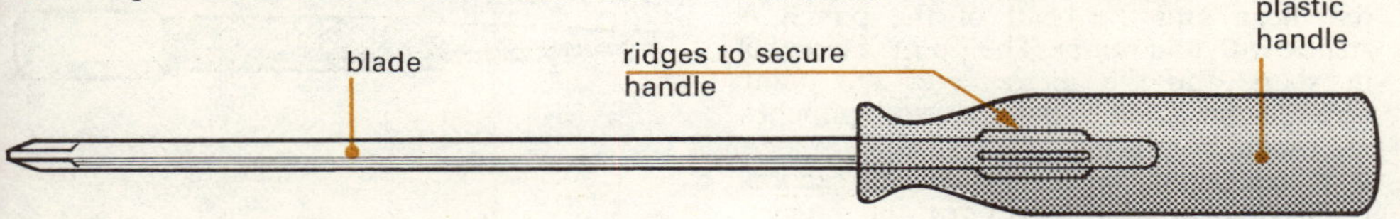

PERCUSSION TOOLS

Claw-hammer

The size of a claw-hammer is given by the weight of the hammer-head, and ranges from 200 g to 925 g. The claw of the hammer is used to withdraw nails. The shaft is made of ash or hickory.

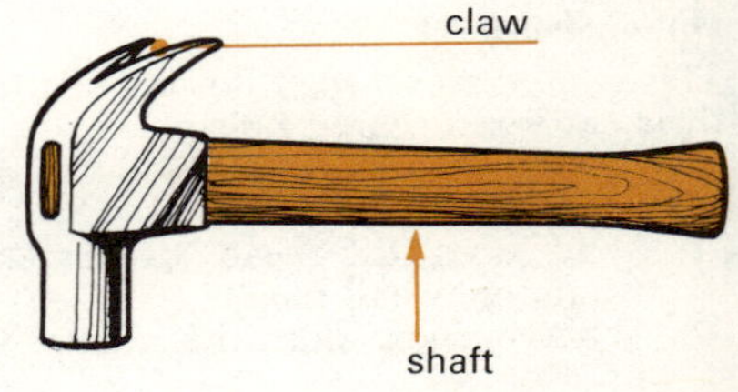

Cross-pein hammer

The cross-pein hammer is light in weight and the size of the hammer-head is given by numbers ranging from 00 to 12. The most popular size of head is number 3, which has a weight of 350 g. This hammer is used for general work, with the cross pein used to start driving in short nails and oval brads. The cross pein can also be used as a veneer hammer to press small strips of veneer or inlay banding into place. The handle is made of ash or hickory.

The shafts of the claw-hammer and the cross-pein hammer have a saw cut across the width of the shaft at the head end. After the shaft is driven into the hammer head a wedge is driven into the saw cut.

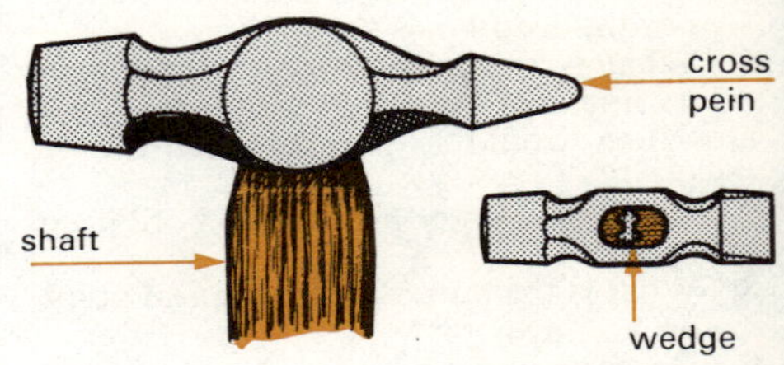

The wedge can be a glued wedge of wood or a manufactured wedge of metal. The purpose of this wedge is to prevent the hammer-head from flying off the shaft when the hammer is in use.

Mallet

The mallet is used for striking chisel handles when heavy cutting is necessary, especially when removing mortises. The head and shaft of the mallet are made of beech, the shaft entering the head through a tapered hole. As the mallet is used, centrifugal force tends to move the head towards the larger end of the tapered shaft and this has the effect of keeping the head tight on the shaft. The striking faces of the head are inclined, ensuring that the mallet blows land square on the chisel handle.

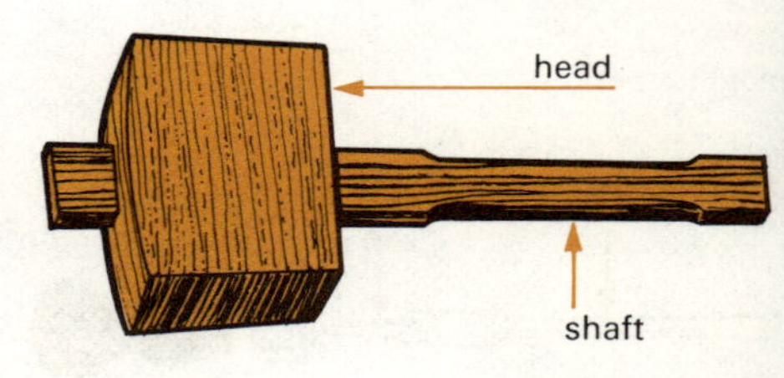

Nail punch

The nail punch is used to drive nail heads below the surface of the wood. The hollowed point of the punch is placed on the nail head and the head of the punch is struck with a hammer. The point is circular in shape and the diameter of the point ranges from 1 mm to 3 mm. Nail punches are made from high carbon steel, hardened and tempered, with the centre section knurled to provide a grip for the fingers.

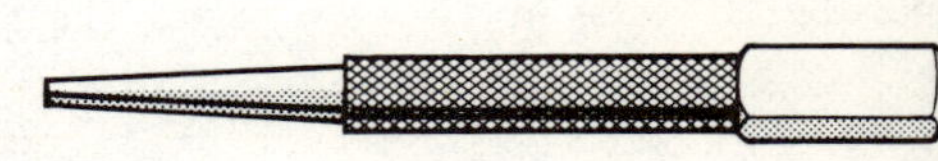

Pincers

Pincers are used to extract nails which have been accidentally bent during hammering. A piece of scrap wood should be placed under the pincer jaw to prevent the jaw from deforming the workpiece. The end of one arm of the pincers is formed in the shape of a claw which can be used as a light lever or as a tack extractor. The most common size of pincers is 150 mm long.

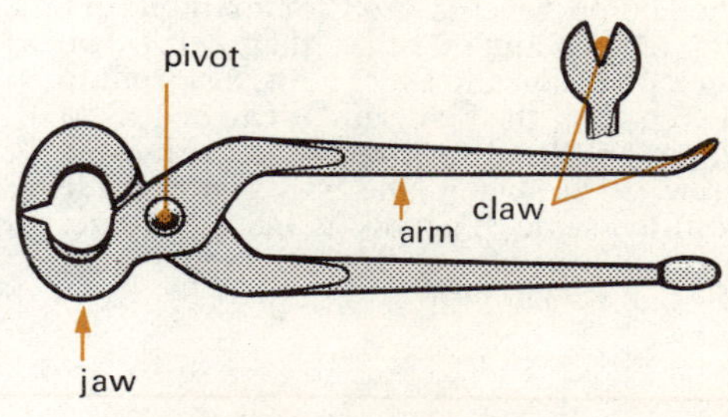

MARKING TOOLS

Try-square

The try-square is used to test if surfaces are square with each other and to draw lines at right angles to a true edge or surface. The blade is made from high carbon steel, hardened and tempered. The stock is made from rosewood, ebony or plastic and faced on the inside with a strip of brass to ensure minimum wear. The sizes of try-squares are based on the length of the blade and range from 100 mm to 300 mm. The square should be tested for accuracy periodically.

Method of testing a try-square for accuracy:
(1) the square is held against a true edge and a line drawn;
(2) the square is reversed and a second line drawn as close as possible to the first line;
(3) if the lines are parallel the try-square is accurate.

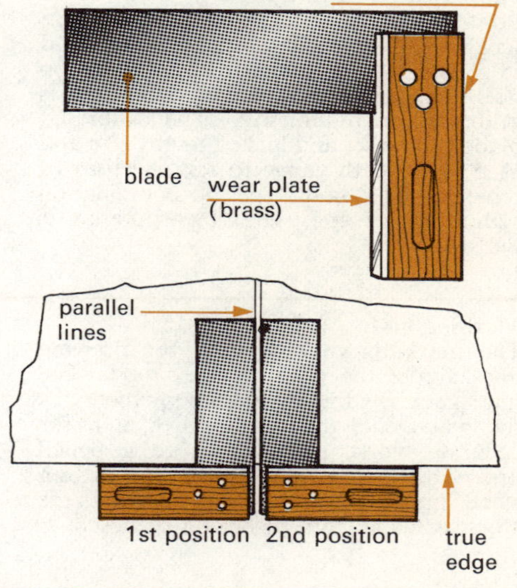

Mitre square (bevel)

The mitre square is used for marking out and testing lines which are at an angle of 45° to a true surface. The blade of the mitre square is rigidly fixed to the stock at 45°. The blade and stock are made from the same materials as the try-square. The sizes of mitre squares are based on the length of the blade and range from 200 mm to 350 mm.

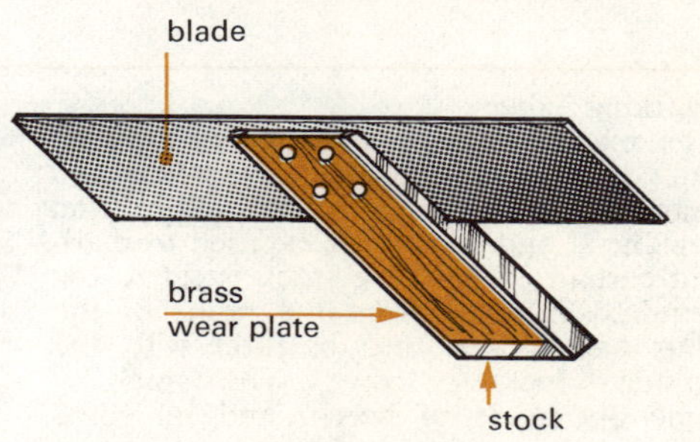

Sliding bevel

The sliding bevel is used for marking out and testing angles other than 90°. The stock pivots on and slides along a slot cut in the centre of the blade and it can be locked in any position by means of a locking screw. The blade and stock are made from the same materials as the try-square. Sizes of the bevel blades range from 150 mm to 350 mm.

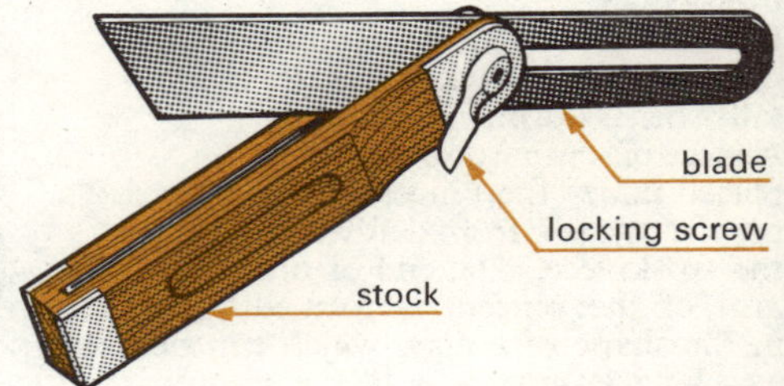

Combination square

The stock of this square is made from close-grained cast iron and the faces are accurately machined to angles of 90° and 45°. The blade is made from high carbon steel, hardened and tempered, and it is calibrated in millimetres. The calibrated blade can be set and locked to any size and used as a depth gauge to test mortises or rebates. The best type of combination square has a spirit-level incorporated in the stock.

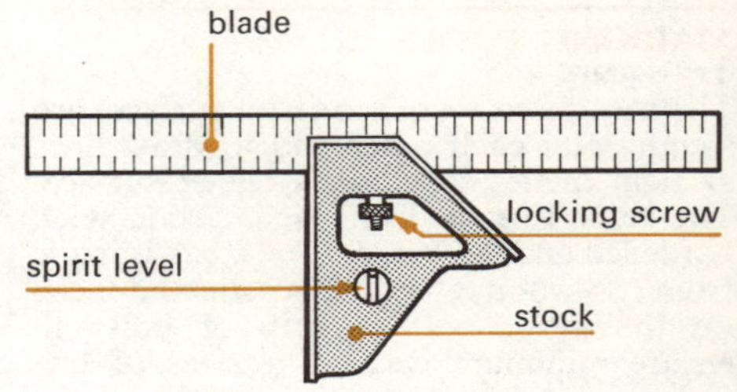

Marking knife

The marking knife is used for drawing lines across the grain of the wood. The line made by the knife is permanent, as the blade cuts the wood fibres and, for accurate work, is preferred to a pencil line. The blade is made from high carbon steel, hardened and tempered, and the stock is made from rosewood or beech.

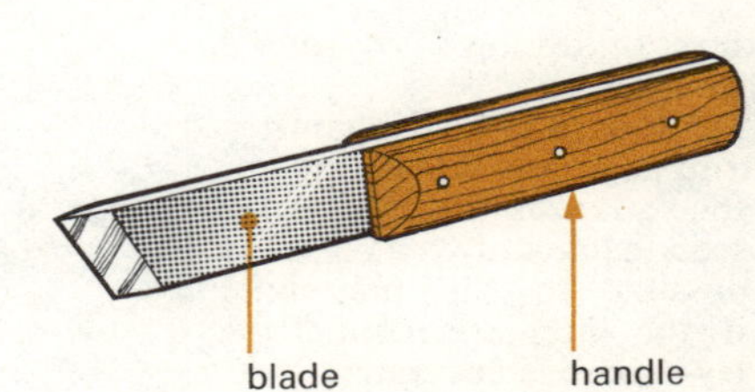

Marking gauge

The marking gauge is used for drawing lines parallel to an edge or surface and marking out the correct width and thickness, and it can also be used to mark out certain joints. The stock is set to the required distance from the point of the spur and locked into position with the wooden locking screw. The stock is generally made of beech, and on some gauges the working surface has two brass strips set into it to minimise wear. The locking screw is made of boxwood and the stem is made of beech.

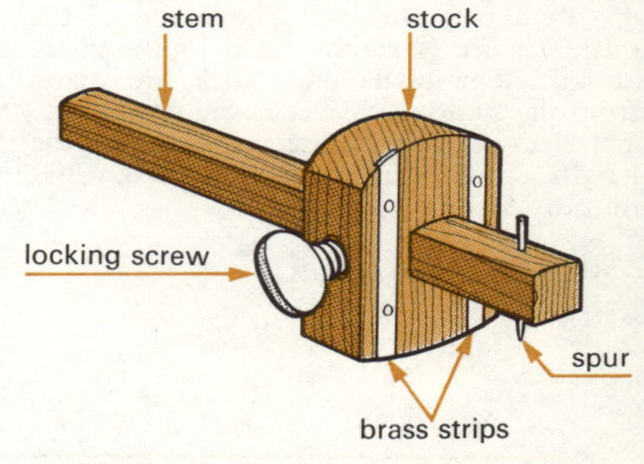

Mortise gauge

The mortise gauge is used to mark out mortise and tenon joints. To set the gauge, the locking screw is slackened and the width of the mortise set to the chisel being used between the spurs, any adjustment being made by means of the thumbscrew at the end of the slide. The stock is then moved along the stem until the required distance from the adjustable spur to the stock face is reached. The stock and slide are both fixed by tightening the locking screw.

The stock and stem of the mortise gauge are made from rosewood or ebony, with the stock having two brass strips inserted in the working face to minimise wear. The slide is made of brass.

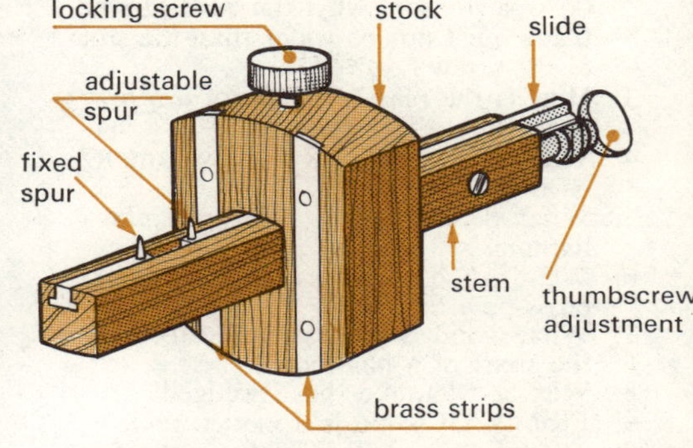

Panel gauge

The panel gauge is used to mark large widths on wide boards. This is a specialist gauge and each workman normally makes his own. Panel gauges are widely used by pattern makers and cabinet-makers. The gauge is set to the required size and the stock is locked in position by means of the wedge.

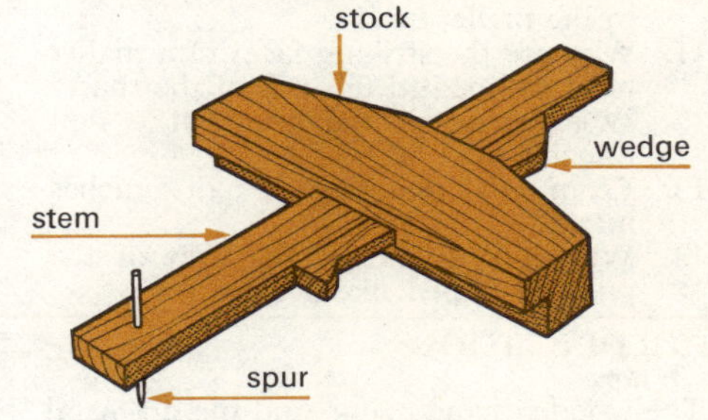

Cutting gauge

The cutting gauge is fitted with a small knife which is held in place in the stem by a small wedge. The gauge is set in the same way as the marking gauge, and it is used for cutting through thin wood, for cutting lines in preparation for inlaying, and to cut veneers. The stock and stem are made of beech, and on some gauges the stock has two brass strips recessed into the working face to minimise wear.

The cutting gauge is especially useful when marking across the grain. On wide boards it can replace the marking knife, as the function of the marking gauge blade is similar to that of the marking knife blade. It should be used across the grain only if the timber has a squared end.

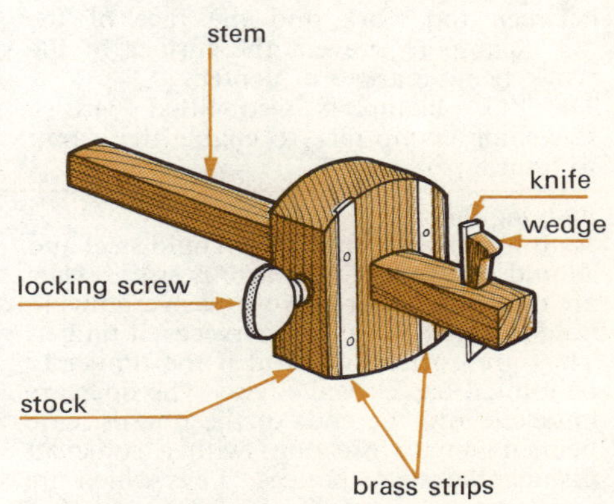

1. Sketch a cabinet pattern screwdriver and name its parts.
2. Give a reason why the screwdriver blade must not be wider than the slot of the screw head.
3. How is the plastic handle of a screwdriver held on to the blade?
4. What is the claw of a claw-hammer used for?
5. What determines the size of a claw-hammer?
6. What is the purpose of the pein on a cross-pein hammer?
7. What wood is generally used to make the shaft of a hammer?
8. Why is a hammer-head wedged?
9. From what wood is a mallet made?
10. There is no wedge in the end of a mallet shaft. How is the shaft fixed to the mallet head?
11. Why are the striking faces of a mallet head inclined to the axis of the shaft?
12. What shape is the point of a nail punch?
13. From what material are nail punches made?
14. Why is one end of the arm of the pincers shaped like a claw?
15. When extracting a nail with the pincers, what precaution should be taken?
16. Describe with the aid of sketches how a try-square is tested for accuracy.
17. Why does a try-square have a brass plate fixed to the inside of the stock?
18. What is the purpose of the mitre square?
19. What tool could be used to mark out angles other than 90° and 45°?
20. Name two advantages of the combination square.
21. What is the marking knife used for? Why is it preferred to a pencil line for accurate work?
22. When would a marking gauge be used?
23. What is the purpose of the brass inserts on the working face of gauges?
24. What is the method of setting a mortise gauge in preparation for marking a mortise?
25. Name two operations for which the cutting gauge is used.
26. What is a panel gauge used for?

HOLDING TOOLS

Clamps

The wooden hand clamp and the all-metal "G" clamp are used to hold down work to the bench top when sawing, chiselling or shaping. These clamps are also used to hold glued components in position while the adhesive sets. The workpiece should have protective pieces of scrap wood placed between the work and the face of the "G" clamp to prevent the surface of the work being marked or dented.

The "G" clamp is also fitted with a swivelling clamp face to enable the clamp to hold tapered work.

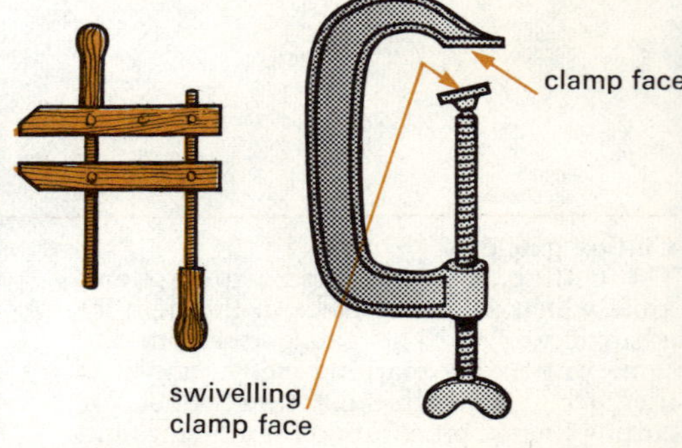

Jointing dog

Jointing dogs are made from mild steel and should be available in various sizes. They are used as an alternative to sash cramps to hold together two or more pieces of timber. They are especially useful if the timber to be jointed has curved edges. The dogs are knocked into the ends of the boards, care being taken to use dogs with a sufficient distance between the legs. Legs which are too near the jointed edge of the timber may cause the boards to split.

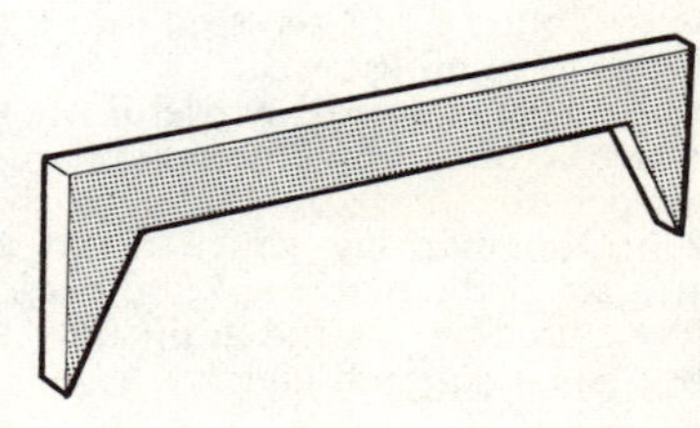

Sash cramp

The sash cramp is used to assemble large work, such as window sashes, cabinets, doors and framed constructions. Sash cramps have a capacity of 450 mm to 2 metres. For larger work an extension piece is used.

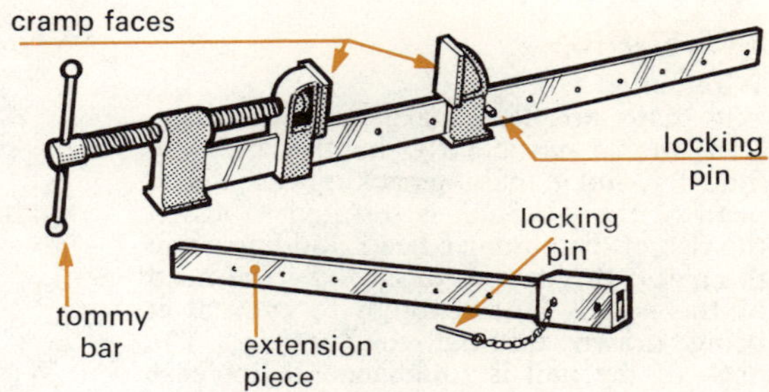

Mitre cramp

There are two main types of mitre cramp. One type holds the joint from the inside with one cramp, and the other holds the joint from the outside with two cramps. The clamping surfaces of the second type are accurately machined and the body is provided with holes so that the cramp may be screwed to the bench.

The design of both types of mitre cramp makes it possible to glue and nail mitre joints on picture frames, trinket boxes, etc., under pressure. They hold the joint at an exact angle of 90°. In addition, mitre cramps have many general purposes and are used by pattern makers.

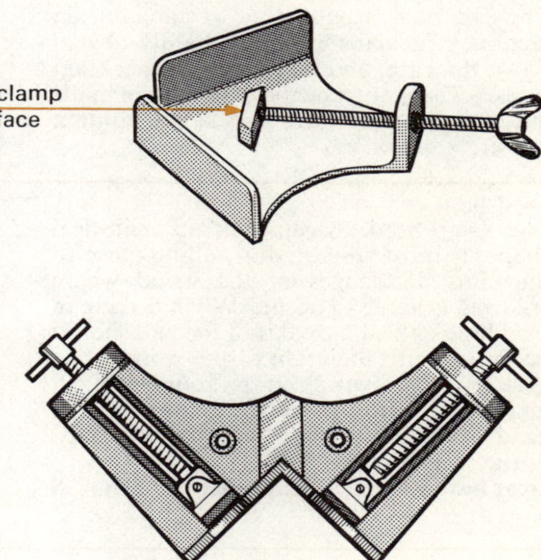

Bench holdfast

The bench holdfast is an alternative to the "G" clamp for holding work to the work-bench when planing rebates and mouldings and when sawing and chiselling. The bench holdfast is not normally used to hold glued components.

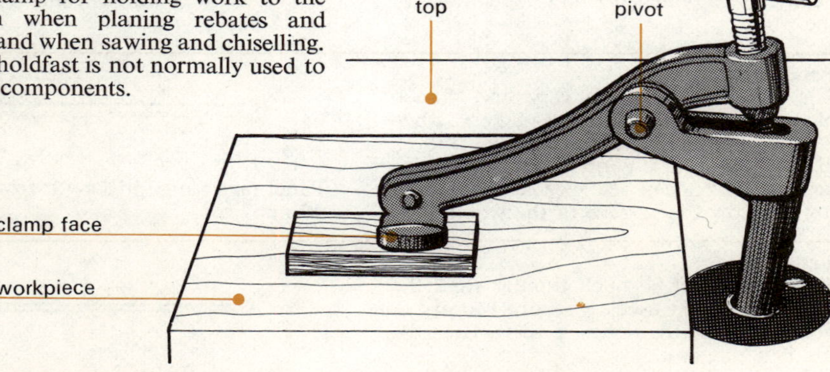

FASTENINGS

Wire nail

Wire nails are used for general construction work, particularly in the building industry, and in making packing-cases. The head of the wire nail is serrated to lessen the risk of the hammer-head skidding when the nail is driven into the wood. The head of the nail is large enough to prevent it being drawn through the timber. The neck of the nail is roughened to increase its grip in the wood.

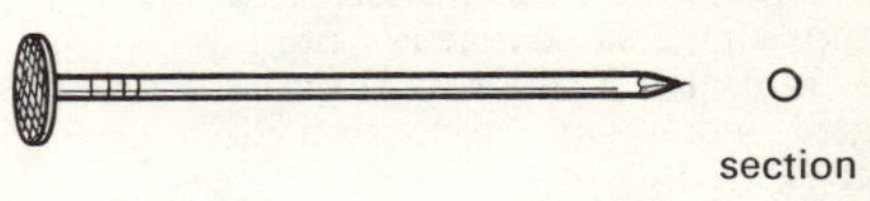

Wire nails range in length from 18 mm to 150 mm.

Cut nail

The cut nail is square or rectangular in section. Cut nails are used mainly to nail down flooring, and when making packing-cases. They are cheaper than wire nails but they do not have the same holding power.

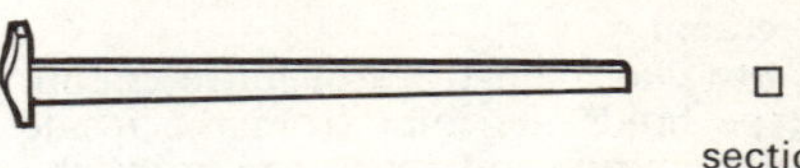

Cut nails range in length from 18 mm to 150 mm.

Oval brad

The oval brad, because of its elliptical shape, is most suitable for nailing close to the ends and edges of the wood where splitting is liable to occur. When driving in oval brads, the major axis of the nail should be in line with the grain of the wood. The neck of the oval brad is roughened to increase its grip in the wood, and the nail head is easily punched below the surface of the wood.

Oval brads range in length from 12 mm to 65 mm.

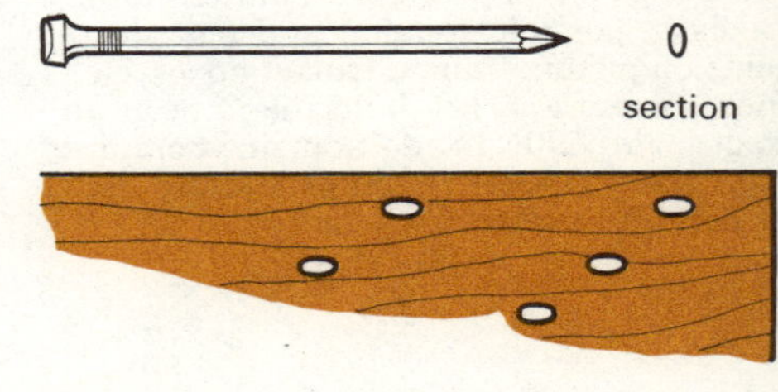

Lost-head nail

This is a fine wire nail, circular in section. It is used for the same purposes as the wire nail. It has the advantage that its head can be punched below the surface of the wood.

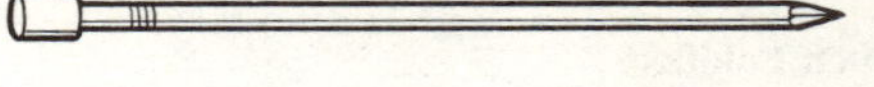

Lost-head nails range in length from 18 mm to 75 mm.

Panel-pin

The panel-pin shank is very fine. Panel-pins are used by cabinet-makers when fixing mouldings, cabinet door frames, picture frames or any other fine work. The head of the pin can be concealed by punching it below the surface of the wood.

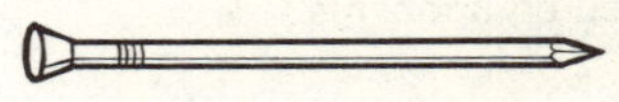

Panel-pins range in length from 8 mm to 40 mm.

Veneer pin

The veneer pin is much thinner than the panel-pin. It is used to secure veneers in position while the adhesive sets. Then the pin is withdrawn.

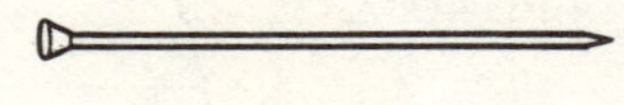

Clout nail

The clout nail has a short shank and a large diameter head. It is used to fix roofing felt and canvas, the large head of the nail preventing holes or tears developing in these materials. The clout nail is galvanised to prevent rusting when it is used outdoors.

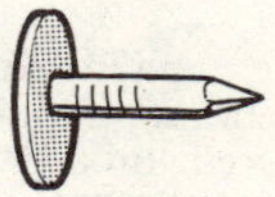

Clout nails range in length from 12 mm to 40 mm.

Upholstery nail

Upholstery nails are used to fix leather, cloth, tapestry and similar materials to wood, e.g. on an upholstered stool. The nail has a large dome-shaped head, and the head and shank are made of mild steel plated with bronze, brass or nickel.

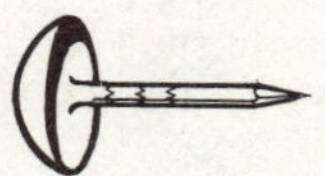

Upholstery nails are 12 mm long.

Escutcheon pin

Escutcheon pins are made of brass and are used to fix keyhole plates on door locks. The pins have an ornamental effect, and cannot rust, so they are often used in bathroom, kitchen and outside door locks.

Escutcheon pins range between 12 mm and 30 mm in length.

Corrugated fastener (wiggle nail)

Corrugated fasteners are used to fix pieces of wood which are butt jointed and to fix frames which have to be covered with hardboard or plywood.

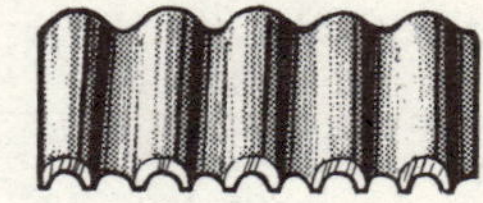

Points to note when nailing

(1) Select the proper nail for the job.
(2) For greatest holding power, always nail the thinner piece of wood to the thicker piece.
(3) Do not place nails in a straight line as this tends to split the wood. The nails should be placed in a staggered pattern.
(4) When nailing thin material which splits easily, holes to accommodate the nails should be made with a bradawl.
(5) The holding power of nails is greater if the nails are driven into the wood at an angle. This is known as dovetail nailing.

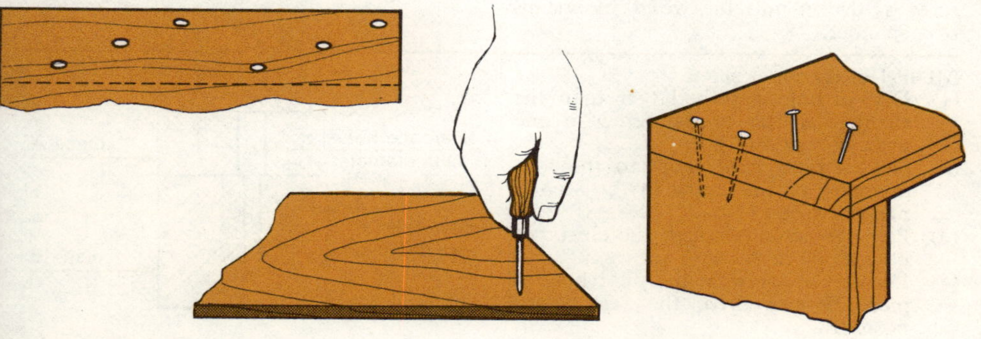

Screws

Wood-screws are made from brass, chromium-plated brass, aluminium, mild steel, black-lacquered mild steel, brassed mild steel and stainless steel.

The shape of the head of the screw determines the type of screw. The shank of the screw is pointed and it is threaded for two-thirds of its length. The thread of the screw pulls the screw into the wood.

Countersunk screws

Countersunk screws are used when a flush-finished surface is required. The head of the screw is countersunk to lie slightly below the surface of the wood.

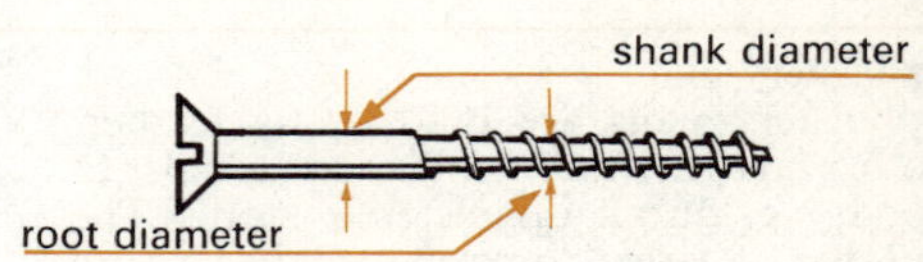

Round head screws

Round head screws are painted with black lacquer to prevent rusting. They are ideal for use where they will be exposed to the weather, e.g. for screwing hinges to garage doors, for garden gate latches, etc.

Raised countersunk screws

Raised countersunk screws are usually chromium-plated. They are used mainly for decorative work.

Phillips and Pozidriv screws

Screws are now being manufactured with the more efficient Phillips or Pozidriv heads. These heads are designed to give more positive positioning of the screwdriver, eliminating screwdriver slip.

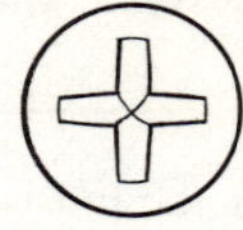
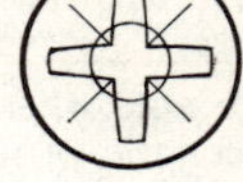

Coach screw

The coach screw is much stronger and heavier than other screws. It is made of mild or galvanised steel and is used for outside work, such as gate hinges, railway carriages and coach-building. The coach screw is driven into the wood by means of a spanner.

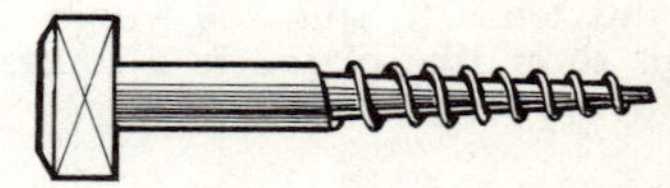

Method of driving a screw

(1) Drill a hole slightly larger than the shank diameter of the screw in one piece of wood (A).
(2) Drill a pilot hole equal to the root diameter of the screw in the second piece of wood (B).
(3) Pass the screw through the clearance hole in piece A.
(4) Locate the screw in the pilot hole in piece B and drive the screw into position.

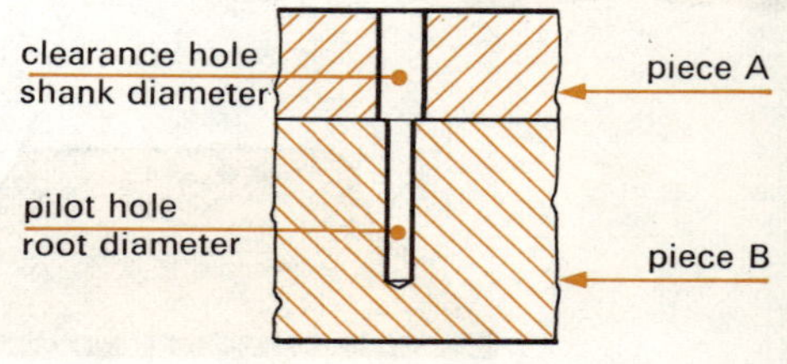

Points to note

(1) When screwing two pieces of wood together, the thinner piece of wood should be screwed to the thicker piece.

(2) The length of the screw used should be at least twice the thickness of the thinner piece of wood.

(3) When screwing acidic woods, such as oak, brass screws should be used. Damage to the heads of brass screws by the action of the screwdriver can be prevented by first screwing a steel screw into the prepared hole.

(4) When driving screws into hardwood, the point of the screw can be coated with a lubricant, such as tallow or wax.

(5) Make sure the screwdriver is in the proper condition, otherwise damage to the screw head and to the surface of the work may occur.

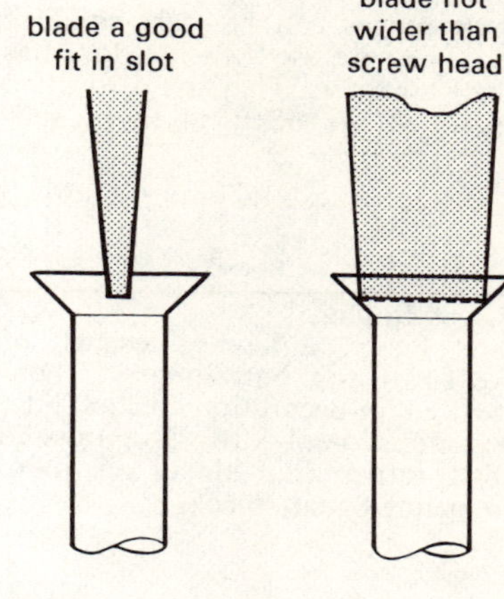

FIXTURES AND FITTINGS

Butt hinge

Butt hinges are most commonly used when making lidded boxes and cabinets. They may be made of brass, steel, plastic or nylon. The hinges are recessed into the door of the cabinet, leaving an unbroken line on the cabinet edge. Butt hinges are available in lengths of 20 mm up to 150 mm.

Back-flap hinge

Back-flap hinges are used mostly on the fronts of writing bureaux and on the leaves of drop-leaf tables. They can be recessed into the surface, or simply screwed directly on to the surface. They can be made of steel or brass, and are available in lengths of between 20 mm and 75 mm.

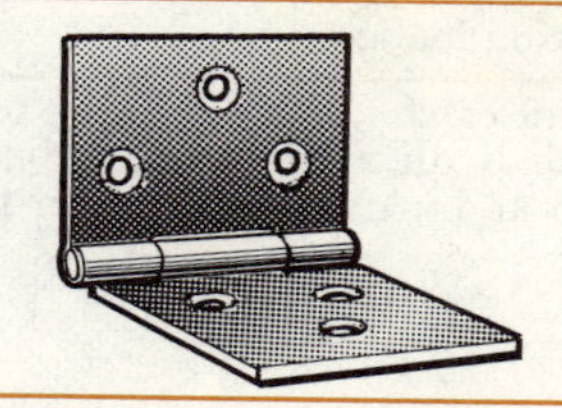

Strap hinge or tee hinge

Strap hinges are used when hanging garage doors, garden shed doors and wooden gates of light construction. They are made of mild steel and are protected for outside use by being coated with black lacquer. Strap hinges are available in lengths of between 50 mm and 300 mm.

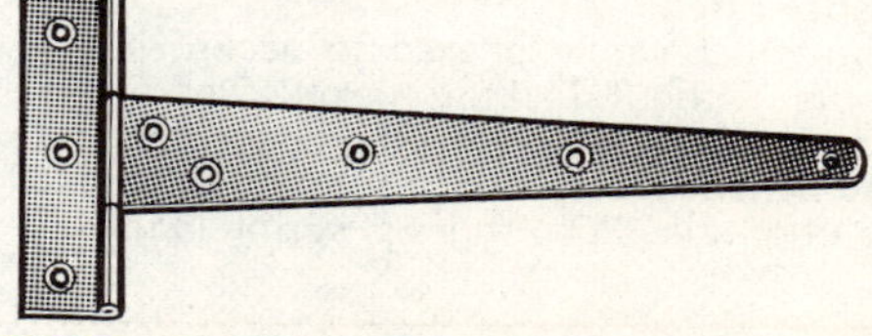

Hook and band hinge

These hinges are made of mild steel and are used for hanging heavy gates and doors, such as the drop doors on railway wagons. They are made to individual specifications.

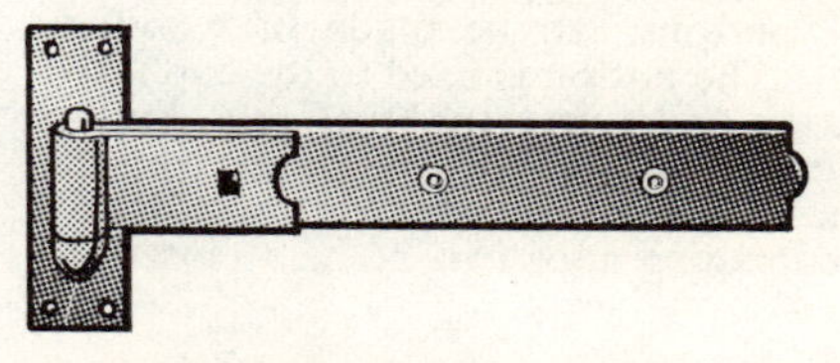

Rising butt hinge

Rising butt hinges can be right-hand or left-hand. They are used when a door has to rise over a carpet. They are also fitted to doors which are designed to be self-closing.

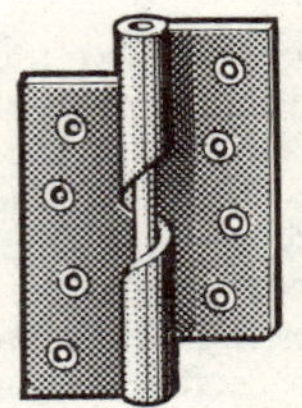

Decorative strap hinge

There are many different designs of decorative strap and butt hinges. These hinges are used for decoration on chest lids, wardrobes, some cupboards and outside doors. Decorative strap hinges on doors are often painted matt black.

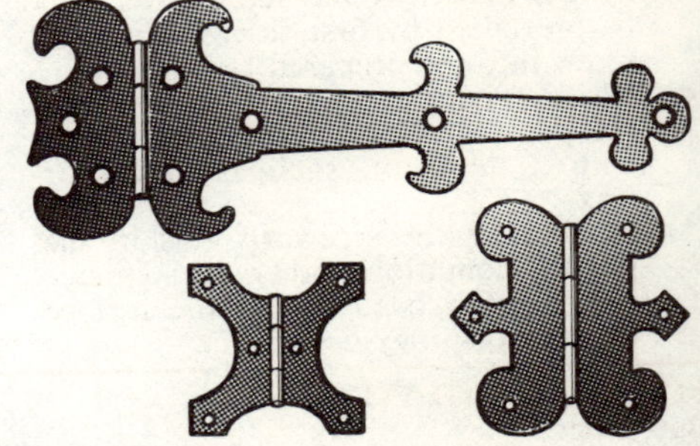

Ball catch

The ball catch secures cupboard doors without locking them. The catch provides a quick release when opening or closing the door. The ball housing is recessed into the door edge, and the plate is recessed into the cupboard carcase. The ball is spring loaded.

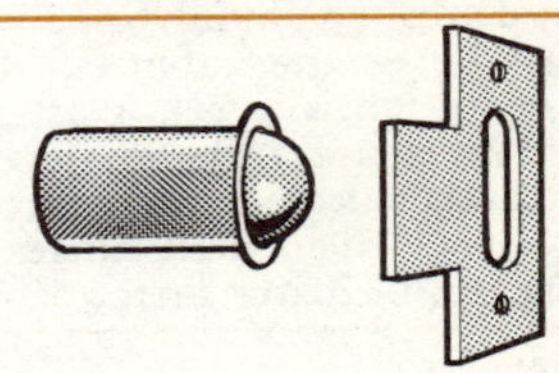

Double ball catch

This catch is an alternative to the single ball catch and provides a stronger grip.

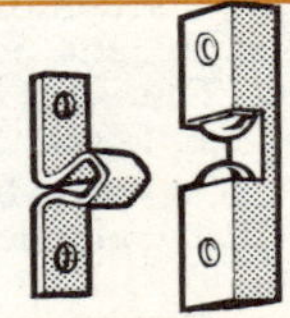

Roller catch

The roller catch is used to secure heavy doors without locking them. The roller housing is recessed into the door edge and the plate is recessed into the cupboard side or door stile. The roller is spring loaded.

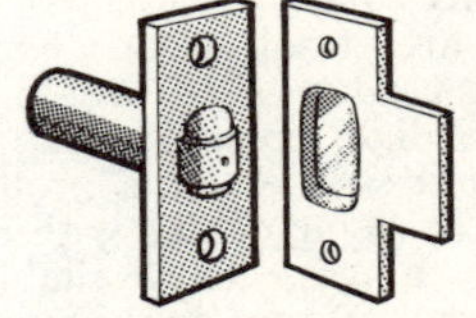

Turn button

Turn buttons can be made of wood or metal. The button is fixed to the cupboard carcase and, by turning the button vertically, the cupboard door can be opened. By turning the button horizontally, the cupboard door can be held closed.

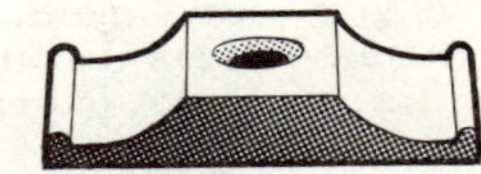

Magnetic lock
This type of lock or catch is used mainly on wardrobe doors, but it can also be used on any other small cabinet such as a record cabinet. The magnet is screwed on to the inside of the wardrobe at the top and bottom and the metal plate is screwed on to the inside of the door.

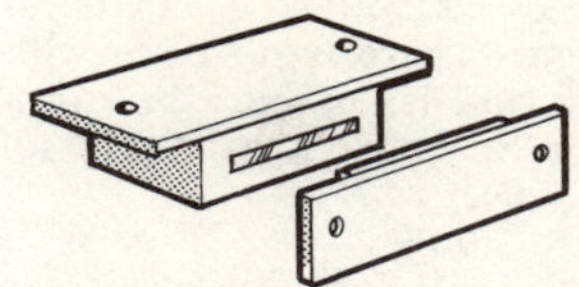

Spring catch
The spring catch is another alternative to the ball catch and is used on small cupboard doors. It is cheaper and does not need to be recessed into the door, which makes for easy fitting.

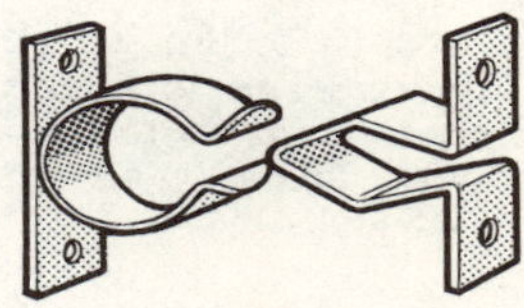

Barrel bolt
This bolt is used to secure doors from the inside. The bolt is fixed on to the door and the bolt housing screwed on to the stile of the door-frame.

Trigger catch
This type of catch is used mainly on cupboard doors. It secures one door without locking it. The trigger catch is fixed to the inside of the door and the latch to the underside of the most convenient shelf. The trigger is depressed to release the catch.

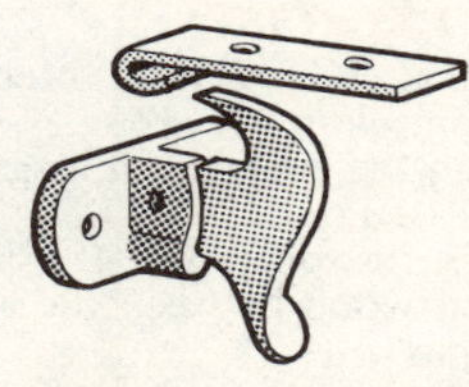

Cupboard lock
This lock is used to secure cupboard doors. The lock is not recessed into the door, but screwed on to the inside of the cupboard door. There is no plate with this lock. A mortise is cut into the cupboard edge to house the tongue of the lock.

Desk lock
This lock is used to secure drop flaps in writing-desks or lids on trinket and jewellery boxes. The lock is recessed into the inside of the box front or drop flap, and the plate is recessed into the lid.

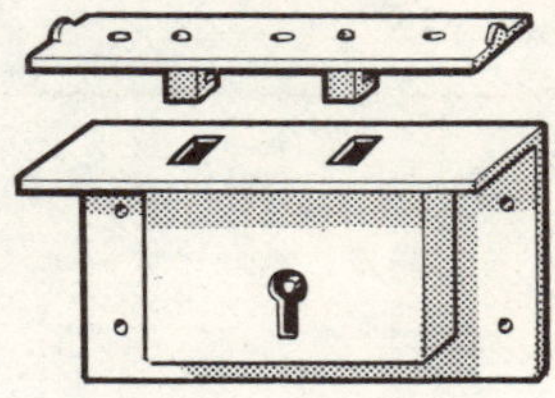

Drawer lock

This lock is used to secure a drawer. The lock is recessed into the inside of the drawer front. There is no plate with this lock. A mortise is cut into the rail above the drawer to house the tongue of the lock.

Rim deadlock

This lock is used to secure garage and garden shed doors. The lock and box staple are simply screwed on to the inside face of the door. There is no need to recess this type of lock.

Mirror plate

Mirror plates are used to secure mirrors, cupboards, etc., to inside walls. The plates are screwed to the back of the fitment, with the single hole in the plate projecting above the fitment. The fitment is then secured to the wall.

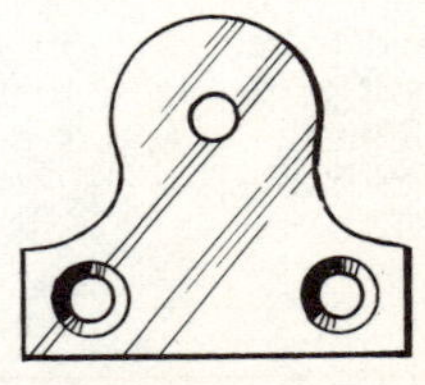

1. Why is a "G" clamp fitted with a swivelling clamp face?
2. How can the capacity of a sash cramp be increased?
3. What is the purpose of using scrap pieces of wood between the work and the clamp?
4. What is a disadvantage of the bench holdfast?
5. What is the purpose of the mitre cramp?
6. Why is the neck of a wire nail roughened?
7. What precaution should be taken when driving oval brads?
8. For what purpose is the cut nail used?
9. Why is the head of a wire nail serrated?
10. When would a panel-pin be used?
11. From what material is a clout nail made, and why?
12. Why is an escutcheon pin made of brass?
13. Write down four points to be observed when nailing.
14. Why are some screws coated with black lacquer?
15. What is the main purpose of the raised countersunk screw?
16. How is a coach screw driven into wood?
17. When would a coach screw be used?
18. How can a screw be driven more easily into hardwoods?
19. What is the advantage of the modern screw head?
20. Show by means of simple sketches the method of screwing two pieces of wood together.

JOINTS

SIMPLE JOINTS

Butt and nailed joint
The end of one piece of wood butts against the side of the second piece of wood and the joint is fixed by glue and nails. Generally used in making simple boxes.

Rebated butt joint
The end of one piece of wood fits into a rebate cut on the second piece. The rebate provides more gluing area and two surfaces which can be nailed. This joint is used when making boxes, cheap cabinets, drawer corners and box constructions which will have a veneered finish.

Tongued and trenched joint
This joint has a tongue sawn on the end of one piece of wood which fits into a trench cut out of the second piece. This joint is stronger than the rebated butt joint but its uses are similar. This joint is fixed by glue and nails.

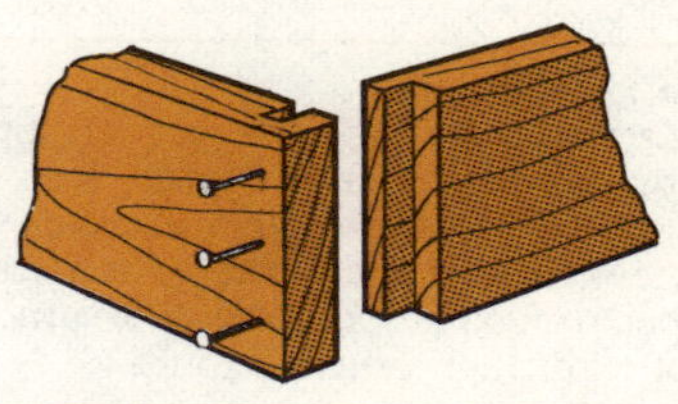

Mitred joint
This is the simplest method of jointing wood at a corner without showing any end grain. This joint is fixed by glue. It provides little strength, but it can be reinforced by cutting grooves in the mitred ends and gluing a tongue, or feather, of wood into the grooves.
An alternative method of strengthening the joint is to saw part way through the corner of the joint and insert glued pieces of veneer or thin slivers of wood into the saw cut.

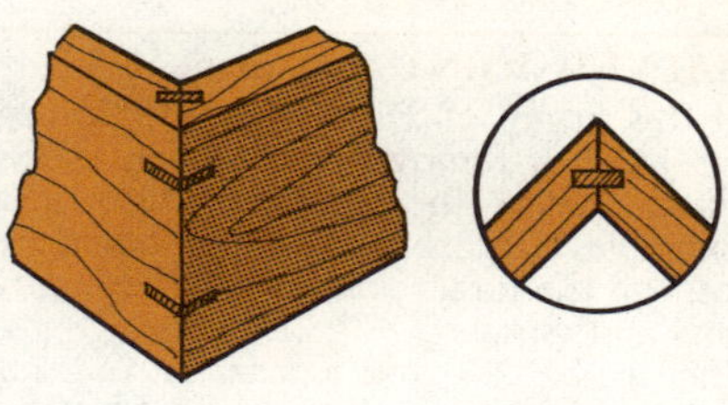

Mitred joints are used to join skirting-boards in the corners of rooms and for joining the corners of picture frames.

Rebated and mitred joint
Both pieces of wood have a rebate and mitre cut at their ends. The rebates provide the joint with two nailing surfaces. This joint does not show any end grain. It is used when making boxes and the plinths of cabinets.

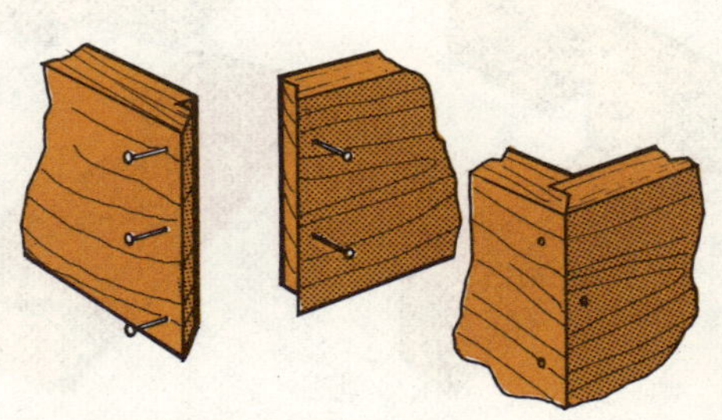

HOUSING JOINTS

Through housing joint
The through housing joint is used when
fitting shelves in bookcases and inserting
partitions in cabinets and in box constructions.

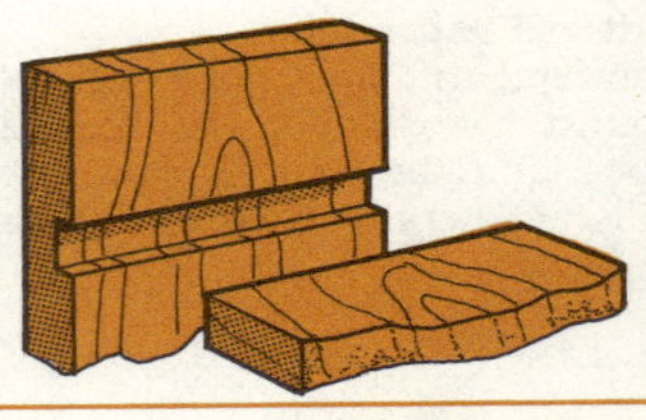

Through dovetail housing joint
The through dovetail housing joint is used
for the same type of construction as the
plain housing joint. This joint has greater
holding power than the plain housing
joint, as it is extremely difficult to force the
end piece away from the taper of the
dovetail.

Stopped housing joint
The stopped housing joint can be either
plain or dovetail. This joint has the
advantage of presenting an unbroken line
when viewed from the front. The uses of
a stopped housing joint are the same as
those of a through housing joint.

HALVED JOINTS

In this group of joints, half the timber of
the joint is removed from each piece of
wood, hence the name "halved joint".
Examples of cross-halved joints can be
seen on the under frames of tables, garden
huts and garages.
The tee-halved and corner-halved joints
are used when making light frames for
doors. The dovetail-halved joint is used
in constructions where an outwards strain
has to be taken.

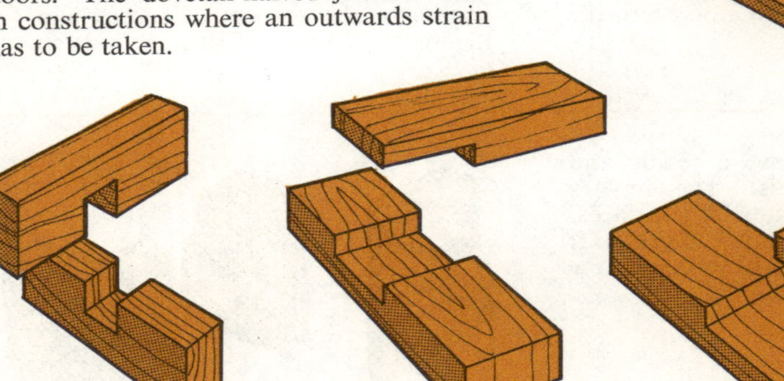

BRIDLE JOINTS

This group of joints offers a stronger joint than the halved joints. The corner and angle bridle joints are sometimes used in place of the mortise and tenon joints. Bridle joints are used to make light frames.

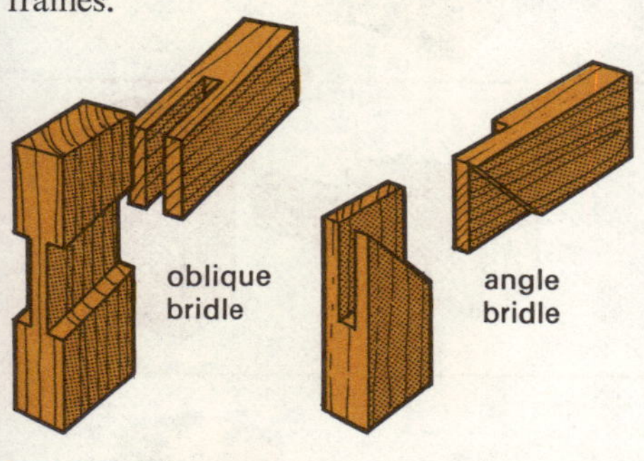

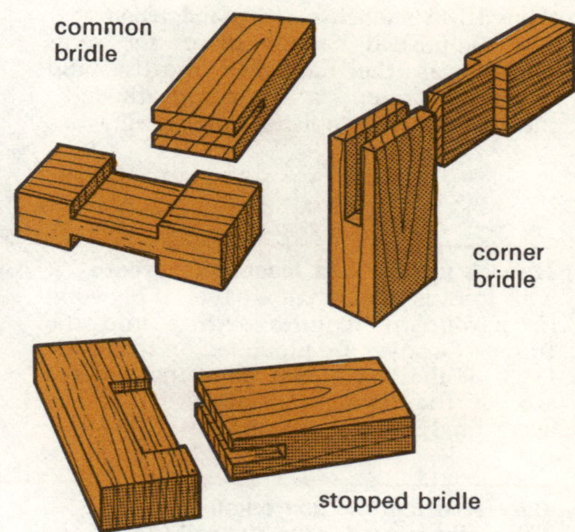

MORTISE AND TENON JOINTS

Mortise and tenon joints are more widely used than any other joint by carpenters, joiners, cabinet-makers and builders. The strongest mortise and tenon joints have the thickness of the tenon exactly one-third of the thickness of the timber. They can be strengthened by the insertion of wedges into the joints. The top and bottom of the tenon are slightly tapered to accommodate the wedges. Glue is applied to the wedges which are then driven into position.

Common mortise and tenon

This joint is used to join the middle rail to the stiles when making framed doors. It is also used when making cabinets which are built on frames instead of from the solid.

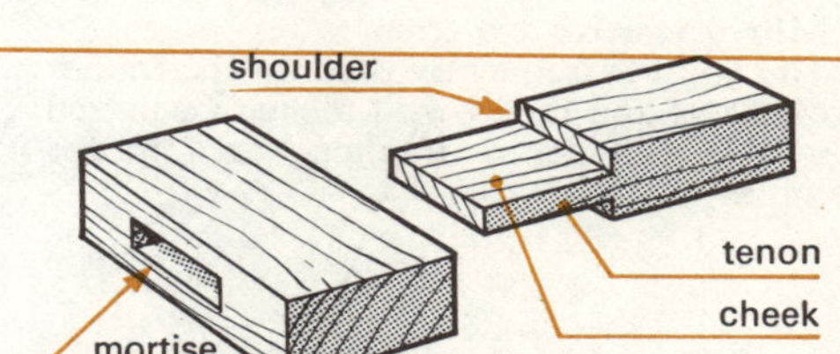

Stub mortise and tenon

The stub mortise and tenon joint is used where it is undesirable to show the end grain of the tenon on the surface of the joint.

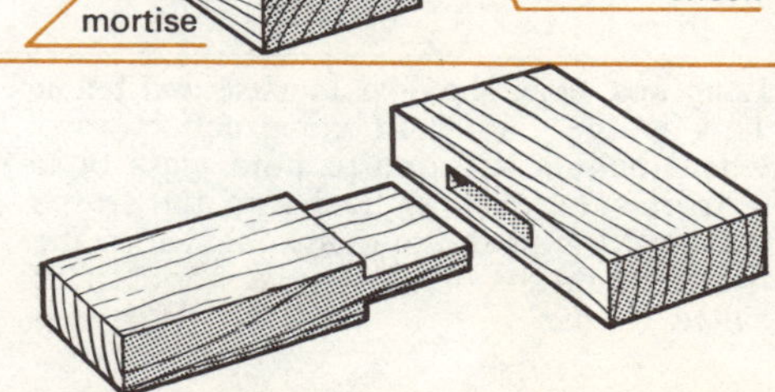

Haunch mortise and tenon

This joint is used at the corners of frames. Part of the tenon is sawn away and a short haunch is formed which fits into a groove cut into the mortise. This prevents the two pieces of the joint from twisting and gives added gluing area. Where it is undesirable to expose the haunch for the sake of appearance, the diminished haunch is used.

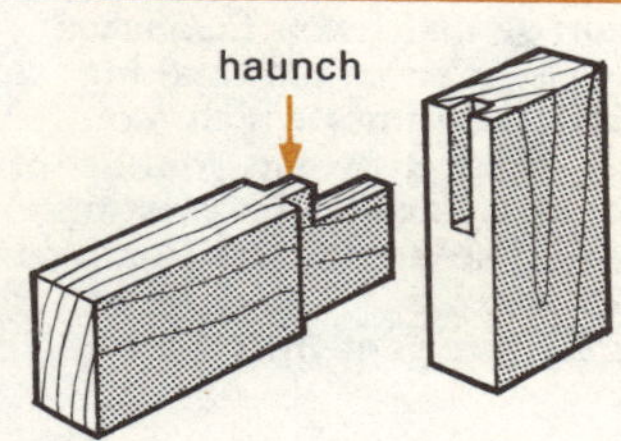

Diminished haunch mortise and tenon

The diminished haunch serves the same purpose as the haunched mortise and tenon but presents a better appearance as the haunch is completely concealed.

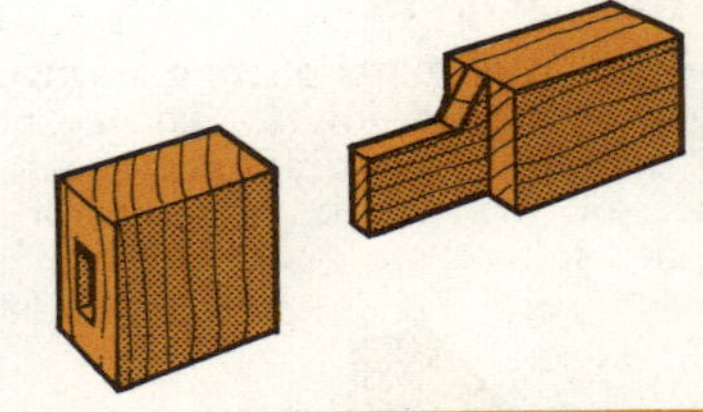

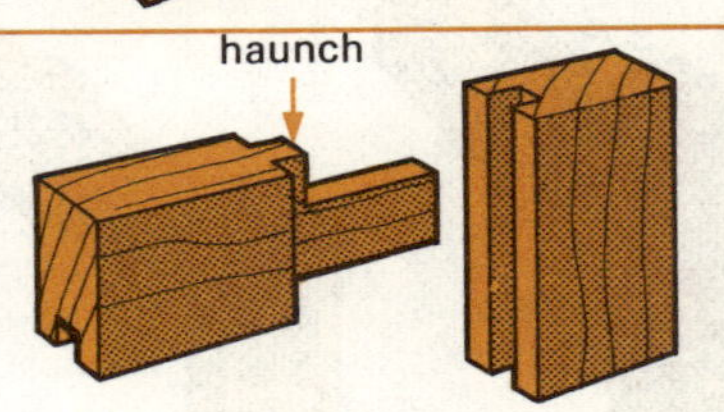

Haunch mortise and tenon with groove

This joint is used when a panel of plywood or hardboard requires setting into the frame. Grooves are ploughed on the inside faces of the frame and allowance on the size of the tenon and mortise is made accordingly.

Barefaced mortise and tenon

This joint is used when the rail (horizontal member) is thinner than the upright, as happens in some tables and stools. The tenon is cut half the thickness of the rail and it has only one shoulder. Where the rails meet inside the upright the tenons are mitred.

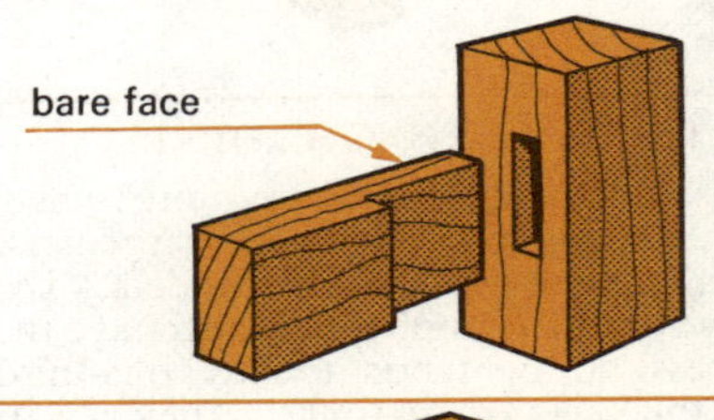

Mitred mortise and tenon

This joint is frequently used on the frames of stools and tables with the tenons mitred to give full depth of gluing area to the joint.

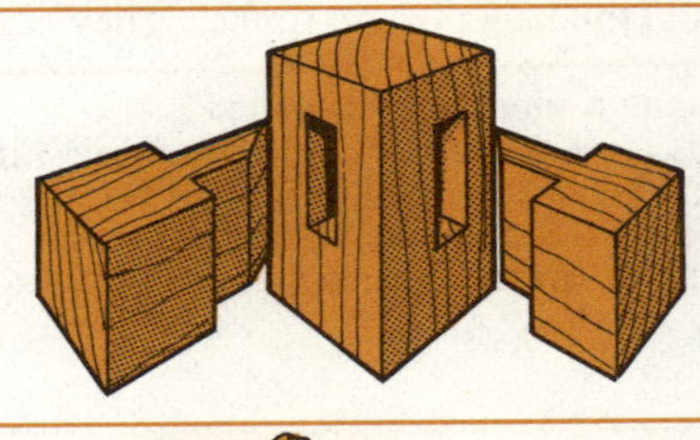

Long and short shoulder mortise and tenon

This is the joint and construction used when making a frame to hold glass or a mirror. The glass is held into the frame with putty and the mirror is held into the frame by means of decorative wood strips called beads.

Double mortise and tenon (haunched)

This joint is used when making stools, tables and door-frames which require wide rails. The tongue in the middle of the tenon prevents warping or twisting.
Through mortise and tenon joints can be wedged if desired. The driving in of wedges ensures a tight-fitting joint.

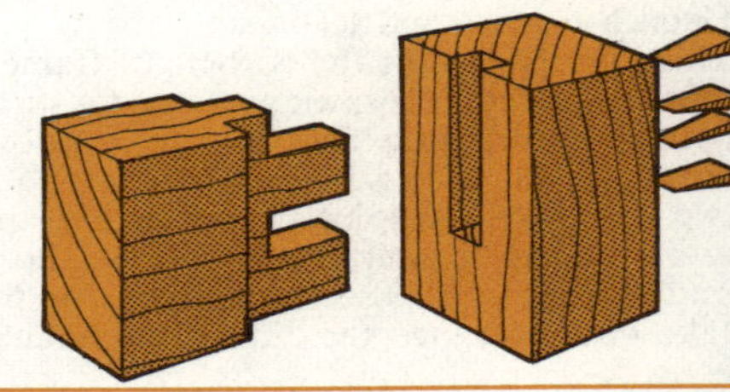

Method of sawing tenons
To ensure accuracy when sawing tenons
the saw cuts are made in a definite
sequence.
The wood is held at an angle in the vice.
Part of the cheek of one side of the tenon
is sawn on the waste side of the line down
to the shoulder line.

The wood is turned in the vice to face the
opposite direction and a second saw cut
is made on the waste side of the same line
down to the shoulder. The wood is angled
in the vice as before.

The final saw cut is made with the wood
placed upright in the vice. The cheek is
completely sawn down to the shoulder line.
The waste wood on the other side of the
tenon is sawn down to the shoulder line
in the same way.

The complete removal of the waste wood
is done on the sawing board. The saw is
positioned on the waste wood side of the
shoulder line and the wood is sawn down
to the cheek of the tenon.
To enable the saw to be accurately placed
for sawing down to the cheek of the tenon,
a wedge of timber can first be removed
from the waste wood at the shoulder line.

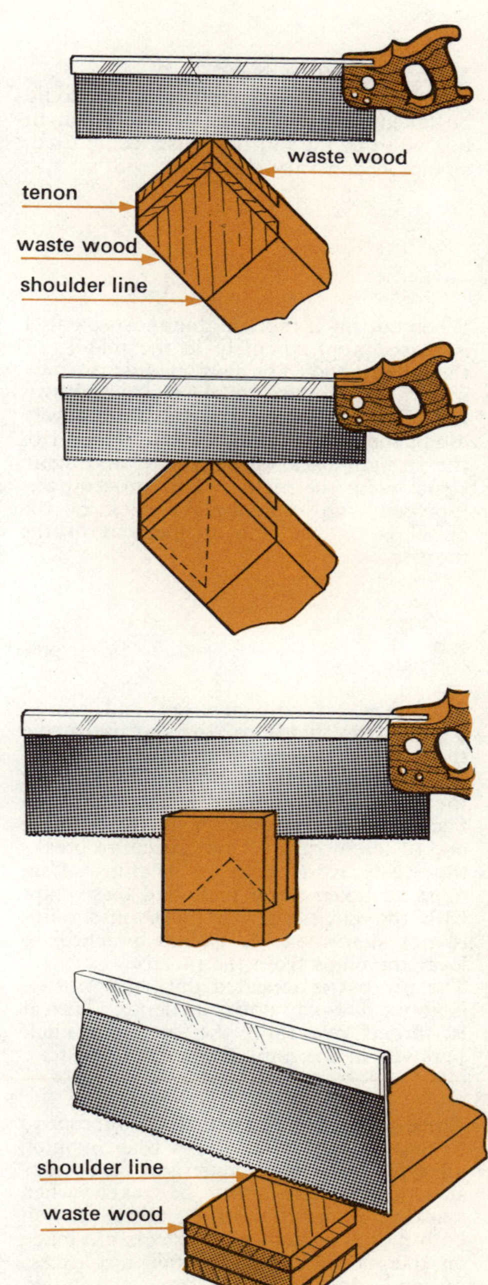

Method of cutting mortises

When marking out mortises, care should be taken that the mortise gauge is set to the width of the mortise chisel being used, as chisels can vary slightly in width.

When cutting a mortise, the mortise chisel is placed approximately in the middle of the waste wood. The chisel handle is struck with a mallet, then the chisel is withdrawn from the wood and moved a little way along the waste wood, in the direction of the straight back of the chisel, and again struck with the mallet. This procedure is repeated until the straight back of the chisel is on the line at the end of the mortise.

The chisel is now reversed and moved back to the middle of the mortise where the first cut was taken. The same process of striking the chisel and moving it along the mortise is carried out until the chisel back again touches the line at the opposite end of the mortise. This procedure breaks the waste wood into small chips. Care must be taken when removing these chips with the chisel so that the shoulder line is not deformed. It is bad practice to lever the chips from the mortise.

The process is repeated until the mortise is about half-way down its depth. Then it is turned over and the remaining half removed in the same way as the first half.

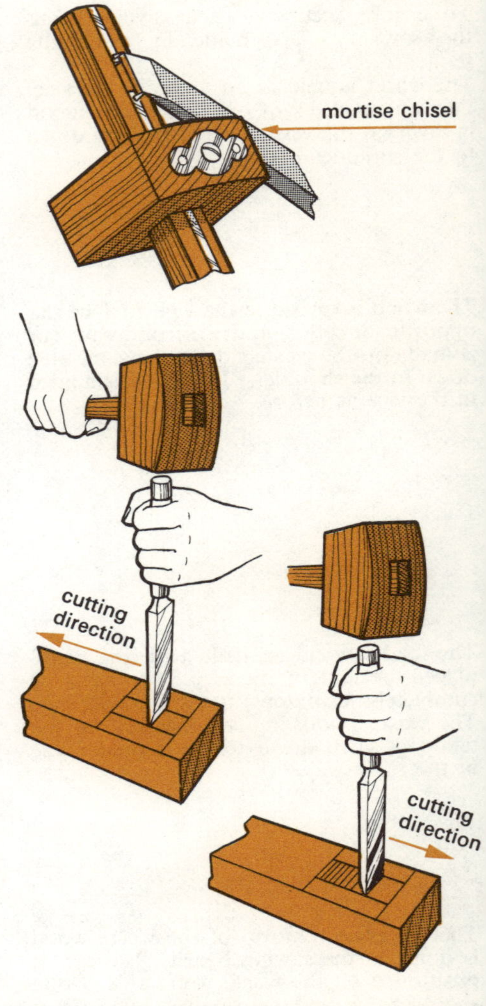

These joints can be used as an alternative to mortise and tenon joints when making all types of frame, chair and stool constructions. Care must be taken when marking the position of the dowel pins on both pieces of timber. Saw cuts are made on the dowel pins to permit any excess air and glue to escape from the holes.

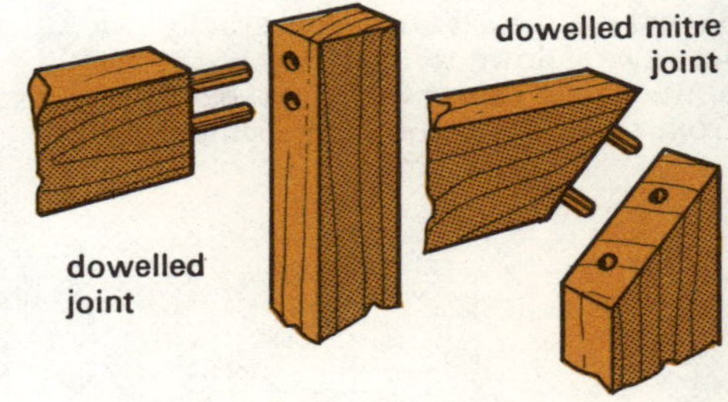

DOVETAIL JOINTS

Dovetailing is a method of fixing pieces of timber together by cutting tapered tails on one piece of wood to interlock with corresponding sockets on the second piece of wood.

Single through dovetail joint
This joint is used when joining together narrow pieces of timber which are at right angles to each other. It is commonly used when making wall brackets, the sides and ends of tea-trays, and in cabinet construction.

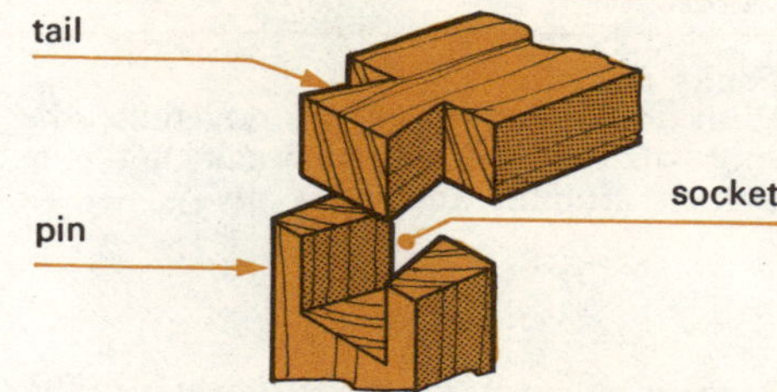

Common through dovetail joint
The common through dovetail is used in box constructions, cabinets, and on the back panels of drawers.

Lapped dovetail joint
This joint is similar to the common through dovetail joint but the lapped dovetail joint conceals the end grain of the piece of wood which carries the tails. It is used in cabinet work and when joining the sides of a drawer to the drawer front.

Double lapped dovetail joint
This joint is also known as the secret dovetail as the joint is not visible from any outside surface. It is used extensively in cabinet-making of high quality.

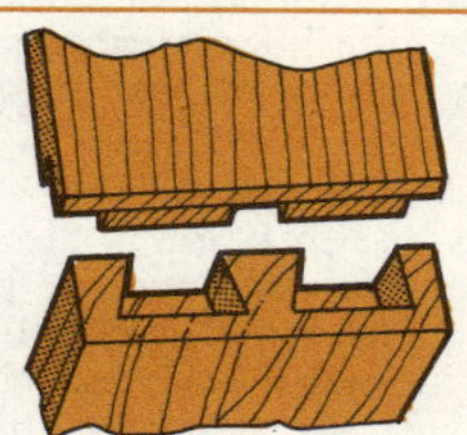

Secret mitre dovetail joint
When this joint is assembled the mitres conceal all end grain, giving the appearance of a plain mitred joint. This joint is used in high-class cabinet-making and when making boxes whose appearance is the first consideration.

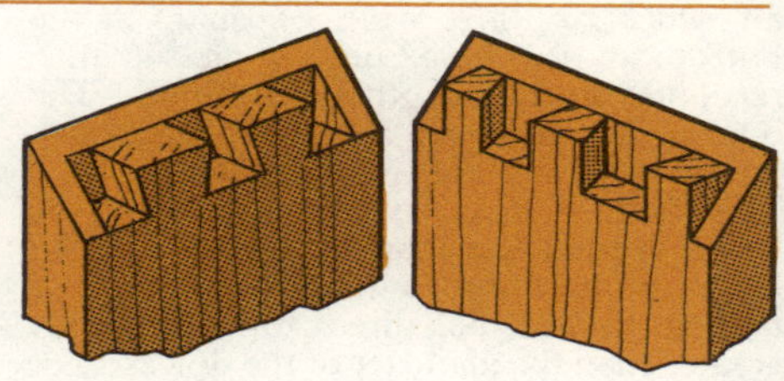

Points to note

To give the joint maximum strength, the amount of taper on the dovetail should be 1 in 6 for softwoods and 1 in 8 for hardwoods.

The dovetail and socket should be equal in area to obtain the maximum gluing surface.

Faulty dovetails

With too much taper on dovetails, the root of the dovetail is weak and the corners crumble and break away.

With insufficient taper on dovetails, the dovetail could easily be forced out of the socket.

JOINTS TO OBTAIN INCREASED WIDTH

Glued and rubbed joint

This joint is used when joining short lengths of timber. One edge of each board is planed straight and square to the face side. The face side marks indicate the true edges. One piece of timber is held in the vice with the true edge upwards. The edges of both pieces of timber are coated with glue and brought together, the top piece being rubbed along the piece in the vice to remove surplus glue. The surplus glue is wiped off the wood with a damp cloth and the glued boards are placed upright against a support until the glue sets. After gluing, the boards can also be held together by means of sash cramps until

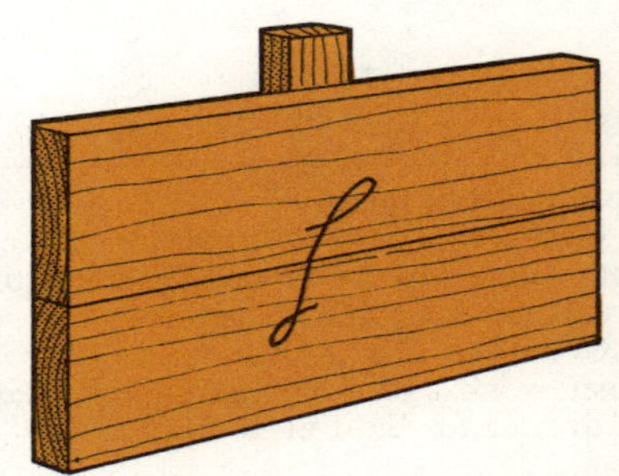

the glue sets. Jointing dogs can be used, but the boards have to be cut much longer than required so that the holes left by the dogs can be sawn off.

Glued and dowelled joint

When making this joint, accuracy in marking out the positions for the dowel pins is of great importance. Before the dowel pins are glued and inserted into the hole, saw cuts are made in the pins to allow the escape of glue and compressed air which would provide a cushion at the bottom of the hole, preventing the pins reaching the full depth of the hole. The boards are cramped together with sash cramps and left until the glue sets.

This joint is suitable for joining boards which are not less than 10 mm thick. The length of the dowel pins in each piece of timber should be three to four times greater than the diameter of the dowel used.

Rebated joint

One edge of each piece is rebated, giving more gluing area than the ordinary glued and rubbed joint. The joint is glued and cramped with sash cramps until the glue sets.

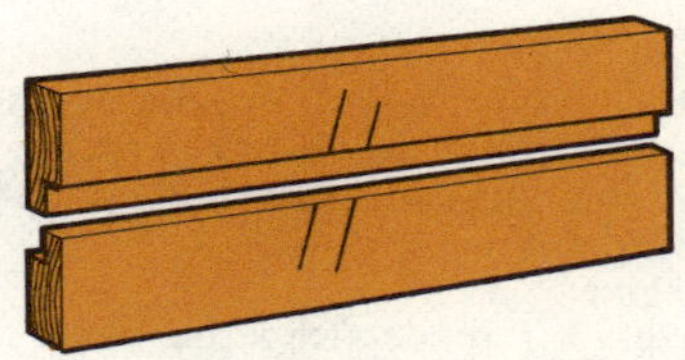

Tongued and grooved joint

This joint is commonly used for floor boards. A groove is worked in the edge of one board and a tongue is worked in one edge of the second board. The joint is glued and cramped with sash cramps till the glue is set.

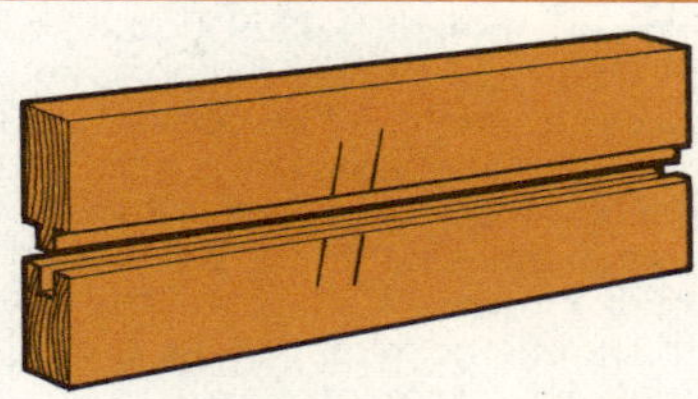

Tongued or feathered joint

In this joint the edges of both boards are grooved using a plough plane, and a strip of wood or tongue is glued and inserted in the grooves. The joint is cramped with sash cramps until the glue sets.

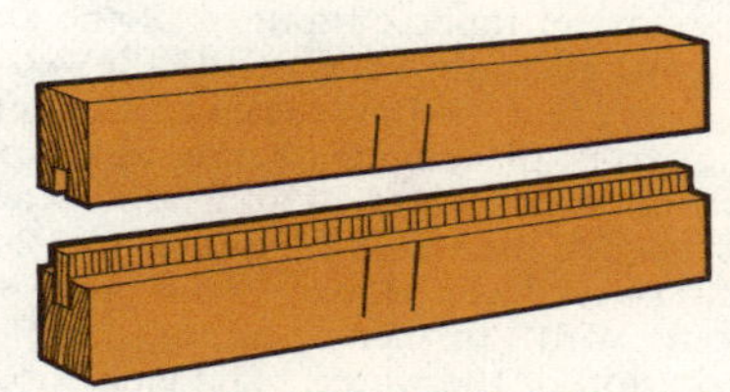

Slot screwed joint

In this joint, screws are driven into one edge of one piece of timber, while keyhole slots to accommodate the screw heads are made in the edge of the second piece of timber. The round hole accommodates the head of the screw and the slot is made to take the screw shank. When the piece of timber containing the slots is driven forwards, the screw heads cut a dovetail slot along the bottom of the hole. The joint is then taken apart, the screws tightened one half turn, and the edges glued and finally assembled.

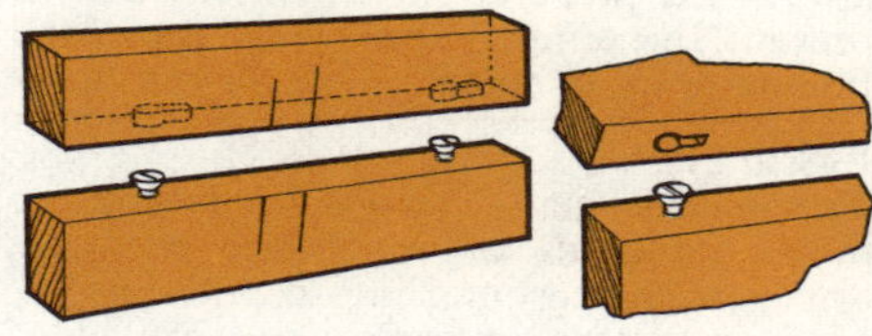

REVISION EXERCISES

1. What is the purpose of a haunch on a haunched mortise and tenon joint?
2. Name and describe a joint used to obtain greater width.
3. What advantage has a stopped housing joint over a through housing joint?
4. What advantage is there in using a rebated butt joint in preference to a butt and nailed joint?
5. Sketch two halved joints.
6. Sketch a single through dovetail joint and name its parts.
7. State the dovetail slope (*a*) when using a hardwood and (*b*) when using a softwood.
8. What is the advantage of the mitred dovetail joint?
9. Sketch the joint used when making a frame with an inset panel.
10. Where would a mitred mortise and tenon joint be used?
11. What is the purpose of wedges in a mortise and tenon joint?
12. What are the ideal proportions when marking out dovetails? Give a reason.
13. What is the purpose of slotting dowel pins before gluing and inserting them in position in the holes?
14. Show, by means of sketches, two methods of increasing the strength of a plain mitred corner joint.

ADHESIVES

The three main types of adhesive used when assembling woodwork articles are Scotch glue, casein glue and polyvinyl acetate (P.V.A.).

Scotch glue

Scotch glue is made from the bones and hides of animals. The bones and hides are cleaned and boiled. The liquid which results from the boiling cools into a brown-coloured jelly. This jelly is cut into blocks which are placed on a wire netting grill and allowed to harden. Supplied in cake form, the glue must be broken up into small pieces. When breaking up the glue, it should be wrapped in a cloth to prevent flying fragments.

The pieces of cake glue (or glue pearls) are placed in the inner container of the glue-pot, covered with water and allowed to soak overnight. After soaking, the inner container is placed inside the outer pot, which contains water, and heated slowly until the glue melts. If the glue is too thick it can be watered down. Thin glue will thicken with further heating, due to evaporation of the water. The glue should always be prepared in a double pot to prevent the temperature rising above the boiling-point of water.

The glue should be used hot, and the work completed quickly, before the glue begins to cool into a jelly consistency. Constant reheating causes deterioration of the glue, a condition which can be recognised by the dark brown colour of the glue. When the glue reaches this state a fresh supply should be prepared.

Scotch glue is now manufactured as small pearls, or beads, and this speeds up the preparation of the glue.

Casein glue

This glue is made from soured skimmed milk, the curds of which are removed, dried out and ground into a fine powder. Lime and borax, or sodium salt, are added to the milk powder. The lime gives the glue water resistance, and the borax or sodium salt makes the powder soluble in water.

The glue is made by mixing the powder with water until it becomes a stiff paste. The paste is set aside for a short period before use. Casein glue is resistant to excessive heat and damp, but it can cause staining of the wood if it is carelessly applied.

Polyvinyl acetate adhesive (P.V.A.)

This is the most recent development in the range of adhesives. It is made by reacting acetic acid and acetylene and then mixing with water to produce an emulsion. The adhesive is white in colour and the consistency of thick cream. The adhesive is supplied ready for use. It is suitable for use in the home, as it is easy to apply, non-staining, and soluble in water.

N.B. Acetylene is a gas produced by mixing calcium carbide and water.

SYNTHETIC RESIN ADHESIVES

Urea formaldehyde

This adhesive is supplied in two separate parts, the adhesive itself, which is a viscous liquid, and a hardener which is also a liquid. The adhesive on its own remains viscous and will not set. The hardener causes a chemical reaction which allows the adhesive to set. One surface of the work is coated with the viscous adhesive (urea formaldehyde resin) while the other surface is coated with the hardener. The joint is then brought together and allowed to set. The setting time is approximately thirty minutes.

With another form of urea formaldehyde adhesive, the hardener is applied to one surface and allowed to dry. The viscous adhesive is then applied to the other surface and the joint is brought together and allowed to set.

Urea formaldehyde adhesive can now be obtained in a powder form. This powder contains both the adhesive and the hardener, with the hardener remaining inert. The addition of water to the powder activates the hardener, which causes the chemical change to take place in the adhesive. The surfaces are then coated and the joint is brought together and allowed to set.

Phenol formaldehyde

This adhesive is used when making plywood waterproof. The adhesive is not affected by hot or cold water. It is widely used in industry, but difficult to use in schools because the setting of the adhesive is dependent on precise control of temperature.

Resorcinol formaldehyde

This adhesive is used mainly for marine construction and boat-building. It is a gap-filling adhesive and its setting temperature is less critical than that of phenol formaldehyde, although the cost of the adhesive is high.

ABRASIVES

Abrasives are sheets of paper or cloth coated with various abrasive materials. They are used when preparing an article for staining, polishing or painting. The use of abrasives is not a substitute for tool finish; proper tool finish is essential before an abrasive is applied. An abrasive wears away the surface of the timber by the cutting action of the abrasive crystalline grit. The grit is deposited on the sheet of cloth or paper which has been coated with adhesive. Grits are graded according to the fineness of the mesh screen through which the grains of abrasive will pass, e.g. number 60 is 60×60, that is, there are 3600 holes in every 25 mm square of mesh through which it will pass.

Types of grit
Glass

This grit is simply crushed glass. It is soft and rather slow-cutting, with the grades ranging from number 3 (the coarsest) in half-numbers down to number 00, which is known as flour grade. It is used mainly for hand finishing.

Garnet

Garnets are semi-precious stones used in making jewellery. The smaller and poorer qualities are used in the manufacture of garnet paper. Garnets are much harder than glass and the abrasive can be used for both hand and machine finishing.

Aluminium oxide

This is a manufactured grit and is one of the hardest of all abrasives used in woodwork finishing. The aluminium oxide is manufactured from the mineral *bauxite*, from which the metal aluminium is extracted. This abrasive is specially valuable for machine sanding hardwood. It has the disadvantage of clogging when used on softwoods.

Silicon carbide

This grit is obtained by heating a mixture of coal and quartz in a furnace to produce carborundum. This is the hardest and, due to the processing, the most expensive of the abrasives. It can be used wet or dry for polishing hard substances such as paint, glass, stone, brass and copper.

Backing papers and cloths

(1) Paper which has a high tensile strength. Abrasives with this backing paper can be used by hand or on a machine.

(2) Woven cotton. Abrasives intended for machine sanding have a woven cotton backing.

(3) Vulcanised fibre. Drum and disc sanding abrasives are backed with vulcanised fibre.

(4) Cloth. The cloth is costly, but lasts longer, and can be used to back abrasives to be used for hand and machine sanding.

Classification of paper and cloth

Papers and cloths are classified by letters marked on the back.

"A" is a flexible paper for hand sanding;

"C" and "D" are medium papers for hand sanding and light machine work;

"E" is a heavy paper used on machine sanders;

"J" is a light cloth which can be used for sanding by hand, or light sanding by machine;

"X" is a heavy, flexible cloth used on machine sanders.

The type of finish applied to an article depends on the kind of timber that has been used and the purpose for which the finished article is intended. Timber is used in many environments, and is open to attack by water, sunlight and chemicals. To preserve it, it is necessary to cover the surface of the timber with a film or coating. Hardwoods of good quality and attractive figure and grain are polished to bring out these qualities and to protect the surfaces from heat, sunlight and spillage. Finished articles which have to be used in moist conditions, such as bathrooms, kitchens and gardens, are given protective coats of paint.

Preparation of surfaces

Any nails used in the construction must be punched below the surface of the wood, and the nail hole filled. The surface is cleaned with the smoothing-plane. The various grades of abrasive paper are then used, starting with coarse paper and working down to fine paper. The surface should be sanded with a sanding cork*, working with the grain to prevent scratching of the surface. Any knots and resinous parts of the timber are treated to prevent the resin from seeping through to the finished surface. A suitable stopper to prevent resin from seeping through is a mixture of shellac and naphtha.

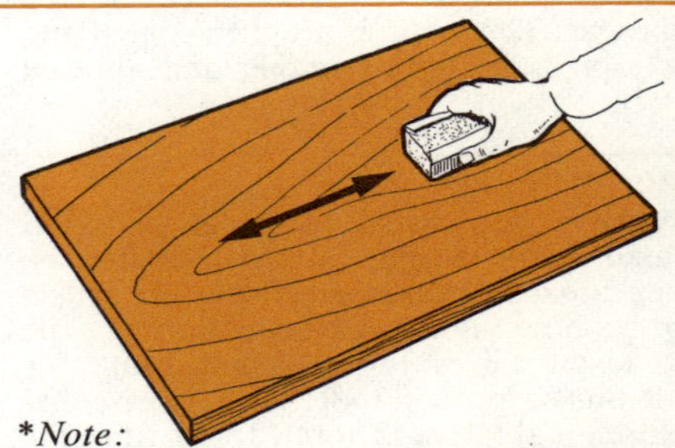

*Note:

A sanding cork is a block of cork, around which the abrasive paper is wrapped. The softness of the cork prevents too rapid wear of the abrasive.

Stains

Wood finishing by staining is now largely out of vogue, finishing timber in its natural colour being preferred. It is applicable, however, where a finished article may have various colours of timber in its construction. Staining does not conceal the grain of the timber; its purpose is to tone the wood to a uniform colour.

1. Water stain

This is made by dissolving water stain crystals of oak, mahogany, walnut, etc. in hot water. The depth of penetration of the stain can be increased by adding a little ammonia to the mixture. The stain is applied by brush, and any surplus deposit wiped away with a cloth. The end grain of wood, when stained, always shows darker in colour than the surface and should be treated with a weaker solution of the stain. The application of a water stain tends to cause the grain of the wood to rise, giving a rough surface. So, before staining, the wood should be dampened with water and glass-papered smooth when dry. When it has been stained it should be burnished with a handful of dry shavings.

2. Oil stain

Oil stain is made by dissolving the colour pigment in turpentine. Oil stains have the advantage of not causing the grain of the wood to rise, but they are likely to fade in strong sunlight. These stains are applied with a cloth or cotton waste.

3. Spirit stain

The colouring agents in spirit stains are aniline dyes (coal tar), dissolved in methylated spirits. They give a wide range of very strong colours. Due to the rapid evaporation of the methylated spirit, these stains dry out very quickly. Like oil stains, they do not cause the grain of the wood to rise.

4. Chemical stain

Chemical stains include bichromate of potash dissolved in water. This stains timber having a tannic acid content (e.g. oak). Dilute ammonia was widely used in staining mahogany, while oak exposed to the fumes of ammonia gives the once popular fumed oak finish.

Grain filling

When the surface has been prepared, and stained if required, the grain is filled, using a filler made from a mixture of powdered whiting, turpentine and a little gold size. It can be coloured by mixing in one of the many powdered pigments. A filler is used to close the pores of the timber, so that both time and polish are saved by cutting down the number of layers of polish which would be required. The filler paste is rubbed into the grain with a cloth crossways and the surplus wiped off with the grain. It is then set aside to harden overnight. The surface is rubbed down lightly with a fine grade glass-paper, ready for polishing.

French polish

The basic ingredient of french polish is *sticklac,* which is a secretion produced by the lac insect. This insect lives on trees in South-East Asia, and the sticklac secretion is mainly wax and resin which, when it is refined, is known as shellac. The polish is made by dissolving the shellac in methylated spirit, producing colours ranging from browns to reds. White polish is obtained by bleaching the shellac before dissolving it in the methylated spirit.

Cellulose polish

This polish is made by mixing dewaxed shellac with ethyl cellulose, to give a mixture which has improved toughness and a higher degree of resistance to abrasion than french polish. It is applied in the same manner as french polish, but a special thinner is used in place of methylated spirit. The surface is brought to a high gloss using a burnishing cream supplied for this purpose (brand name, *Excellac*).

STAGES WHEN POLISHING

Fadding

The initial coats of polish, which seal the pores of the wood and create a hard and smooth surface for further polishing, are applied by means of a "rubber". The rubber consists of a wad of unbleached cotton wool, wrapped in a piece of linen. The shape of this rubber is important, as it has to be capable of working into corners and confined spaces. It is formed like a foot, with a pointed toe which is able to cover all areas.

The rubber is charged by pouring a small measure of polish inside the cloth on to the cotton wool, and it is then applied to the work in straight strokes along the grain of the wood. Very light pressure is placed on the rubber at the outset, but as the polish is deposited, pressure is increased to keep up the flow of polish from the rubber. When the reservoir of polish has been exhausted, the rubber is recharged and used until the surface has been completely sealed. The polish is then allowed to harden completely, usually for about twelve hours, after which

time it is rubbed down lightly with a fine grade abrasive paper, ready for the next stage.

Bodying

This is the stage when a body of polish is built up on the work. The rubber is charged with polish as before, and a spot of polishing oil applied to the sole of the rubber to lubricate its passage over the work. The rubber is held as before and the polish applied, using a circular over-lapping motion for the first coat and parallel strokes with the grain for the second coat. The circular movement of the rubber pulls over any ridges that may have been formed in the fadding stage. A number of layers of polish are deposited in this fashion until a full body of polish has been applied, each charged rubber being worked until it is fairly dry, using the smallest amount of polishing oil.

When the work has a full body of polish, it is set aside to harden. When the polish is hard, it is rubbed down lightly with well-worn glass-paper ready for the final or finishing stages.

Finishing

This stage is often referred to as "spiriting off". Its purpose is to eliminate the polishing oil and to burnish the surface to a high gloss. The rubber is charged with 50% polish and 50% methylated spirit. This mixture can be made up and kept ready in a separate jar. The rubber is passed over the work in large circular movements, changing to oval, and finally straight strokes parallel to the grain. The rubber is then charged with a little methylated spirit only, and the procedure repeated, until the bulk of the oil is removed. Finally, a new rubber is formed, charged with a few drops of methylated spirit, and worked over the surface with light strokes parallel to the grain until a bright, shiny surface is obtained.

WAX POLISHING

Wax polishing gives a satin, or eggshell, finish which is most attractive. The polish is made by dissolving shredded beeswax in turpentine. A good quality polish can be made by shredding beeswax into a container which is standing in hot water, and gradually adding turpentine until the mixture achieves the consistency of soft margarine. A harder polish can be made by adding one part of carnauba wax to six parts of beeswax.

Procedure for wax polishing

The surface to be polished may be stained or left in its natural colour. If an oil stain has been used, the turpentine in the wax will tend to dissolve the stain in places and leave a patchy surface. To prevent this, an oil-stained surface should be sealed by applying two coats of french polish to the surface, sanding down the first coat before applying the second. The wax is applied by a cloth and rubbed well into the grain of the wood. It is then laid aside to allow the turpentine to evaporate, leaving a film of wax on the surface of the wood which is burnished with a soft cloth. Successive applications of wax can be given until the desired finish is obtained.

Carnauba wax

This type of wax is a product of the palm tree, its main use being the polishing of turned work. When the work has been glass-papered, two or three coats of french polish are applied and rubbed down, between each coat, to a smooth matt finish. The work is now revolved in the lathe, and the carnauba wax applied by holding it against the work and slowly moving the wax over the surface. The heat generated by the friction melts the wax and deposits a layer of wax on the article. With the work still revolving a cloth pad is passed over the coating of wax polish, spreading it evenly over the surface. Finally, this coating is burnished to a gloss finish, using a soft rag.

Teak oil
This finish is used on furniture made from teak, afrormosia and similar timbers. The article is finished by the usual processes, and a thin coat of teak oil is applied using a non-fluffy cloth. This coat is allowed to dry, normally in four to six hours. The surface is lightly rubbed down with well-worn glass-paper, and two further coats of teak oil are applied. When absolutely dry, the surface is polished with a dry cloth. Teak oil penetrates and is absorbed by the wood, therefore it cannot peel or crack. Any marks left on the wood by spilled liquids, spots or finger-marks, are removed with a damp cloth and then polished dry.

STAGES IN PAINTING

1. Primer coat
The purpose of the primer is to seal the grain of the wood, thus preventing the bare wood soaking up the successive coats of paint.

2. Undercoat
The undercoat is applied to complete the sealing of the wood and to cover the grain and figure. Two undercoats may be required to achieve this.

3. Gloss coat
This coat is applied to provide a gloss finish and to complete the protection of the wood. Two coats are recommended. Each coat should be well brushed in, both with the grain and across the grain. For the best quality finish, the work should be sanded down with a fine grade paper between each coat of paint.

High gloss paint
This paint has a large percentage of varnish in its composition which gives it a high gloss finish. When using this type of paint, the manufacturer's undercoats should be used, and there should be no delay beyond that recommended between applying undercoat and finishing coat.

Cellulose paint
Cellulose paints give a fine, smooth finish with rapid drying time between each coat. Cellulose paints do not yield with timber movement and, in consequence, are likely to show crinkles after a time. Normally, cellulose paint is applied by spraying, but brushing types are also available.

REVISION EXERCISES

1. Describe the preparation of Scotch glue.
2. Sketch a cross-sectional view of a glue pot.
3. Constant re-heating of Scotch glue can cause deterioration. How is this condition recognised?
4. What is the advantage of pearl or bead glue over cake glue?
5. Name two advantages of casein glue.
6. What is the disadvantage of casein glue?
7. Name two advantages of polyvinyl acetate.
8. What is the disadvantage of phenol formaldehyde when used in schools?
9. What is the basic difference between synthetic resin adhesives and other forms of glue?
10. What is an abrasive?
11. What is the purpose of using an abrasive?
12. How does glass-paper differ from garnet paper?
13. Name three backing materials for abrasives.
14. Give reasons for applying a surface finish to woodwork articles.
15. Describe how an article is prepared to receive a surface finish.
16. When would an article be french polished and when would it be painted?
17. Describe, stage by stage, how you would gloss paint a small kitchen cupboard.
18. What is the function of an undercoat?
19. Name an advantage and a disadvantage of cellulose paint.
20. What is the purpose of staining an article made from wood?
21. What is the advantage of using an oil stain as opposed to a water stain?
22. Describe how a good wax polish can be made.
23. What is the main use of carnauba wax?
24. What is the advantage of teak oil?
25. What is the purpose of a grain filler?
26. How is white french polish obtained?
27. Describe how a french polishing rubber is made.
28. Why is polishing oil used when french polishing?
29. What is the purpose of "spiriting off"?

There are four basic principles which govern the design of any article:
(1) it must be fit for the purpose for which it is intended;
(2) its proportions must be correct;
(3) the correct method of construction must be employed;
(4) it must be made from suitable materials.

Fitness for purpose

This is the first consideration of good design. The article must fulfil the purpose for which it is designed, whether it is a work-bench, dining-room chair or kitchen cabinet. The function of the article determines its dimensions, e.g. the height of the work-bench, the height of the chair seat or the height of the working surface on the kitchen cabinet.

Proportions

The main dimensions of an article are determined by the use for which it is designed. Other dimensions are calculated in proportion to these main sizes. The heights of tables and chairs must be related to each other. Shelves in bookcases and drawers in chests should increase in depth from the top of the unit to the bottom, to give a balanced appearance and to make it easier to use the shelves or drawers. The proportions of the width and thickness are selected, bearing in mind the strength factor of the article.

Method of construction

A knowledge of the methods of joining materials is essential. The joints selected must give the required strength and rigidity, and also ensure that unnecessary work is eliminated. The methods of construction and assembly must be considered, as some kinds of work are better polished or painted before they are assembled.

Material

Due to the growth characteristics of timber, articles made from wood are mainly confined to straight lines. The natural beauty of timber, with its different grains and colours, should be displayed to greatest advantage. Featureless timbers can be stained or painted. Dark woods and veneers tend to create a heavy appearance. The use of different woods and veneers on the same article should be avoided, as this is not restful on the eye. Choose timber carefully. The beauty of the wood can be displayed to the best advantage by exercising care in both finishing and polishing the article.

After an article has been designed, a list of the required materials is made. When the article is to be made of wood, the list of materials is known as the "cutting list". The cutting list is necessary to identify the parts of the construction and to specify the kind of timber to be used.

The sizes given on the cutting list are the finished, or net, sizes, therefore allowances must be made for planing to the finished widths and thicknesses.

Allowances for finishing must be made:

1. on the length when the timber is planed all round (P.A.R.)
2. on the length and width when the timber is planed two sides (P.2.S.)
3. on the length, width and thickness when the timber is rough sawn (R/S).

When a mortise has to be cut on the end of a table or stool leg, sufficient allowance should be made to give added strength to the timber to avoid splitting the leg when the mortise chisel is being used. It is common practice to allow about 25 mm at the end of the leg for this purpose. This allowance is removed after the legs and rails have been assembled.

small stool

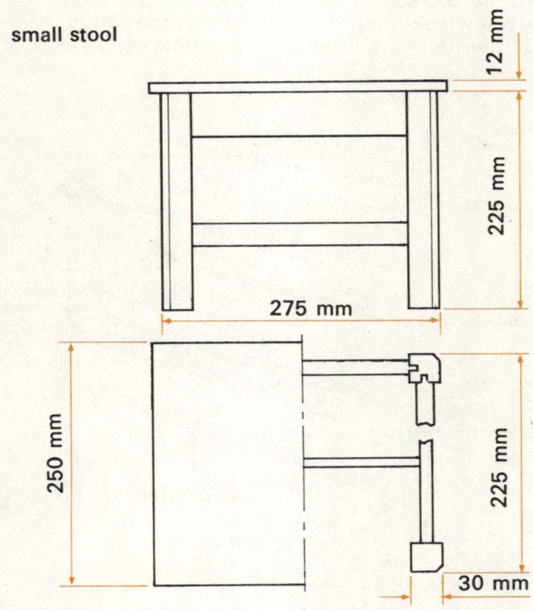

CUTTING LIST

Legs	4 off	225	× 30	× 30 mm	oak
Long Rails	2 off	265	× 56	× 15 mm	oak
Short Rails	2 off	215	× 56	× 15 mm	oak
Long Stretcher Rail	1 off	255	× 25	× 12 mm	oak
Short Stretcher Rails	2 off	215	× 25	× 12 mm	oak
Top	1 off	300	× 250	× 12 mm	oak
Buttons	10 off	30	× 25	× 12 mm	deal

10 wood-screws 18 mm × 6 countersunk mild steel to secure buttons

All sizes are net.

Cabinet and frame construction

The joints used in the construction of the cabinet carcase should be chosen to give maximum strength, to show as little end grain as possible, and to present unbroken lines on vertical edges.

The top of the cabinet should be fixed to the cabinet sides by means of double lapped dovetail joints or secret mitre dovetail joints. When the double lapped dovetail joint is used the minimum of end grain is shown. When the secret mitre dovetail joint is used all the end grain is concealed. The bottom of the cabinet can be fixed to the cabinet sides by using single lap dovetail joints. The end grain on the bottom of the cabinet sides will not be seen if the base of the cabinet is below eye-level.

The vertical cabinet division and the cabinet shelf are fixed to the cabinet carcase by using stopped housing joints. The stopped housing joint presents unbroken lines on the cabinet sides and the cabinet division.

The frame on which the cabinet sits is constructed in the same manner as a table or stool frame. Haunched mortises are cut on the top of the legs and the rails have tenons cut to fit into the mortises.

The railed shelf is fixed to the legs of the frame by using stopped mortise and tenon joints. The cross members of the shelf are fixed to the shelf rails, using stub mortise and tenon joints. The use of stopped mortise and tenon joints and stub mortise and tenon joints means that no end grain is visible on the legs or on the shelf rails.

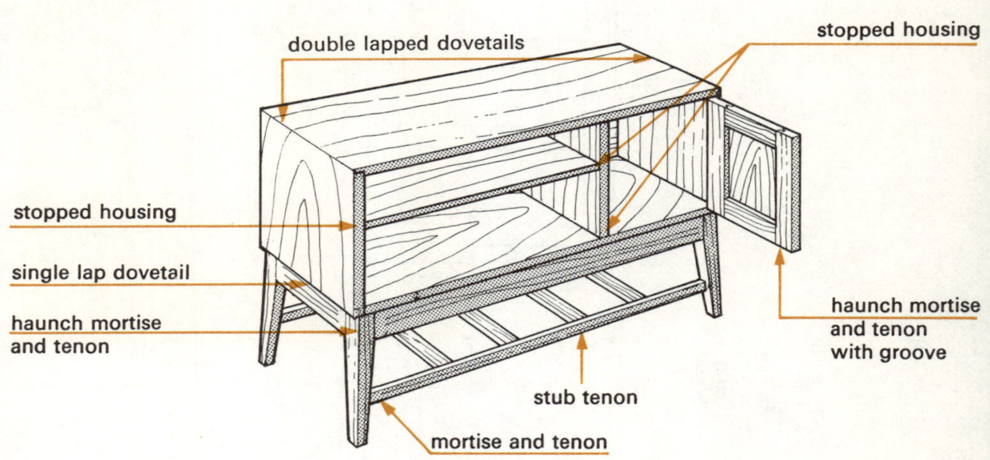

Door construction
Garage or hut door

This door-frame is assembled by using mortise and tenon joints. The frame is fitted with diagonal braces to give rigidity and support. Tongued and grooved battens are nailed or screwed on to the door-frame. The door is hinged using strap or tee hinges, and care must be taken to hinge the door from the correct stile (housing stile). The door must be hung so that the diagonal braces help to support the weight of the door and prevent distortion.

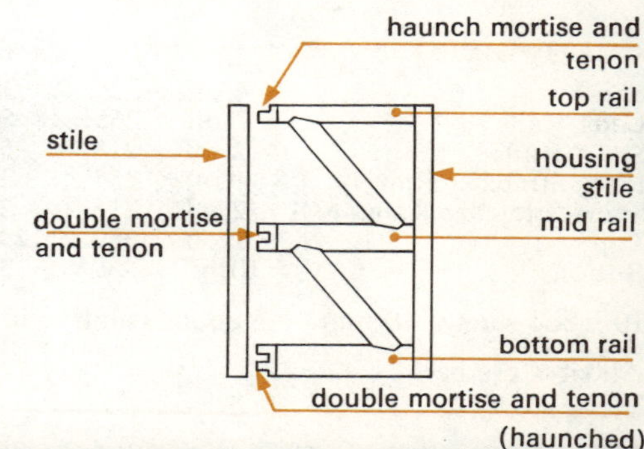

Edge treatment of doors

Some form of treatment of door edges is required in order to conceal any end grain showing on the door-frame construction, or to conceal the laminations of doors made from plywood or laminated board.

The end grain of timber and plywood laminations are concealed by gluing and pinning wooden strips, called lippings, on to the door edges. These lippings are mitred at the four corners of the door so that no end grain is visible.

Lippings are made to the required length, with the width of the lipping the same as the thickness of the door. The thickness of the lipping should be no less than 6 mm and no more than 10 mm.

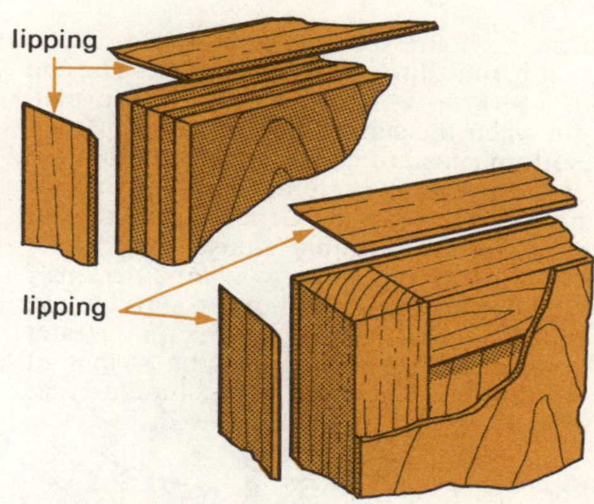

Cabinet door

This door-frame is fitted together using haunched mortise and tenon joints. The inside edges of the frame are grooved to accommodate the panel. The grooves to hold the panel are cut after the mortises are marked out, so that the edge of the mortise can be made level with the bottom of the groove. If the end grain needs to be hidden, the door is made smaller than the inside of the cabinet, and lippings are glued and pinned to the door edges.

Drawer construction

The sides of the drawer are fitted to the front by means of lapped dovetail joints. This presents an unbroken surface on the drawer front. The sides of the drawer are fitted to the back by means of modified common through dovetail joints.

The back of the drawer is set down below the level of the sides so that it does not scrape the underside of the carcase.

The bottom is screwed directly on to the edge of the drawer back with the grain running from side to side. Slotted screw holes are cut on the drawer bottom to allow for bottom movement due to shrinkage. When plywood is used to make the drawer bottom there is no need to slot-cut the screw holes, as plywood has virtually no shrinkage.

The groove cut on the inside of the drawer

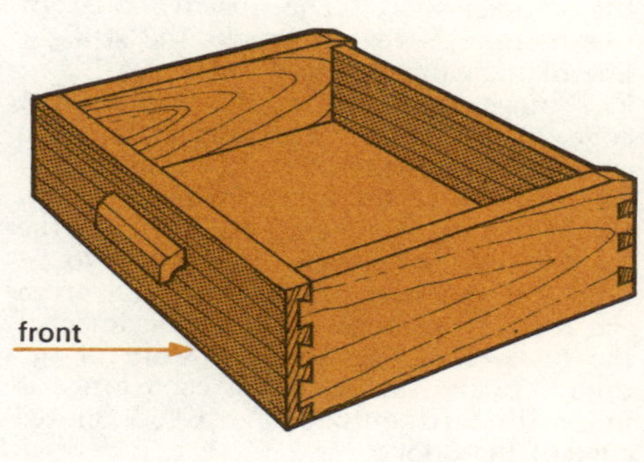

front to house the drawer bottom is cut so that it runs into a dovetail socket. The end of the groove is hidden by the dovetail pin when the side of the drawer is fitted. Bottom slips are used to house the bottom of the drawer in preference to grooving the sides of the drawer. Grooving the drawer sides would certainly house the drawer bottom but the sides would be seriously weakened. The use of bottom slips has the added advantage of giving a greater bearing surface to support the weight of the drawer. There are two common types of bottom slip that can be used.

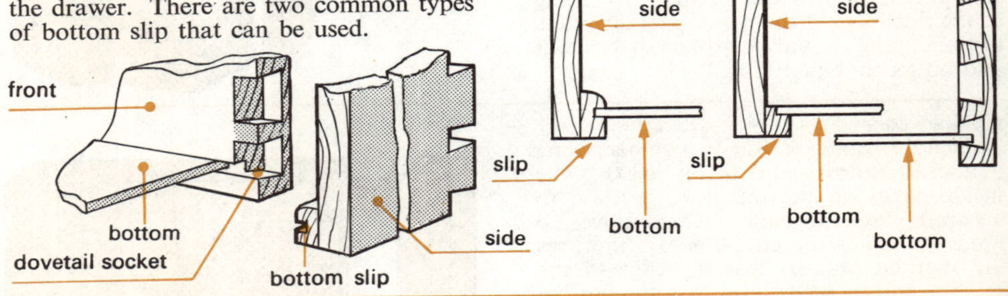

Fitting a hinge

There are two methods of fitting a hinge to a cabinet door and the cabinet side.

In the first method, the thickness of the knuckle is recessed into the edge of the door. Sloping recesses are cut into the door and the side of the cabinet to allow the hinge flanges to sink in flush with the cabinet door and the cabinet side. This method presents an unbroken edge on the cabinet side, and is preferable to recessing the flanges into the door and the cabinet side.

Using the second method, the flange thickness is recessed into the door edge and the cabinet side. The disadvantage of this method is that it breaks the straight line of the cabinet side.

The hinge is placed in position on the edge of the door, with the door edge running through the centre of the hinge pin. The distance of the hinge from the top of the door is approximately the length of the hinge itself. Where two hinges are to be used, the distance of the top hinge from the top of the door, and the distance of the lower hinge from the bottom of the door, are the same. When each hinge is in position its outline is marked on the edge of the door.

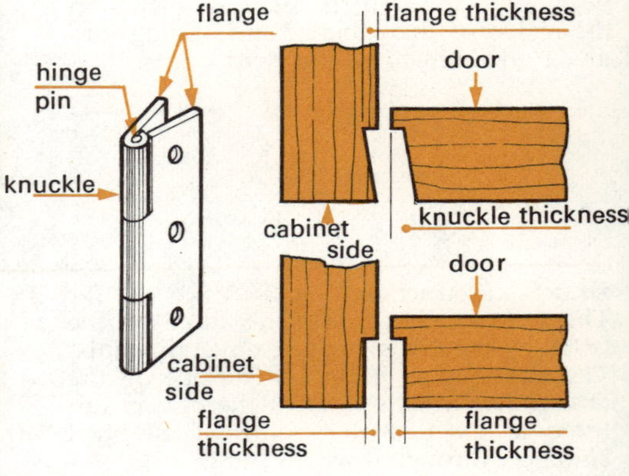

The depth that the hinge is let into the door is the thickness of the knuckle of the hinge. This size is set on the marking gauge from the hinge and marked across the face of the door.

The gauge is now set from the edge of the hinge to the centre of the pin and this size is marked across the door edge. This determines the amount of hinge which is set into the edge of the door.

To remove the waste wood, first saw down each end of the hinge recess with a tenon-saw or dovetail saw. Several saw cuts can be made along the length of the hinge recess to aid the removal of the waste wood.

The saw must be held so that it does not cut straight across the edge of the door, but at an angle to meet the gauge lines on the door face and the door edge.

After the recess has been sawn, the waste wood is removed with a bevelled-edge chisel. The chisel is held vertically at each end of the recess and the chisel handle struck with a mallet. This is to sever the fibres at the ends of the recess where they have not been cut by the saw. This prevents splitting when the waste wood is removed.

The chisel is now placed vertically on the gauge line marked along the door edge for the flange width. The chisel handle is pressed so that the cutting edge deepens the gauge line. The handle of the chisel is not struck with a mallet in this operation as this would tend to split the wood.

The chisel is now held horizontally and the waste wood is pared away. As the waste wood is removed the chisel may be held at an angle to allow for the taper necessary when fitting the knuckle of the hinge into the door edge.

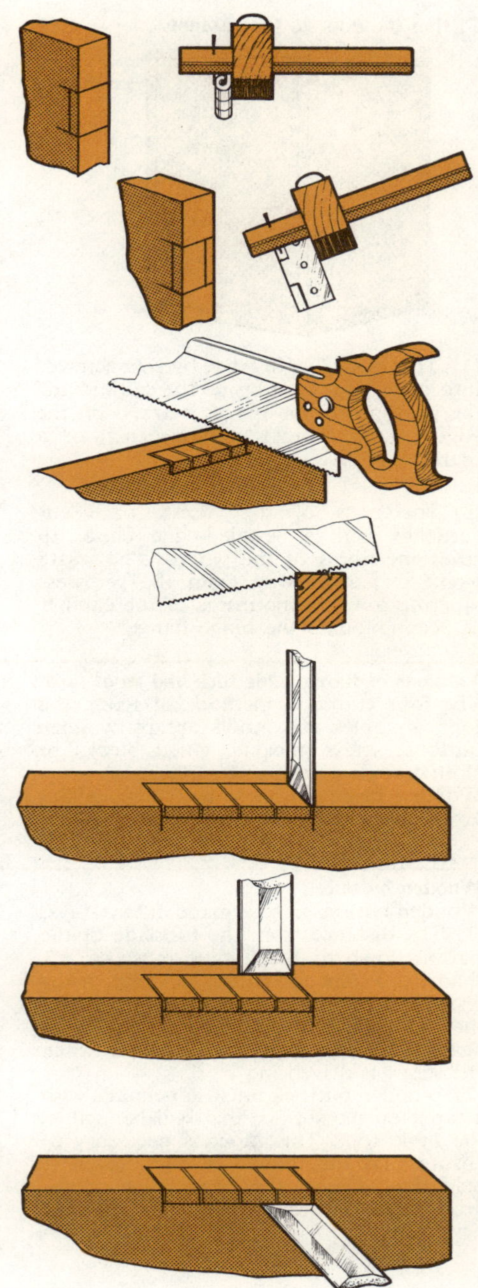

Fitting the door to the cabinet

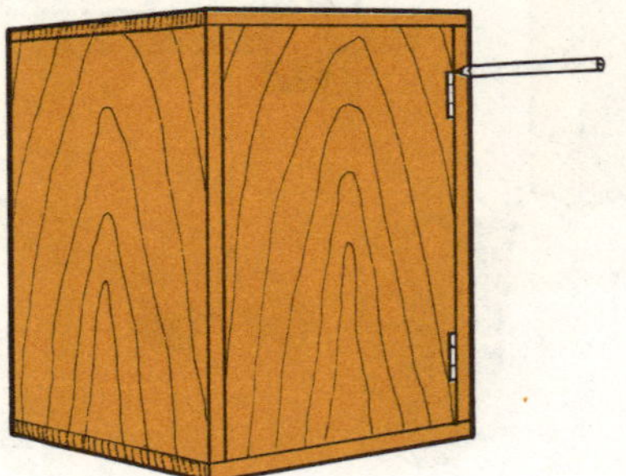

(1) The door, with the hinges screwed into place, is placed inside the cabinet and the position of the hinges marked on the edge of the cabinet with a pencil or a marking knife.

(3) The ends of the recesses are cut vertically with a bevelled-edge chisel to sever the fibres of the wood. The waste wood is pared away from the recesses, tapering towards the inside of the cabinet to accommodate the hinge flange.

(2) The door is removed from inside the cabinet and the mark locating the hinges is squared across the cabinet side and edge with a pencil or marking knife and a try-square.

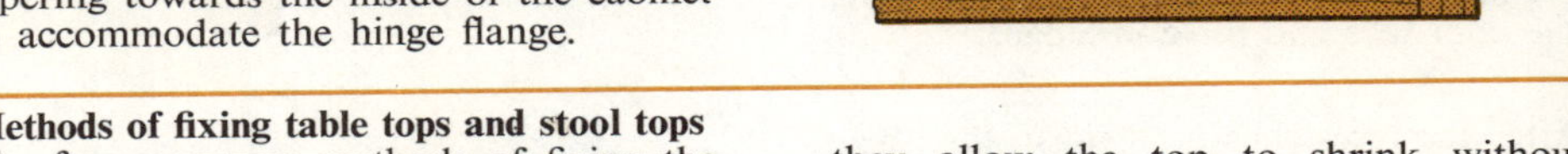

Methods of fixing table tops and stool tops

The four common methods of fixing the tops of tables and stools are by wooden buttons, screw pockets, glued blocks or slotted angle plates.

Wooden buttons and slotted angle plates are perhaps the most effective methods as they allow the top to shrink without splitting.

Screw pockets and glued blocks are ideal when the top is made from plywood, blockboard or lamin board, when shrinkage is negligible.

Wooden buttons

Wooden buttons can be made in two ways.
(1) The distance from the top side of the button down to the tongue must be less than the distance from the top edge of the groove to the top of the rail. This ensures that the tongue of the button is held tight against the top edge of the groove when the screw is driven in.
(2) Wooden buttons can also be made with a taper on the surface that will be against the table top. This taper is necessary to ensure that the tongue of the button is held tight against the upper edge of the groove in the rail when the screw is driven in.

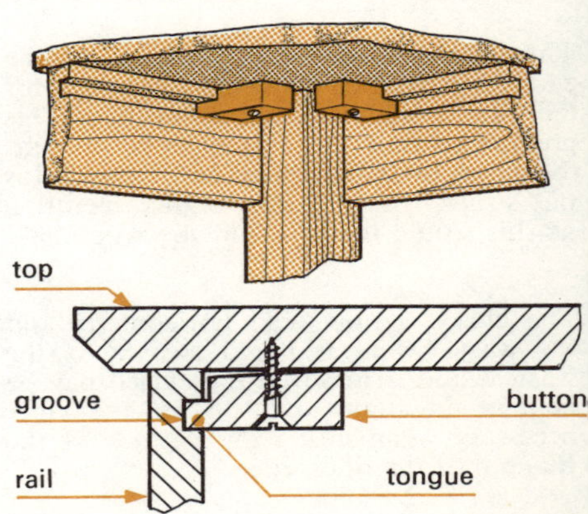

Screw pockets

When making screw pockets, the pilot hole for the screw is bored from the edge of the rail at the required angle until the bit appears through the inside of the rail. A scribing gouge is used to taper-cut the inside of the rail at the same angle as the bored hole. This permits the head of the screw to be housed in the rail.

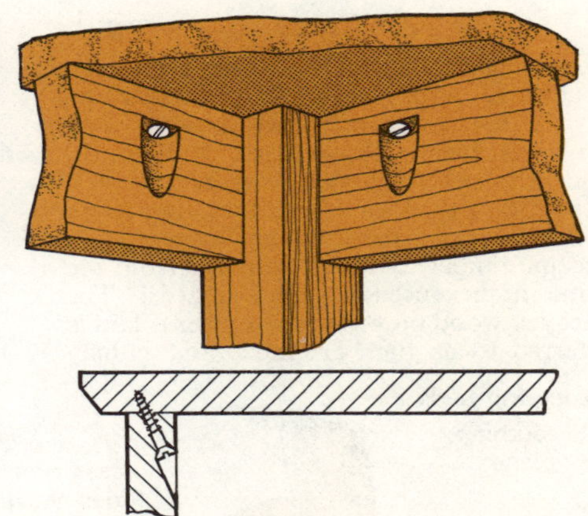

Angle plates

Angle plates have two slotted screw holes on one side of the angle plate and one plain screw hole on the other. The slotted screw holes are cut at 90° to each other. This enables the angle plate to be used on either the side rail or the end rail. The purpose of the slots is to allow the screw to move with the timber in the direction of shrinkage. This avoids any possibility of distortion or splitting of the top. The angle plate is screwed on to the rail, keeping the plate tight against the table top, then the angle plate is screwed on to the top.

Glued blocks

When using glued blocks, the edge of the block against the rail and the edge against the top must be at 90° to each other. The position of the block is marked on the rail and the top and Scotch glue applied to this area. The squared surfaces of the block are coated with glue and the block is placed in position and rubbed to exclude excess glue and air. The work is then set aside until the glue sets.

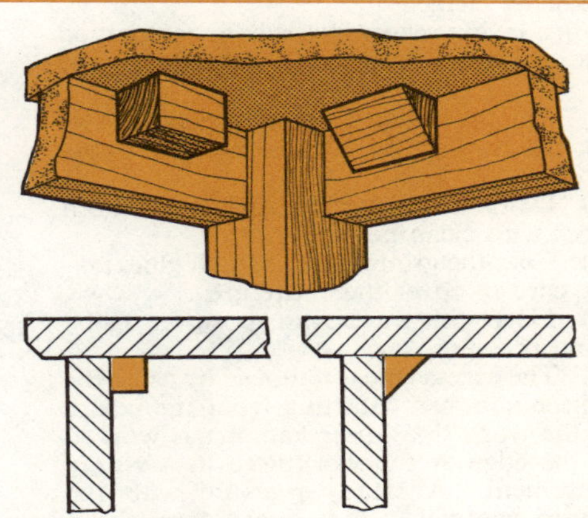

Veneering is the art of improving the decorative appearance of an article by laying thin pieces of choice figured wood on its surfaces. On average, between 30 and 40 sheets of veneer can be obtained per 25 mm thick of wood, therefore more articles can be made using veneers of a specific timber than can be made from the same timber used as solid boards. The cheaper wood on which the veneer is laid is referred to as the "ground", and it may be solid timber or plywood, laminated board or blockboard. When veneer is laid on solid timber the glue causes the board to distort or curl as the glue dries out. This tendency for the board to curl can be eliminated by veneering both sides of the board. The use of plywood as the ground means that only one surface of the plywood needs to be veneered, as the plywood ground eliminates warping or curling.

Veneering tools

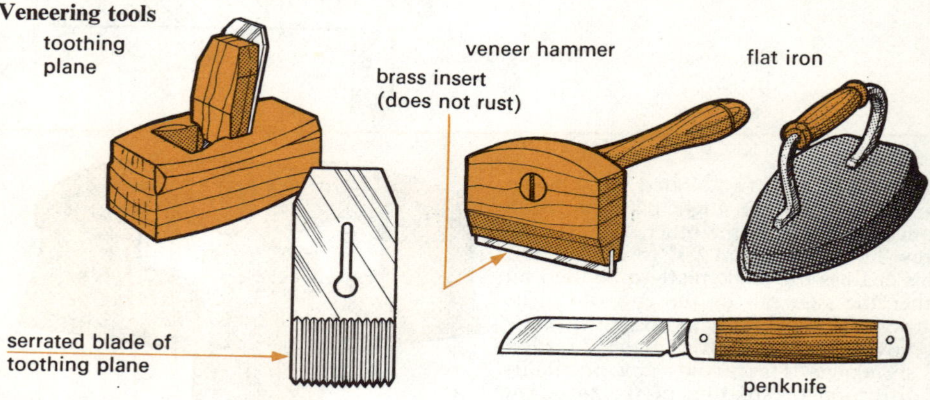

Preparation of the ground

The surface to be veneered should be cleaned and any imperfections removed. The surface is then roughened by using either a toothing-plane or a hack-saw blade diagonally across the surface.

This roughening provides a key for the glue. End grain which has to be veneered should first be given a coat of weak glue (size).

Hammer method

When laying veneer by the hammer method the adhesive used is Scotch glue. The glue should be freshly made and of a proper consistency, thin but not watery.

(1)   Cut the selected veneer to size, allowing an overlap of 10 mm all round the work.

(2)   Dampen the veneer slightly on both faces with clean hot water.

(3)   Coat the ground with Scotch glue, taking care to cover the entire area.

(4)   Place the veneer in position using hand pressure.

(5)   The excess glue is removed by using the veneer hammer. Starting from the centre of the work the veneer hammer is worked to the edge of the workpiece in a zigzag movement. A steady pressure with the veneer hammer is maintained throughout this operation.

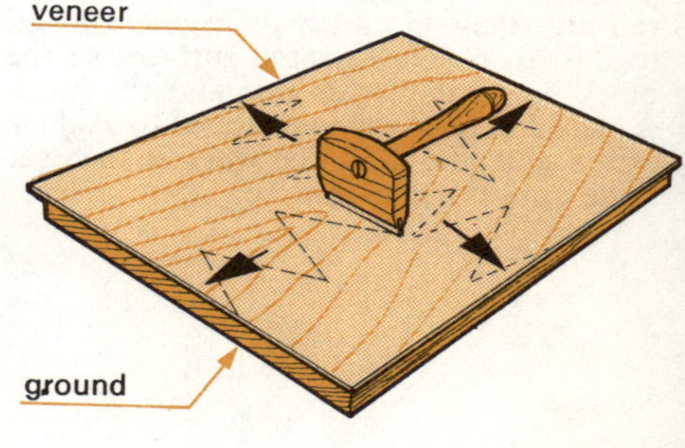

(6) Surplus glue should now show round the edges of the ground. If surplus glue is not present the glue may have been too thick or been allowed to chill. To liquefy the glue the veneer is dampened with clean hot water and a hot flat-iron is passed over the veneer. The moist heat generated will remelt the glue which can finally be forced out with the veneer hammer. The use of the hot flat-iron is simply a convenient way of heating the glue beneath the veneer. If the iron is overheated the veneer may be scorched.

(7) Remove the surplus glue from the work edges with a cloth dipped in hot water. Care must be taken not to soak the edges, as the hot water would then flow under the veneer causing it to lift off the ground.

(8) When the glue has set, the veneer overlap is trimmed off flush with the ground, using a sharp penknife.

(9) If any blisters appear on the surface, due to trapped air below the veneer, these are treated by slitting the veneer with a penknife and inserting a small amount of glue. The veneer is then pressed down into place.

Heated caul method

This is a simpler method of laying veneer and is the method adopted when laying veneer which has a difficult grain structure. The cauls are pieces of wood of a suitable size, heated and positioned on either side of the ground, with the veneers already glued in position. Paper is placed between the veneer and the caul to prevent the caul sticking to the veneer. Battens are placed across the cauls and pressure exerted by "G" clamps. The battens should be slightly convex in shape, so that the pressure is exerted from the centre of the panel outwards, forcing the glue to the edges.

The heated caul method is also used when veneering curved surfaces. Shaped cauls are made to the same radius as the surface being veneered. When the ground has been coated with glue and the veneer placed in position, paper is placed on the veneer and the heated cauls are clamped in place by means of suitably shaped battens and "G" clamps. The cauls are kept clamped to the veneers until the glue has set.

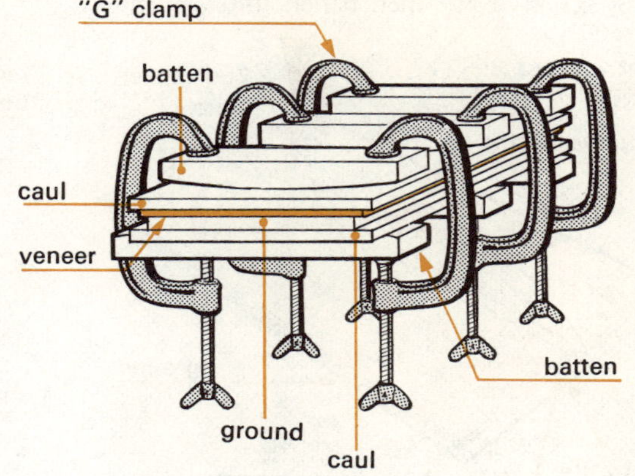

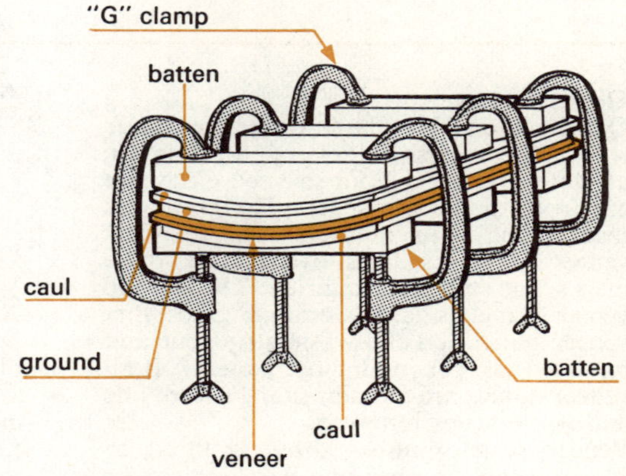

Matching panels

Pieces of veneer which match each other in grain and figure are frequently laid side by side and joined down the centre of the panel. A centre line is first marked on the ground, and the veneers cut with an overlap all round the ground and at the centre. The first veneer is cut to overlap the centre line, and the second veneer is then laid to overlap the first veneer, also at the centre line. A straight-edge is then placed over the veneers on the centre line, and both veneers are cut through using a sharp penknife. The waste strip from the top is removed and then the bottom waste strip is removed by carefully raising the edge of the veneer. Both edges are then pressed down, and held in position by strips of gummed paper, until the glue sets.

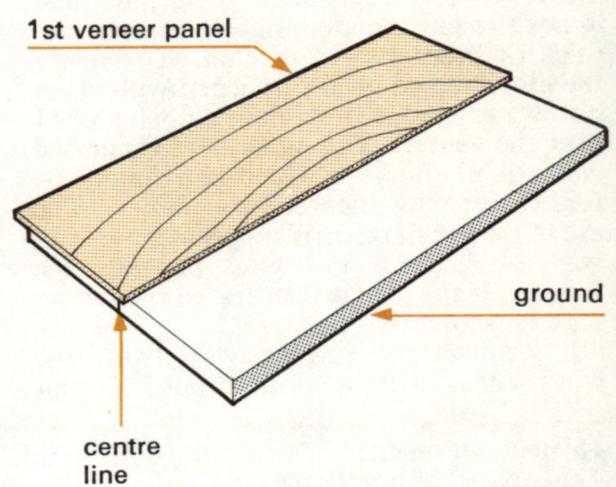

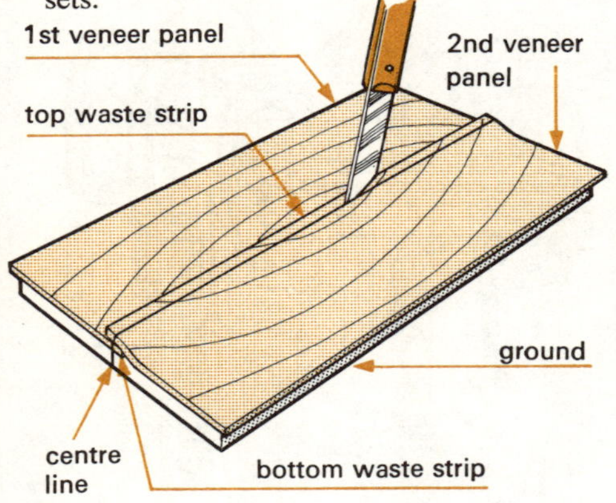

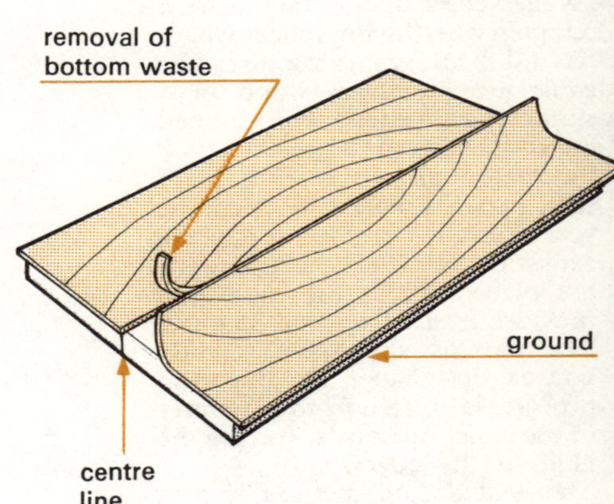

Quartered panels

Quartered panels are used where the veneer sheet offers possibilities of forming an attractive pattern. Four selected pieces are cut from the veneer sheet. The ground is marked off into quarters and the first veneer panel is laid, overlapping these marks, on the first quarter. The second veneer panel is laid overlapping the first veneer panel and the waste strips cut and removed as for matching panels. Both veneer panels are cut across the centre line and waste strips removed.

Veneer panel number three is fitted to veneer panel number one overlapping the centre. The waste strip is cut and removed.

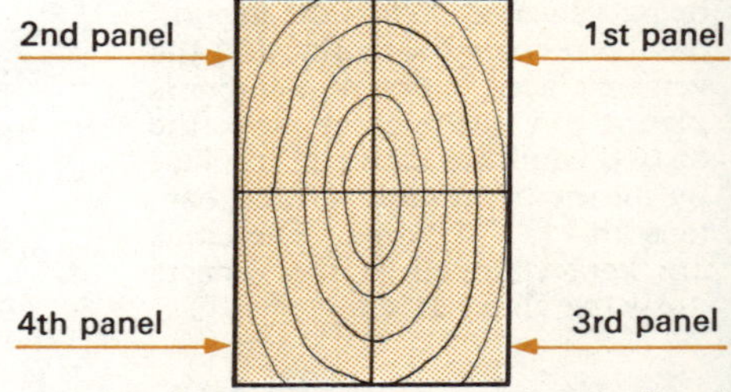

Finally veneer panel number four is fitted to veneer panel number two overlapping the centre line. The overlapping strip is cut and removed. Surplus strips of veneer round the edges of the ground are cut and removed.

Safety precautions when using the lathe

1. Wear an apron and protective goggles.
2. Roll up sleeves and remove necktie.
3. Make sure you know the position of the control switches.
4. When screwing work to the faceplate, avoid placing screws in the same line of grain.
5. Before starting the lathe, rotate the work by hand to ensure that it rotates freely without catching the tool-rest.
6. Remove the tool-rest before sanding and polishing in the lathe.
7. Select a suitable speed according to the diameter of the work and the type of wood.
8. Use the correct tool for the job and hold it firmly with both hands.
9. Make sure you are standing in a comfortable, well-balanced position when working at the lathe.
10. Do not measure or make adjustments to the work while it is turning.
11. Do not try to stop the lathe revolving by pressing your hand on the wood.

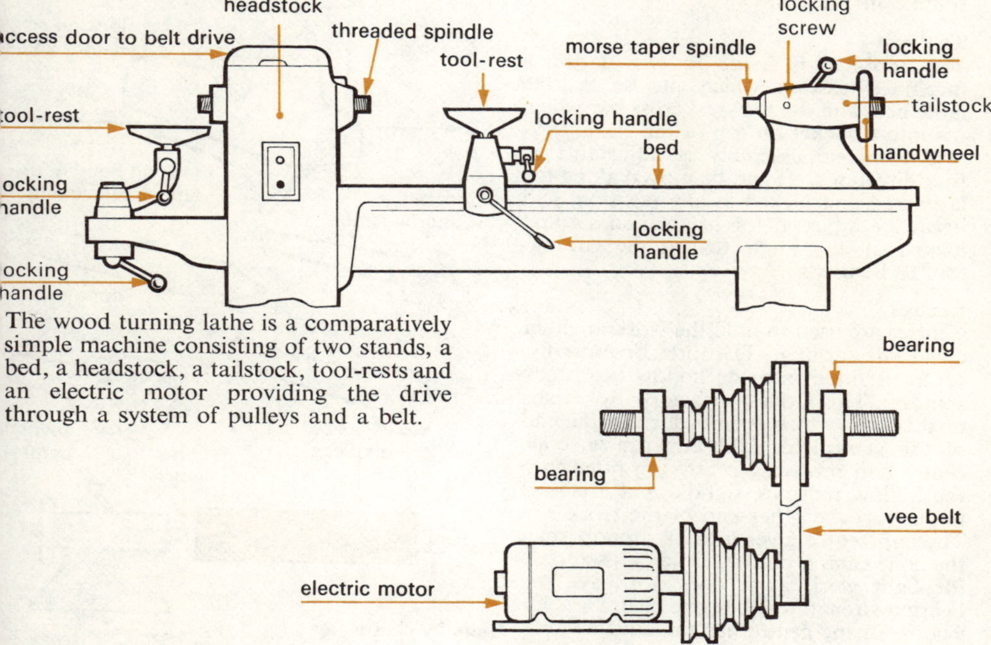

The wood turning lathe is a comparatively simple machine consisting of two stands, a bed, a headstock, a tailstock, tool-rests and an electric motor providing the drive through a system of pulleys and a belt.

Stands

The stands are heavy castings, one at either end of the lathe. One of the stands contains the motor and headstock assembly, the other supports the bed and tailstock unit. Both stands are robust to minimise vibration.

Bed

The bed is a rectangular hollow casting, machined accurately on its top and side bearing surfaces. The bed is bolted to the stands, and carries the tailstock and tool-rest assemblies.

Headstock

The headstock is a threaded spindle carrying the top set of pulley wheels. These pulleys are connected to the bottom pulleys by a belt, the whole assembly being driven by the electric motor. The headstock spindle is threaded on both ends to take the faceplates required for large diameter work. This spindle is supported by, and runs on, roller bearings. It is hollow to accommodate a driving centre which rotates on the work, the other end of the work being supported by the tailstock centre.

Tailstock

The tailstock is made from cast iron and it is machined accurately to fit on to the lathe bed.

The tailstock serves two main purposes:

(1) to support the work by means of the cone-shaped centre;

(2) to drill holes, by means of a taper shank drill inserted in the hollow spindle.

The tailstock can be moved along the lathe bed and locked in any position, the final adjustment being made by turning the handwheel. A locking screw retains the spindle in position.

Tool-rest

The tool-rest is made in two parts: a machined casting which fits across the lathe bed, and the tool-rest cross bar which fits into a socket on top of the casting.

The complete assembly is adjustable in four directions. It can be moved along the lathe bed and locked in any position, and it can be adjusted for height and set and locked at any angle to suit the cutting-tool to be used.

Centres

Centres are used to hold the work at either end while turning. The fork, or butterfly, centre is fitted into the hollow headstock spindle. This drives the work by means of the fork, which is embedded in the end of the workpiece. The cup centre, cone centre and revolving centre are fitted into the hollow tailstock spindle and are used to support the other end of the work.

The cup centre gives greater support than the cone centre, but it should be used only for light work as it does not have the bearing strength of the cone centre.

The revolving centre has the advantage of running on ball races; the centre of the cone revolves with the work and so does not wear or generate heat.

Faceplates

Faceplates are used to hold the wood when making bowls, plates, dishes, etc. The wood is held to the faceplate by means of wood-screws. The faceplate is then screwed on to the threaded spindle of the headstock. A paper or lead washer is placed between the faceplate and the headstock spindle to facilitate removal when the operation is complete. The faceplate used on the outside of the lathe, for large diameter

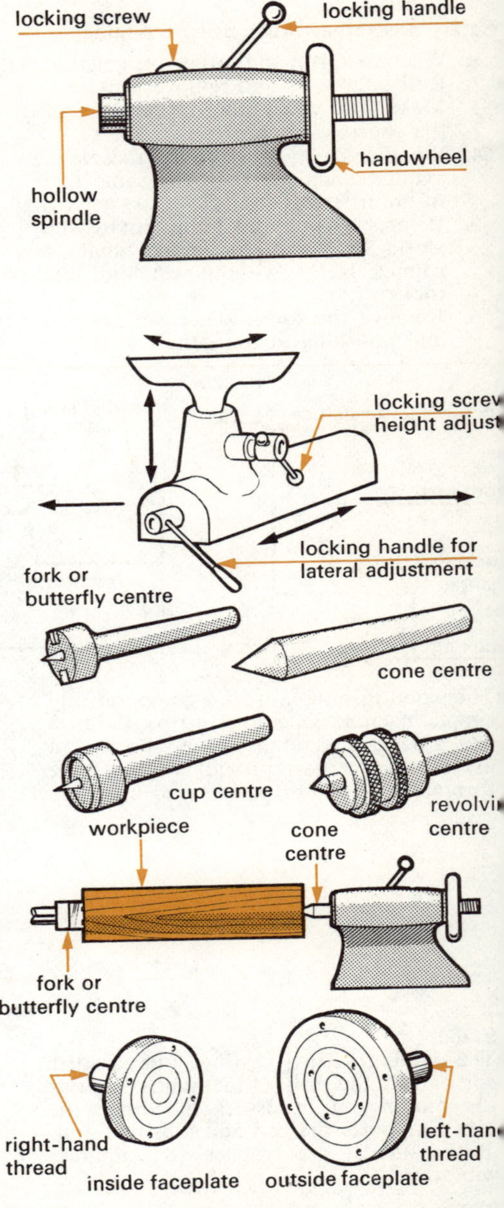

work, carries a left-hand thread to prevent the work from winding itself off the spindle while it is rotating. The faceplates have concentric circles marked on their surfaces as a guide to the correct positioning of the wood in preparation for turning.

Wood turning tools

Two main groups of tools are used when wood turning: cutting tools (gouges and chisels), and scraping tools. Shapes can be formed using scraping tools, but the real skill is developed using the cutting tools. Cutting gouges are made in various diameters, and cutting chisels are made in various widths with skew and straight cutting edges. Gouges are used to cut the work down to size quickly, and chisels are used mainly for decorative cuts. Scrapers should be used to smooth and finish the work, in the same way as the cabinet scraper is used in cabinet-making.

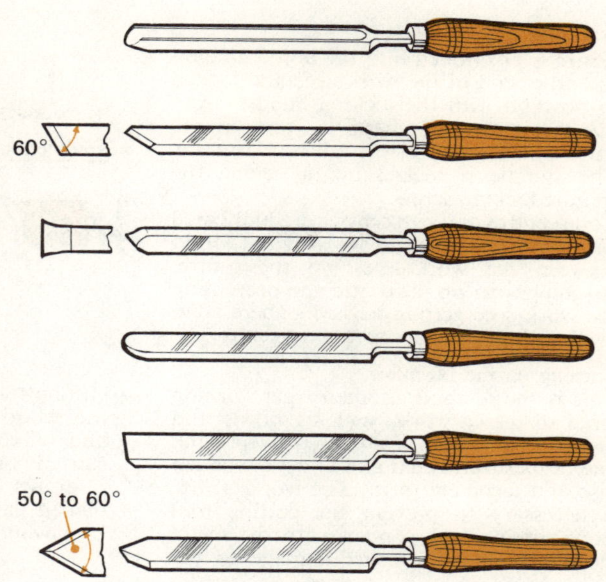

Turning between centres

Setting up work to turn between centres is an operation which presents very little difficulty. The work usually involves turning fairly long cylinders, such as candlesticks, reading-lamp stalks, tool handles, rolling-pins, etc.

The workpiece is prepared by marking out the diagonals on each end, in order to find the centre of the wood along its axis. These centres can be bored with a small diameter drill, to facilitate the mounting of the work. The corners of the wood are usually planed off to make the initial stage of turning easier.

The end of the wood into which the butterfly centre is fixed is prepared by cutting a saw slot across its surface on one of the diagonals to accommodate the blade of the centre. The end of the workpiece with the saw slot is held uppermost and the butterfly centre driven into position with a mallet. The butterfly centre, now attached to the workpiece, is inserted into the headstock spindle. The tailstock

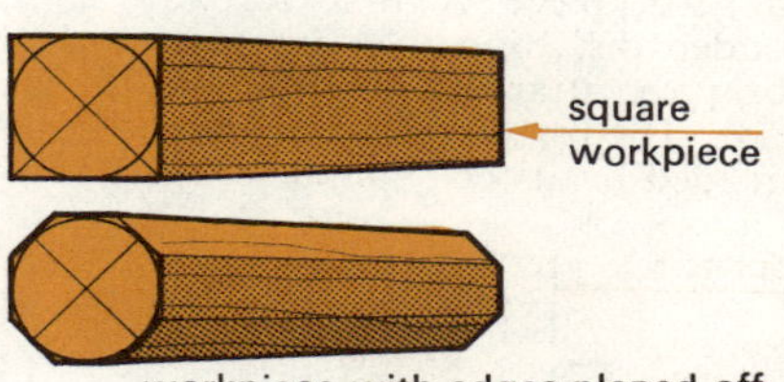

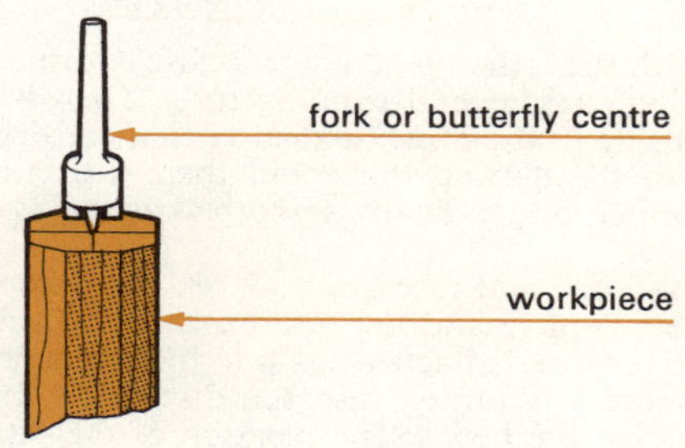

centre is positioned into the bored hole on the other end of the workpiece and locked in position with the locking handle. Any fine adjustment is made by turning the handle on the end of the tailstock spindle. The spindle is locked by tightening the spindle locking-screw.

Cone centres and cup centres are lubricated with tallow or soap. This reduces friction between the workpiece and the centre, lessening wear on the centre and preventing the workpiece getting burned. There is no need to lubricate the revolving centre.

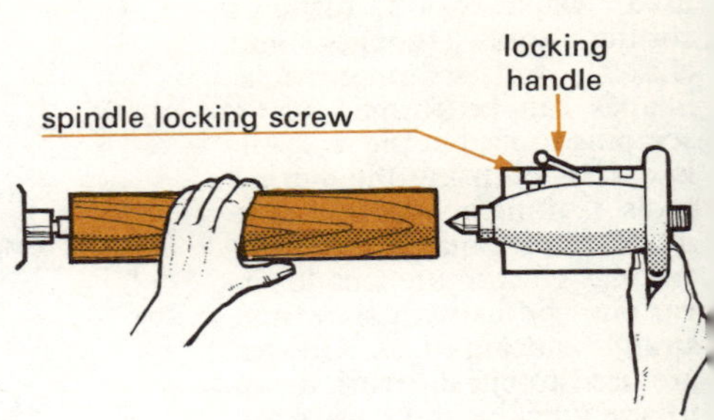

Turning on the faceplate

This is the method adopted when turning large diameter work, such as bowls and dishes. The wood is prepared by planing one of its surfaces flat and fixing a wooden disc and faceplate to it. The wooden disc is necessary to prevent the cutting tool from coming into contact with the metal faceplate and so causing damage to the cutting tool. Failure to plane a surface of the wood flat will mean insecure fixing and off-centre running when the lathe is started. A circle of the required diameter is drawn on the surface which has been planed flat, and the waste wood removed by sawing off the corners.

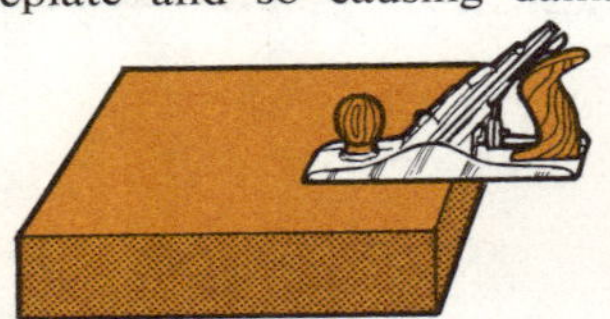  

The workpiece is first screwed to the wooden disc, and then the disc, with the workpiece attached, is screwed to the faceplate. The faceplate is then attached to the threaded headstock spindle.

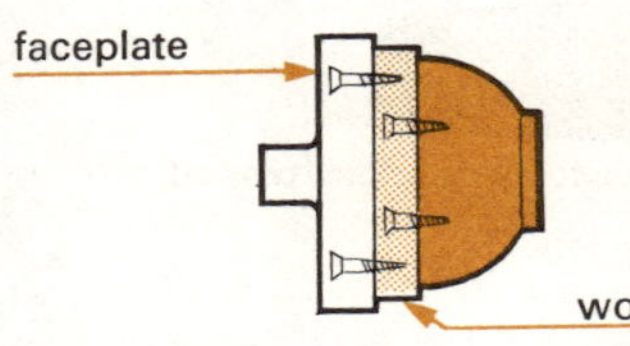

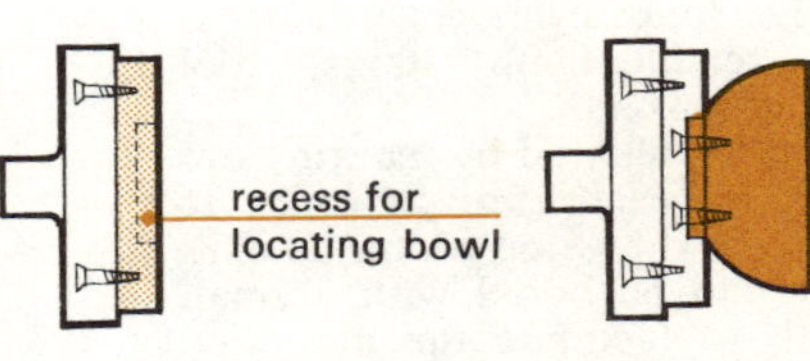

With the lathe revolving, the disc is turned to be circular and running true. Then the outside of the bowl or dish is shaped, first with the cutting tools and then with the scraper, and is finally smoothed with glass-paper.

The bowl and disc are now removed from the faceplate and the disc unscrewed from the bowl and attached again to the faceplate. A recess is turned into the disc to fit the base of the bowl. The position of the disc on the faceplate is carefully marked, the disc again removed from the faceplate, and the base of the bowl fitted into the turned recess and screwed to the disc. The recess is necessary to ensure that the bowl will run true when the disc and bowl are again attached to the metal faceplate. Care must be taken to make sure that the screws holding the bowl to the disc are not too long, otherwise the screws will break through into the bowl as the inside of the bowl is turned. The inside of the bowl is removed first by using the cutting gouge, and then the round-nose scraper, finishing off with glass-paper.

Wood turning using lathe attachment

This headstock spindle attachment can easily be made in the metalwork room. One end of the attachment is bored out and threaded to fit the headstock spindle thread, and the other end is machined down to make a pin 15 mm in diameter and threaded with a die.

Several metal discs of various diameters, each one the thickness of the threaded pin, can be made. Using the correct size of metal disc, a bowl or dish can be turned at one setting without having to reverse the bowl.

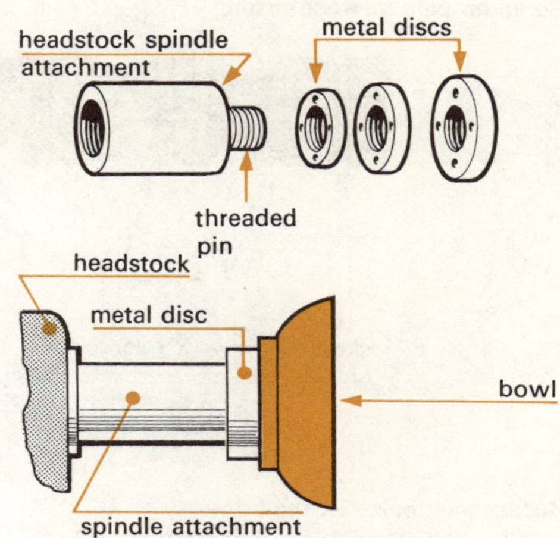

Use of gouge and chisel

The work is first reduced roughly to its diameter using a gouge. The gouge is held firmly on the tool-rest with the left hand. The right hand holds the handle of the gouge at its end, to gain the maximum leverage in order to counteract the pull of the revolving work at the cutting edge. The gouge is passed over the work, removing a series of light cuts. This may leave ridges on the surface of the work, due to the curvature of the gouge, and a slicing cut is used to remove them. This is done by holding the gouge against the work so that the bevel on the gouge rubs the work. The gouge is then slowly turned, keeping the bevel rubbing the work, until the gouge begins to cut. Held in this position, the gouge is moved at a uniform rate along the workpiece. This cut removes any ridges, leaving the finishing cut still to be done with the skew chisel.

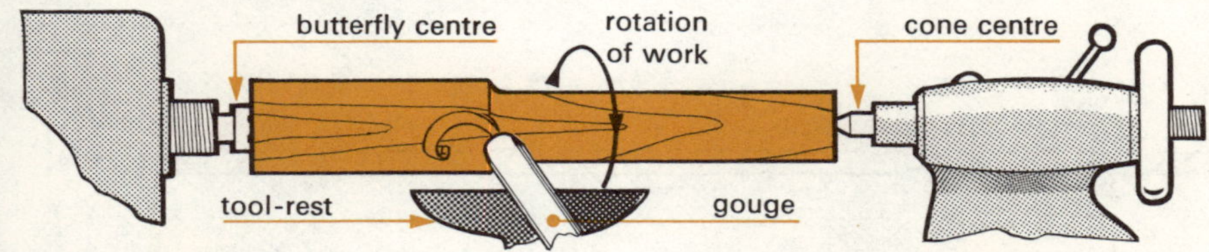

The skew chisel is placed firmly on the tool-rest, and positioned so that the bevel on the chisel rubs on the work. The proper cutting angle is obtained by slowly lifting the handle of the chisel until the chisel starts to cut. This angle is then maintained on the workpiece throughout the cutting process. As the tool is traversed along the work, care must be taken to ensure that the point of the chisel does not dig into the workpiece, as this would spoil the surface.

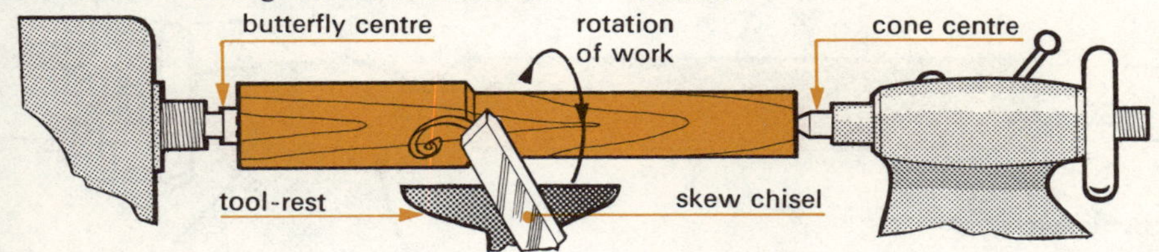

Common cuts in woodturning

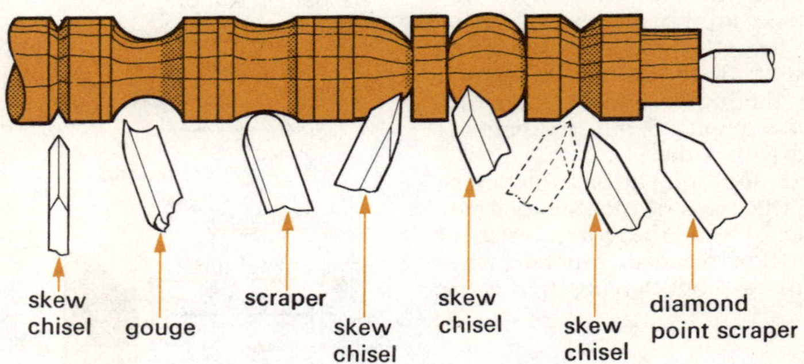

Boring long holes on the lathe

Long holes frequently need to be bored while the workpiece is in the lathe, e.g. the flex holes in reading-lamp and standard lamp stalks. A suitable boring tool can be made by taking an engineer's twist drill and drilling a hole in the end of its shank. A piece of mild steel bar, of any required length, is machined at one end to fit the hole drilled in the shank of the drill, and brazed into the hole. The other end of the mild steel bar is filed to a square, and a handle with a square hole in its centre is attached to the extension piece, either by brazing or riveting. A hollow centre, placed in the tailstock spindle, permits the drill to pass through and make contact with the end of the wood. With the tailstock locked, the lathe is started and the workpiece, which is rotated by the butterfly centre, is bored by pushing the boring tool through from the tailstock end. The boring tool should be withdrawn occasionally to allow the shavings to escape.

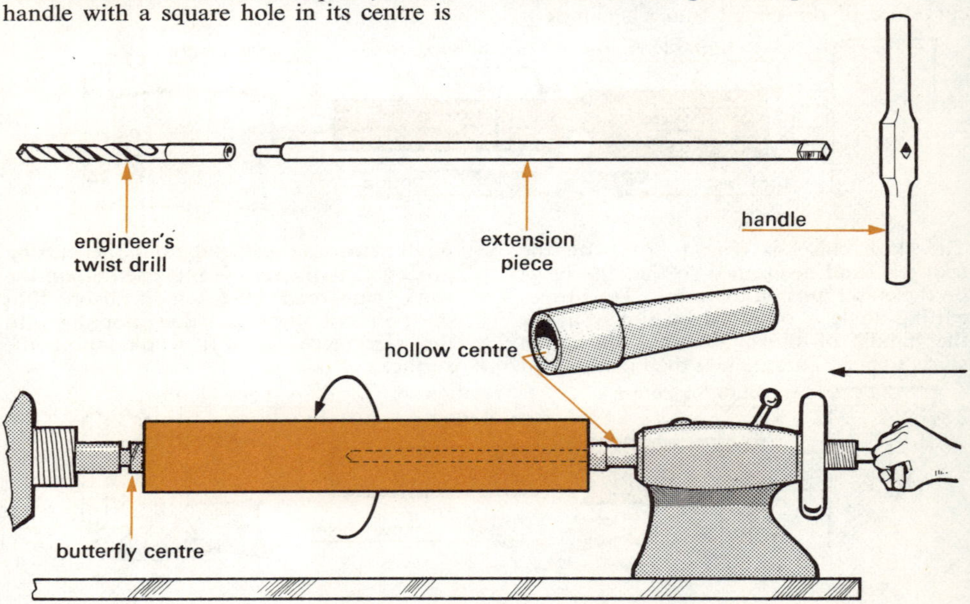

Polishing in the lathe

Articles made on the lathe can be removed from the lathe and finished by french polishing. Many articles are polished while still in the lathe, as this is generally much quicker than french polishing by hand. The grain of the wood is filled by applying a coat of french polish and, when it is dry, rubbing it down smooth with fine grade glass-paper. A second coat of french polish is applied and, when it dries, is again rubbed down smooth with fine glass-paper.

With the work revolving in the lathe, carnauba wax is applied to the surface of the work, so that a thin film of wax is deposited on the surface. This film of wax is burnished with a soft cloth. Care must be taken, when holding the cloth, to ensure that any loose end of the cloth is not caught up in the revolving work. The wax and the cloth are applied to the lower half of the work, to prevent the hand from being snatched as the work rotates.

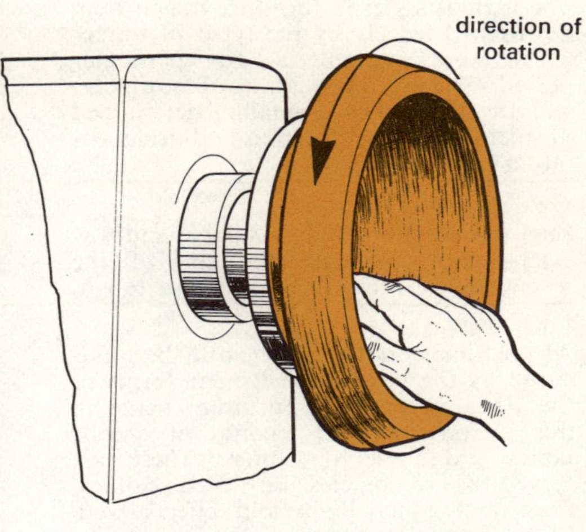

REVISION EXERCISES

1. When veneering a piece of wood, how can you prevent it from curling?
2. What is the purpose of toothing the ground in preparation for veneering?
3. Why is the insert in a veneer hammer made of brass?
4. When veneering, what is an indication that the glue may have been too thick?
5. If the glue was applied when it was too thick, how can this condition be remedied?
6. How can blisters on the surface of the veneer be treated?
7. What method of veneering is used when veneering curved surfaces?
8. Describe briefly how to veneer using the heated caul method.
9. Sketch two types of tailstock centre.
10. What are the main purposes of a tailstock?
11. What is the advantage of the revolving tailstock centre?
12. When turning between centres, how is the workpiece driven?
13. Why is the hollow tailstock centre a necessary part of a lathe's equipment?
14. What is the purpose of the concentric circles marked on a faceplate?
15. Show, by means of sketches, how a piece of wood is prepared for turning between centres.
16. Why is a disc of wood placed between the faceplate and the work?
17. Explain why wood turning tools have exceptionally long handles.
18. In wood turning, what is the purpose of a gouge?
19. Can you give a reason why the point of a diamond scraping tool is ground at an angle of less than 90°?
20. When would a scraping tool be used?
21. Describe the headstock of a lathe.
22. Describe briefly how turned work can be polished in the lathe.
23. What precautions must be observed when burnishing the workpiece in the lathe?

The various styles in furniture design were determined largely by the types of timber which were available at any particular period. The working qualities of the timber, and the tools then available, determined the methods of construction and ornamentation.

With the introduction of new timbers, each having different working qualities, and improvements in tool design, new shapes and forms became possible.

Oak period

English oak was readily available and was extensively used until the end of the seventeenth century. Oak, being a tough, hard timber with a broad grain, was difficult to work. Therefore ornamentation was necessarily simple and restrained.

Early Tudor, 1485—1558

At this time, craftsmen began to be influenced by the Greek and Roman forms of the Renaissance. The furniture made in this period consisted mainly of stools, tables and chests or coffers. These last served as receptacles in which clothes, linen and other household effects were kept. They were fitted inside with various sizes of open boxes or trays. During this period the crude nailed joint was replaced by mortise and tenon joints, with a wooden peg driven through the joint to give it more strength. Craftsmen who employed this type of construction became known as 'joiners', and stools made in this way were called 'joint stools'.

Ornamentation took the form of carvings depicting flowers, leaves, Tudor roses and medallions. A popular decoration was the "linenfold" panel, representing a piece of linen folded upon itself in various ways.

Tudor rose

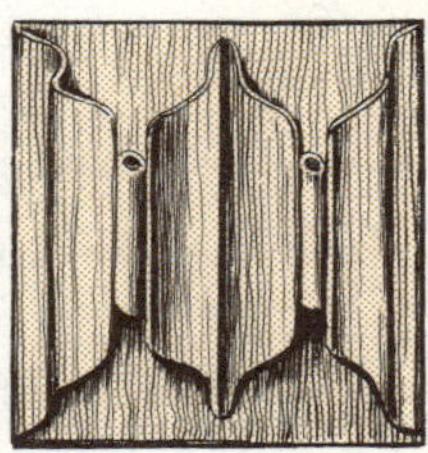

linenfold panel

Tudor chair

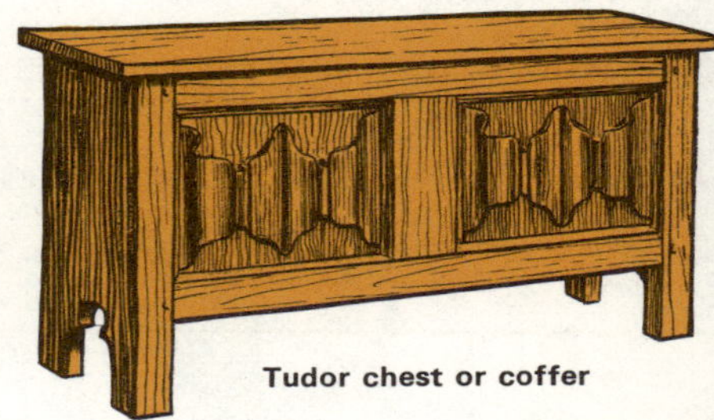

Tudor chest or coffer

This period saw the introduction of the four-poster bed, the draw leaf table and the court cupboard, from which the modern sideboard evolved. Carvings and inlays were extensively used to decorate the articles. The inlays were mostly of holly, the lightest coloured wood grown in Britain. The tables of the period featured legs turned in large, bulbous shapes, ornamented with reeded and carved work; the chairs were of large proportions fitted with low stretcher rails.

turned table leg

carved chair

court cupboard

The Jacobean period encompassed the reigns of James I and Charles I. The rich carvings and overall decoration of the previous era gave way to simpler geometric shapes. During this period, the style of furniture legs changed from the heavy, melon-like, bulbous shapes of the Elizabethan period and became slimmer and more varied in design. Ornamentation featured chip carving and interlacing circles.

Chairs featured padded seats made from leather with punched decorations. The farthingale chair was introduced at this time by James I. This was a low-set, armless chair, designed to accommodate the whalebone crinoline dresses worn by court ladies. The gateleg table, for occasional use, was also introduced during this period.

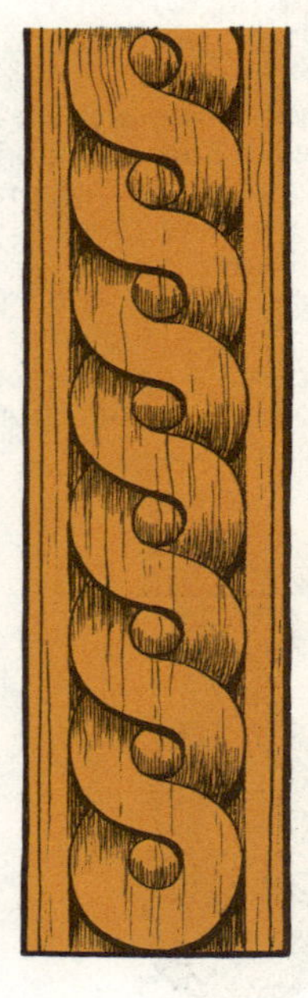

interlaced carving

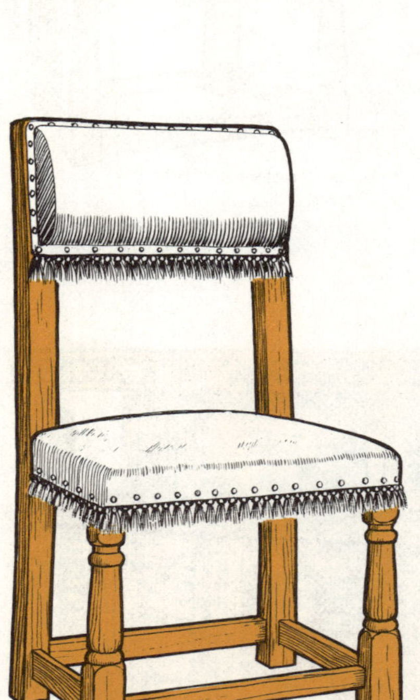

farthingale chair

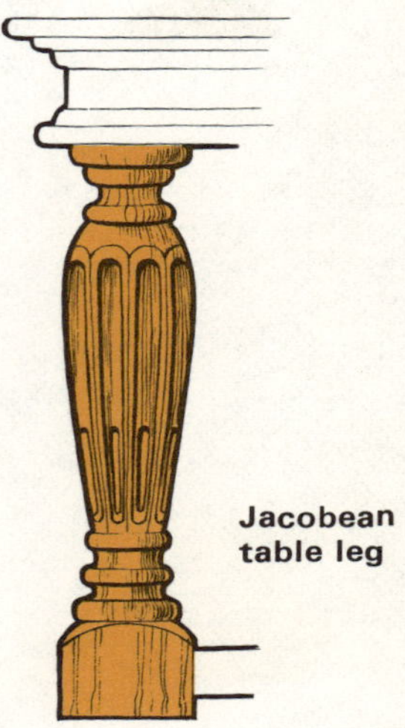

Jacobean table leg

Jacobean chest

Commonwealth, 1650—1660 (Cromwell)

This was the period of puritanism. The ornate carving of previous eras was replaced by a more restrained style of decoration. Carvings and inlays were of the simplest form, but leather upholstery on the seats and backs of chairs was retained.

Twist turning, ball turning and bobbin turning of furniture legs were popular in Europe at this time, and these styles were introduced into English furniture design.

bun foot

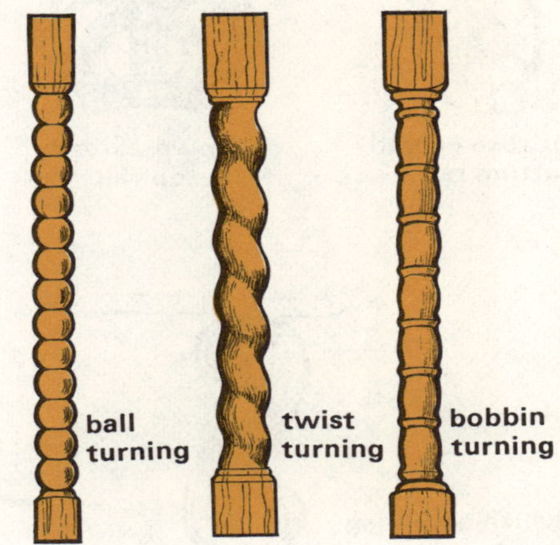

In 1660 Charles II returned from his exile in France. During his travels he had been impressed by French, Italian, Spanish and Flemish furniture design, and on his return to England he encouraged English designers to adopt Continental styles of furniture making. The Continental furniture styles were luxurious, with extravagantly curved shapes, scroll legs and feet, and chairs with "barley sugar twist" uprights.

Veneered work was very popular and this eliminated the panelled construction associated with English oak furniture in favour of flush panels suitable for veneering. Solid walnut and walnut veneer were being used increasingly. Richly carved work was sometimes gilded.

Ornamentation was very elaborate and included cherubs, birds, flowers, fruit, crowns and lions. Linen chests now became chests of drawers. Chairs of Flemish design had high cane backs and cane seats. Many comparatively small pieces of furniture began to appear, such as little occasional tables, small writing bureaux and sofas.

Charles II chair

Tudor rose carved on bottom rail

crown carved on top rail

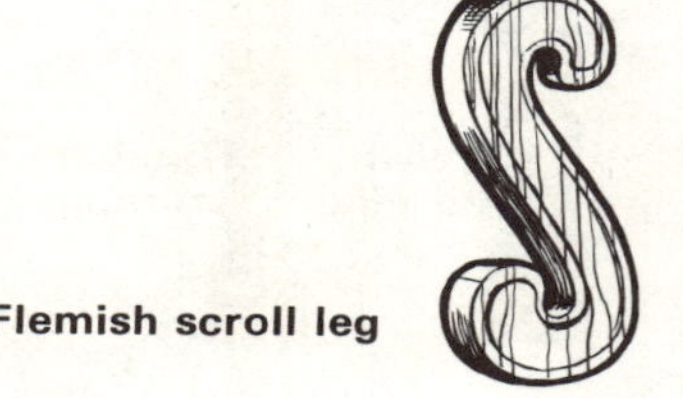

Flemish scroll leg

crown and scroll carved decoration

William and Mary, 1689—1702 (Walnut period)

Dutch styles at this time began to exert great influence on English furniture design. Styles were much simplified, departing from the elaborate pieces of the Restoration period. Pieces of furniture, such as china cabinets, tea-tables and bookcases, were made smaller and lighter, enabling them to be used in the home as well as at court.

This period featured very fine veneered work in curl walnut, and an oyster shell effect obtained by cutting cross-sections of the branches of the laburnum tree. Walnut now dominated in both veneered and solid timber furniture.

Twist turnings, the Flemish scroll leg and the trumpet shape, with inverted cup leg, were retained. Ornamentation depicted stars, fans, flowers and birds.

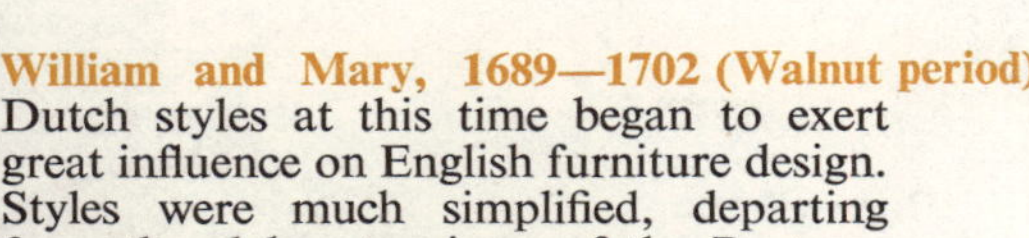

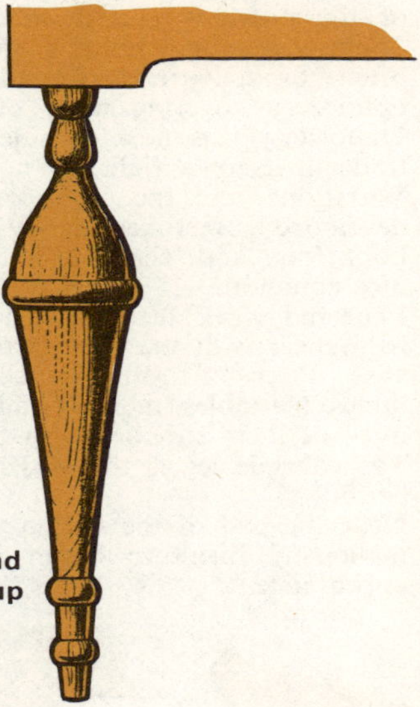

trumpet and inverted cup leg

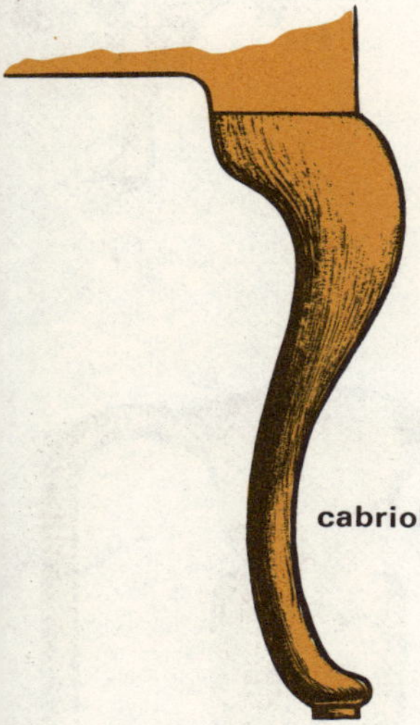

cabriole leg

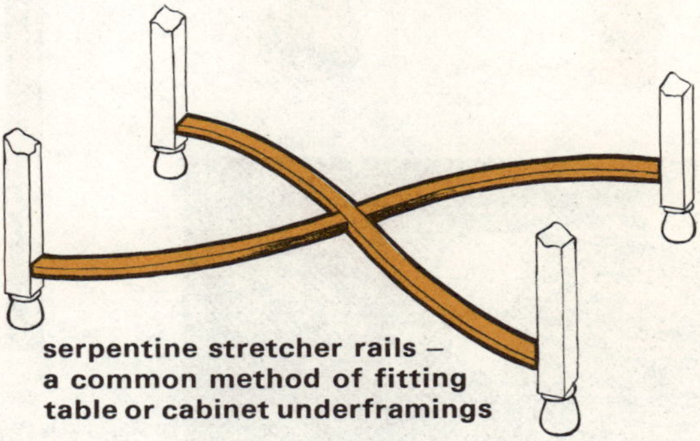

**serpentine stretcher rails —
a common method of fitting
table or cabinet underframings**

Queen Anne, 1702—1714

During the reign of Queen Anne the styles of the previous period were continued. There was great emphasis on upholstery, often ornately embroidered, with the upholstery covering most of the wood. Upholstery was now considered to be a trade in its own right.

Variations of the cabriole leg were developed, sometimes heavily carved. The hoof foot and claw-and-ball foot were also common.

Veneered work featured cross bandings, i.e. veneer with the grain arranged cross-wise. Pieces of furniture included dining-tables, tea-tables, tallboys and easy chairs, most of them supported on cabriole legs. The cabriole leg is the trademark of this period.

Near the end of the Queen Anne period mahogany furniture began to make its appearance.

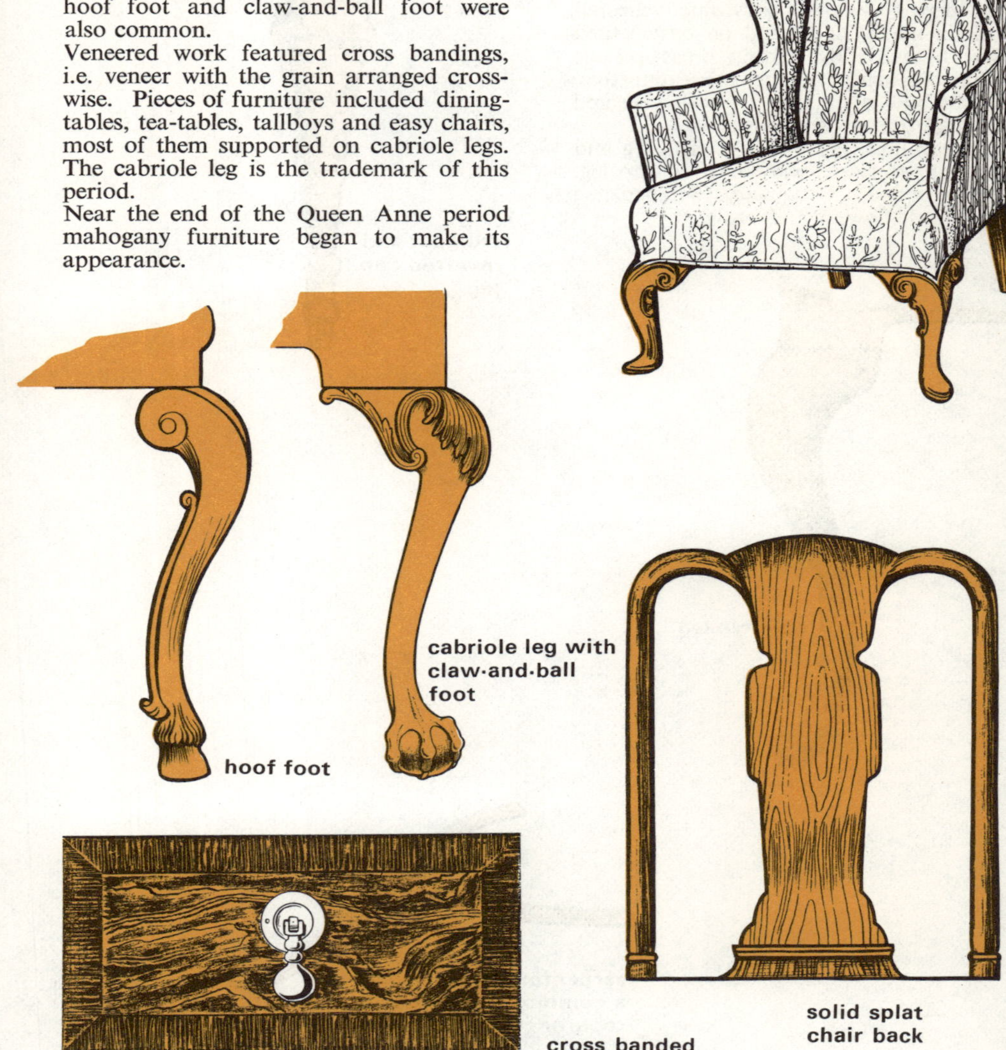

cabriole leg with claw-and-ball foot

hoof foot

cross banded drawer front

solid splat chair back

Georgian, 1714—1840 (Mahogany period)

The initial part of this period was the start of "the mahogany era", although most furniture was still made in walnut. With the cancellation of the import tax in 1733, mahogany became more popular for furniture making and also for interior work, such as wall panelling. The mahogany used was rather featureless and lacked interesting grain pattern. Because of this, ornamentation was added in the form of mouldings and carvings. Mahogany was ideal for ornamentation, and carvings included lions' heads and rock and shell shapes.

The cabriole leg was given a more pronounced sweep, and usually carved to show a lion's head with the bottom of the leg in the form of a ball and claw.

This period is often referred to as the "golden age of cabinet-making", due to the outstanding work of a number of prominent craftsmen who had a great influence on furniture design.

William Kent

William Kent was an English architect who studied in Italy for ten years. When he returned to England he designed many houses and many pieces of furniture. His furniture was big and heavy, with large carvings of animals and mask heads.

Some of Kent's furniture was covered in gold leaf, a process known as "gesso" work. Gesso was a mixture similar to plaster of paris, and it was brushed on to the furniture. When the gesso dried out the gold leaf was applied, the gesso providing a base to which the gold leaf could adhere. The gesso was often brushed, layer upon layer, on to solid panels of timber, and the gesso itself carved and then covered with gold leaf.

carved gilt mirror

typical mask head

William Kent
gesso table

Thomas Chippendale

Thomas Chippendale was the son of a Yorkshire cabinet-maker. From 1745 to 1779 he produced both simple and ornately designed furniture, particularly chair backs. The most common of his chair back designs were the ladder-back, riband back, Chinese slat back and carved-splat back. Some of his chair backs carried complicated pierced designs, in contrast to the solid splat back of the Queen Anne period.

He designed small tea-tables with a raised edge, known as the piecrust edge. By reducing the dimensions of his furniture he was able to introduce his pieces into the smaller, middle-class home.

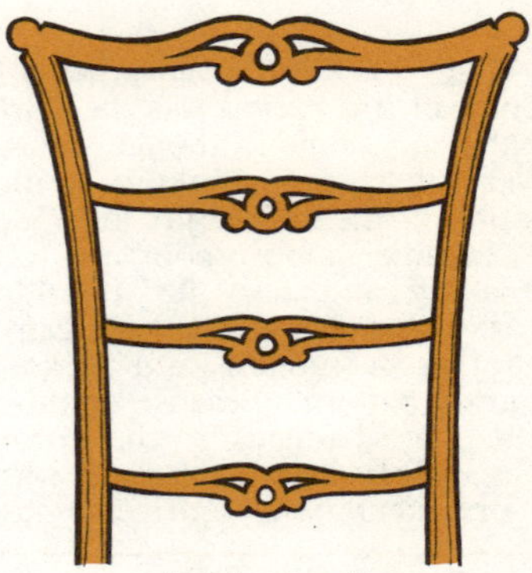

ladder-back

riband back

Chinese-splat back

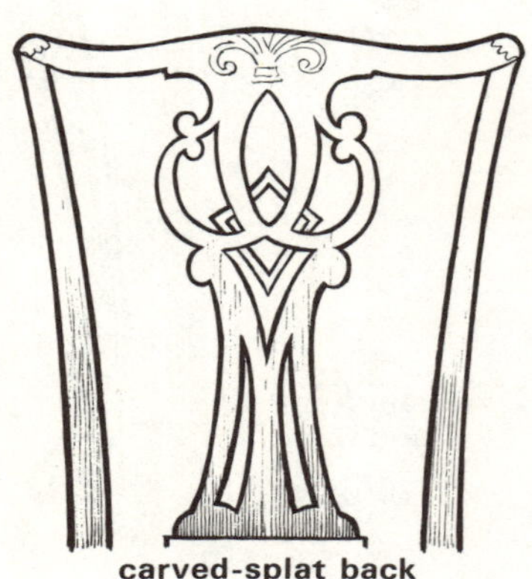

carved-splat back

piecrust
table top

bureau
bookcase

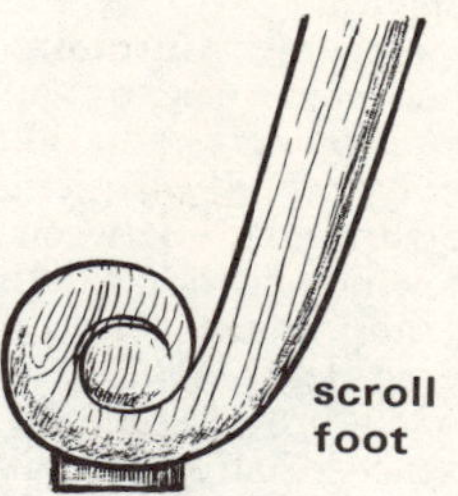

scroll
foot

**Chippendale-splat
Windsor (a country
chair reflecting
fashionable taste)**

George Hepplewhite

George Hepplewhite's furniture is noted for its grace and elegant appearance. Carved decoration was reduced to a minimum to display without distraction the fine form of the furniture. Between 1760 and 1794 Hepplewhite introduced the famous oval-backed and shield back chairs, with square tapered legs inlaid with delicate stringing. A feature of some of his chairs was the absence of stretcher rails.

He ornamented his furniture with delicate carvings depicting flowers, drapery and feathers.

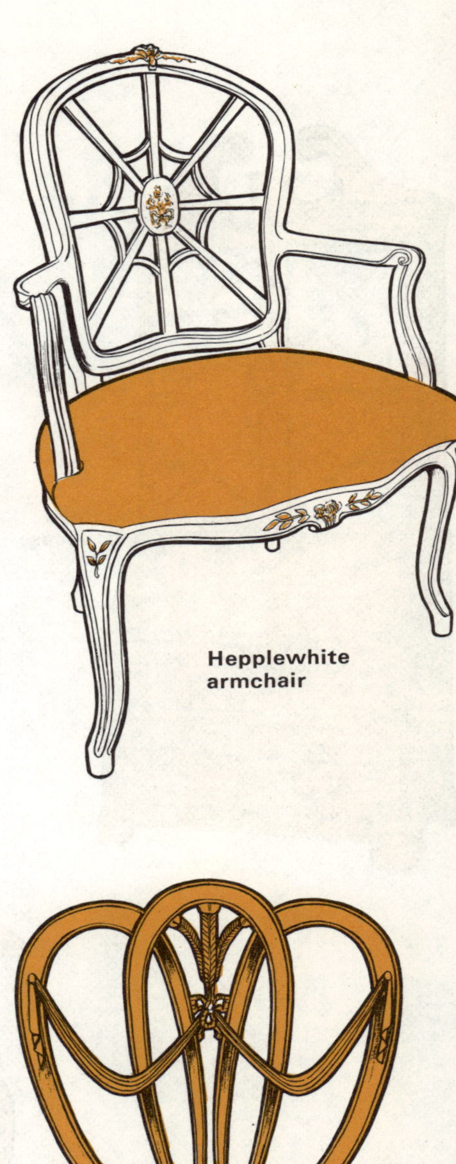

Hepplewhite
armchair

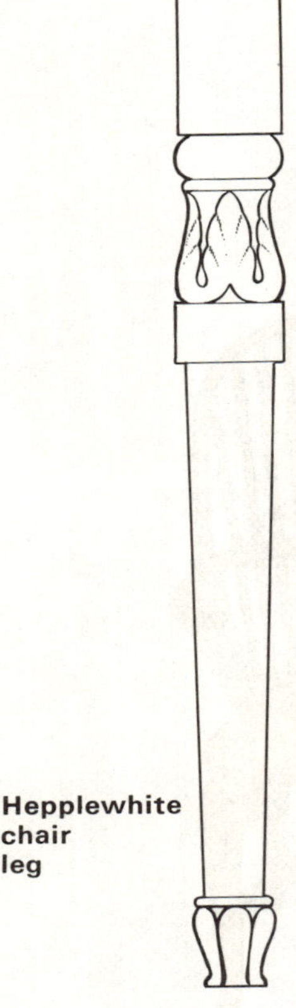

Hepplewhite
chair
leg

heart-shaped
chair back

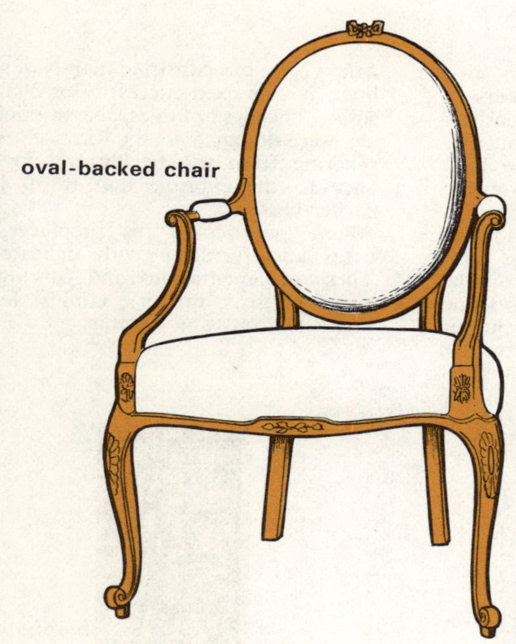

oval-backed chair

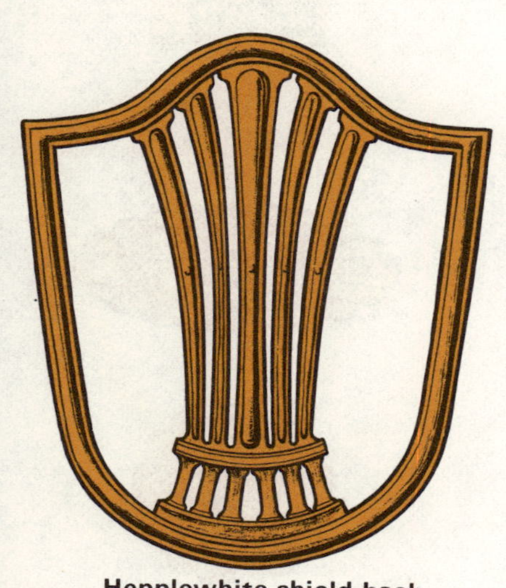

Hepplewhite shield back

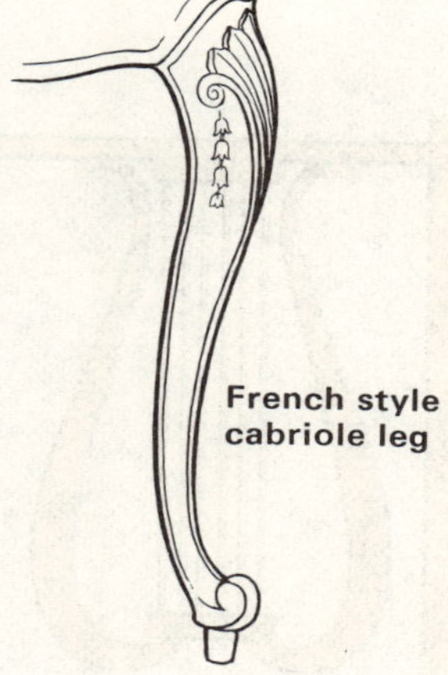

French style
cabriole leg

Robert Adam

Robert Adam was the son of a Scottish architect. He spent a number of years in Italy where he studied the classical designs uncovered at Pompeii and Herculaneum. His work during the period 1762 to 1792 was based on these studies and produced a style of achitecture which became known as the "Adam classical style". Although best known as an architect, he also designed interior furnishings to complement his exquisite porticos, staircases and fireplaces. Many of his designs, including his well-known lyre-back chair, were used by contemporary cabinet-makers such as Hepplewhite and Chippendale.

Adam's designs consisted mainly of straight lines, but he used curves in his chairs and sofas. The legs of tables, chairs, bookcases, etc. were designed in the form of a square, tapering from top to bottom, in preference to the cabriole and scroll legs of earlier periods.

Adam ornamented his fireplaces, staircases and furniture with delicate taste. These ornamentations and carvings consisted of urns, drapery, cupids, festoons, bluebell drops and paterae.

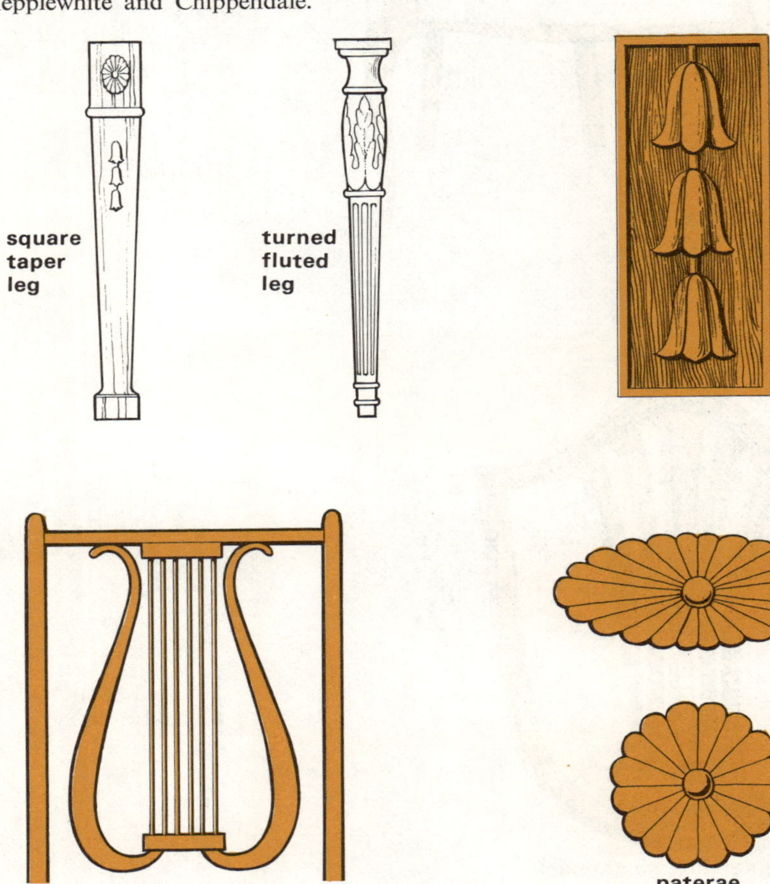

square taper leg

turned fluted leg

bluebell drop carving

lyre-back chair

paterae

urn and drapery carving

**semicircular
Adam side table**

Thomas Sheraton

A feature of Sheraton's furniture was the use he made of different coloured woods, such as rosewood, tulip-wood and satin-wood, to produce intricate marquetry designs. Carved decoration was kept simple and restrained and included circles, ovals, urns, scrolls, fans and drapery. Sheraton also painted and gilded some of his furniture.

Sheraton chairs had the chair arm coming from the chair back in a flat curve. The chair legs tapered gracefully all the way to the floor. The cabriole leg was completely abandoned.

He designed household articles, such as tea-caddies, fireplace screens, sewing tables, etc., as well as furniture. Secret drawers, operated by intricate mechanical arrangements, were also a feature of his work. Perhaps the most interesting example of his work was his design for folding library steps.

Thomas Sheraton's most prolific period was from 1790 to 1806.

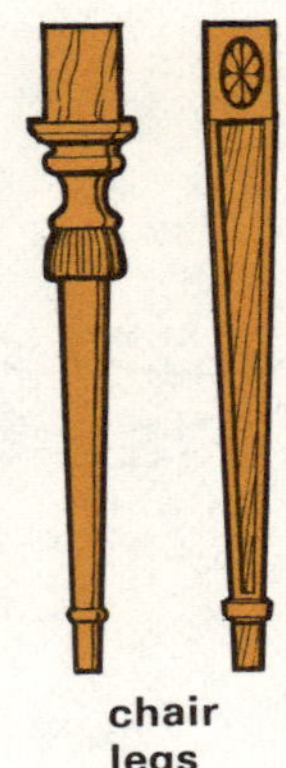

chair legs

stretcher rail

Sheraton chest of drawers

Sheraton Pembroke table

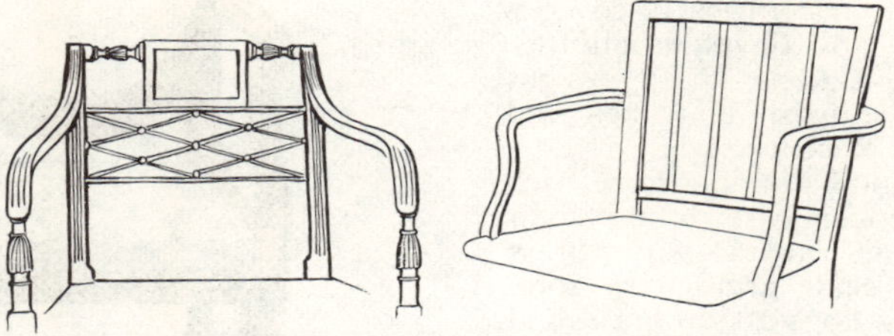

typical Sheraton chair backs

**Sheraton
tambour bureau**

**folding
library steps**

Regency, 1800-1830

This period is also known as the Empire period, after the style of furnishings of the French Empire of Napoleon. The designs, which gradually appeared in England, were based on the archaeological discoveries of Greek, Roman and Egyptian cultures. With slight modifications, these designs were adopted by English craftsmen and became known as Regency style.

Chairs of this period had upholstered back rests, and the wooden parts of the chair were painted and inlaid with brass decorations. The chair arms were somtimes supported on lions cast in brass, and the chair legs were in the form of a sabre. Sofas were designed with outward curving legs. Veneered surfaces were inlaid with brass decoration.

Regency chair with sabre legs

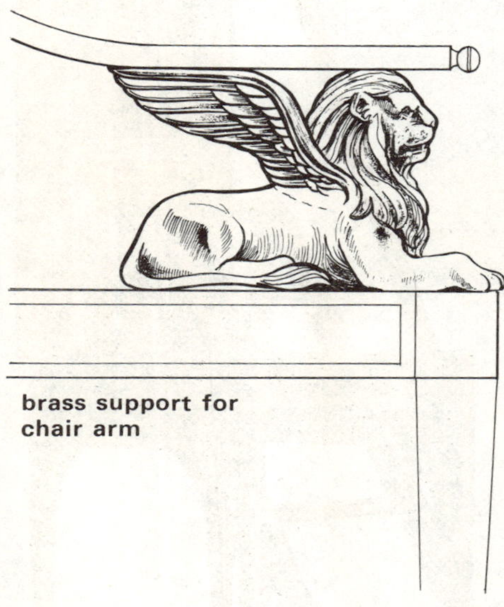

brass support for chair arm

inlaid brass decoration

upholstered
chair

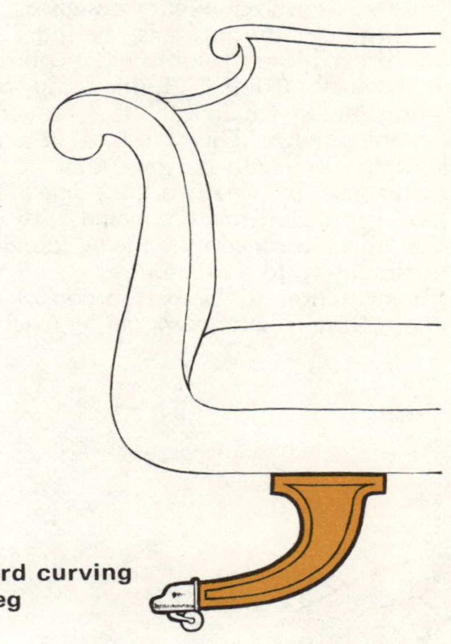

outward curving
sofa leg

sofa table

There was no predominant design or style of furniture during this period. The furniture made at this time was a confusion of Regency, Chinese, Italian and other Continental styles in an effort to create something new. The standard of craftsmanship declined, possibly due to the greater use of woodworking machinery. Rival furniture firms competed with each other and succeeded in reducing individual craftsmanship to a minimum.

Ornamentation at this period consisted of carvings and of scrollwork cut by machines and applied to the pieces of furniture. Victorian sideboards were usually big and heavy and chairs and sofas were thickly padded and of large proportions.

The Victorian era is renowned for the number of smaller items, such as boxes, trays, small tables and novelties, that were made in great profusion during the period. Towards the end of the century, William Morris, the designer, began a campaign to restore high standards and to encourage a revival of interest in earlier elegance and pleasing design.

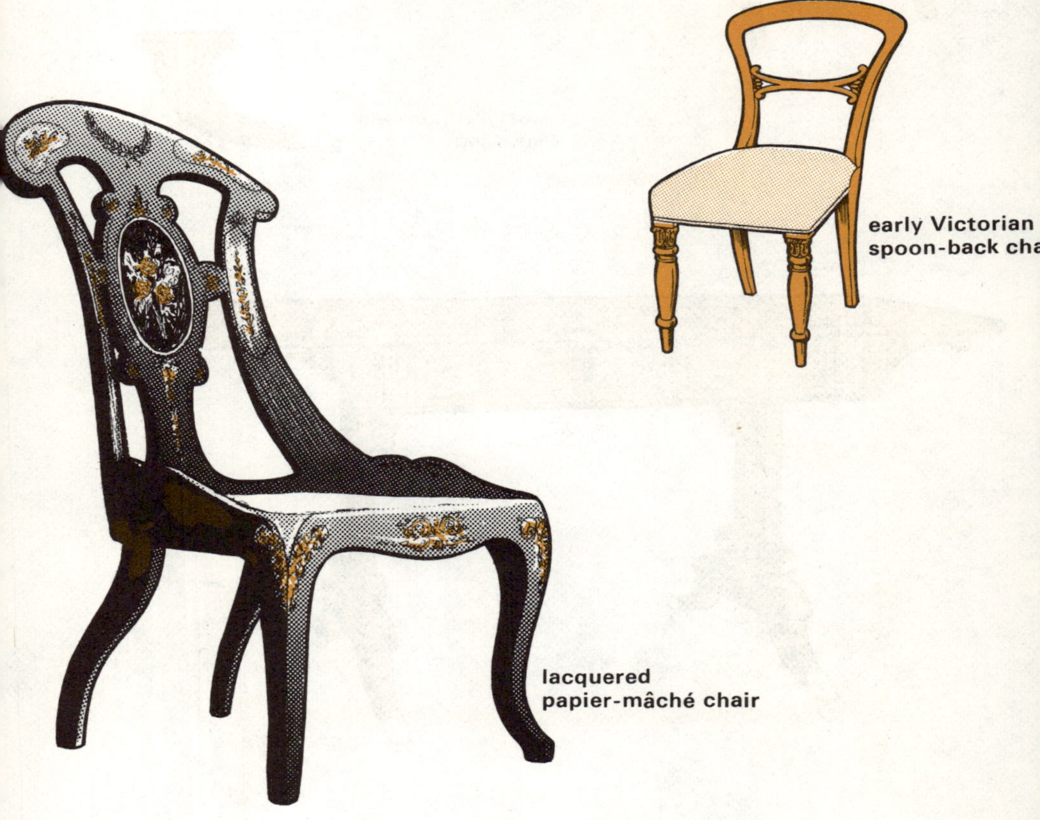

early Victorian
spoon-back chair

lacquered
papier-mâché chair

Victorian sideboard

drawing-room sofa

The authors wish to acknowledge the undermentioned Examination Boards for their kind permission to reproduce the examination questions.
The following abbreviations have been used:

Oxford and Cambridge Schools Examination Board — OCSEB
Welsh Joint Education Committee — WJEC
Middlesex Regional Examining Board — MREB
Southern Regional Examinations Board — SREB
East Midland Regional Examination Board — EMREB
Joint Matriculation Board — JMB

*** For the questions so marked the answers should be written separately. Please do not write in this book.**

TIMBER

1. Name two methods of seasoning timber and describe one of them in detail. Illustrate your answer. Why is seasoning necessary?
   (OCSEB) GCE 1972

2. An oak log is sawn through and through into boards, as shown in Figure 1, and these are then seasoned. With the aid of sketches, show what differences you would expect to find between board A and board B:
   (*a*) in the markings of the grain on the surface of the boards,
   (*b*) due to any natural defects present in the tree,
   (*c*) in the stability of the boards.

Fig. 1

   (WJEC) GCE 1972

* 3. Use five of the given list of names to complete the labelling of the cross-section of a hardwood tree, shown in Figure 2.

Cambium layer	Medullary ray
Cell structure	Pith
Cortex	Annual ring
Grain	Sapwood
Heartwood	

Fig. 2

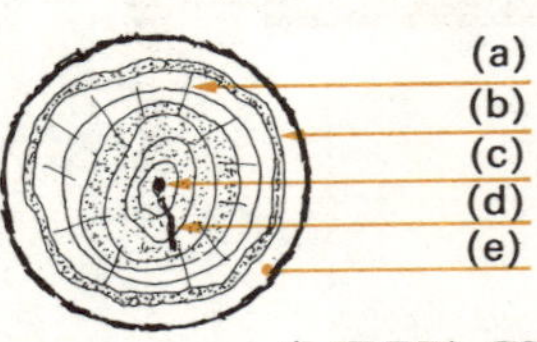

   (MREB) CSE 1973

* 4. Figures 3–7 show defects in logs or boards. Name each of these faults in the spaces provided.

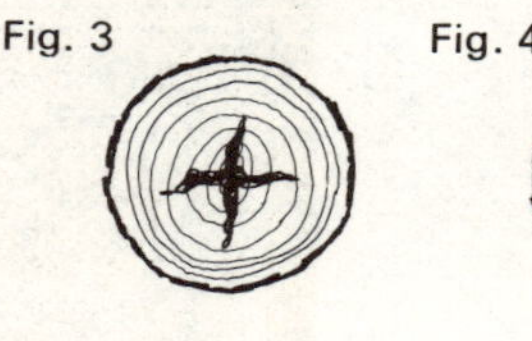

Fig. 3   Fig. 4

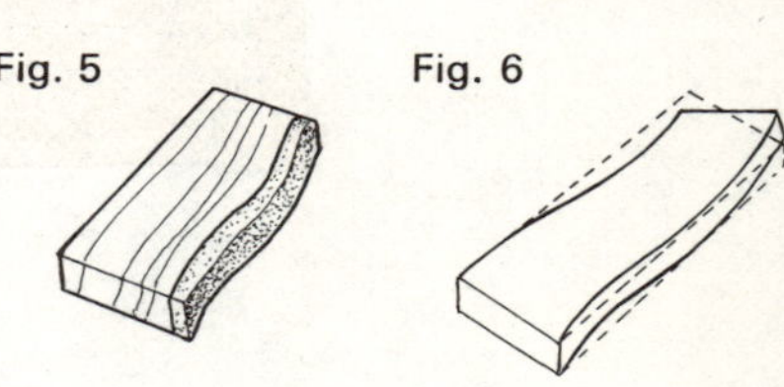

Fig. 5   Fig. 6

Fig. 7

   (MREB) CSE 1973

5. With sketches, write detailed notes on any TWO of the following:
   (*a*) Conversion of timber.
   (*b*) Shrinkage and warping of timber.
   (*c*) A method of seasoning timber.
   (EMREB) CSE 1973

* 6. Place against each of the jobs in list A the timber from list B which would be most suitable for the purpose. Do not use any timber more than once, and note that not every timber in list B will be required.

List A	List B
(*a*) Rabbit hutch	Ash
(*b*) Table top with a Formica surface	Beech
	Chipboard
(*c*) Bowl to hold salad	English oak
(*d*) An axe shaft	Red deal
(*e*) Wooden jack-plane	Teak

   (MREB) CSE 1973

* 7. By shading carefully, show clearly the end grain edges of the layers of wood on the drawing of the 3-ply sheet.

Fig. 8

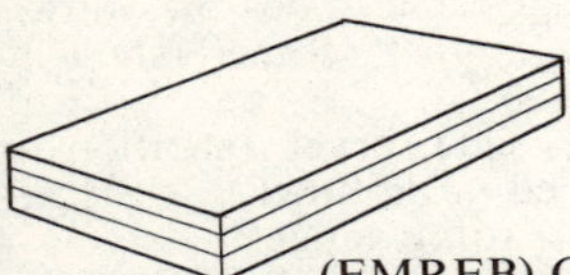

(EMREB) CSE 1973

* 8. Figure 9 shows a cross-sectional sketch of a tree trunk. Write in the names of the parts on the lines alongside the arrowheads.

Fig. 9

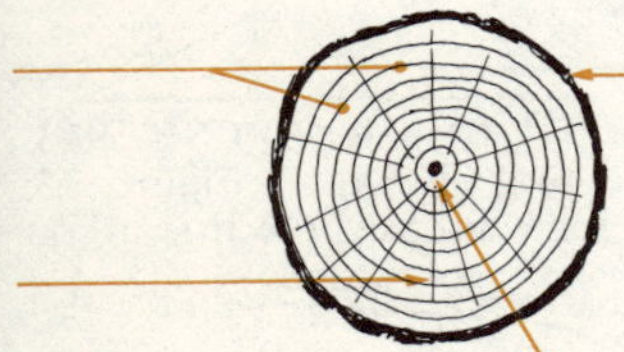

(SREB) CSE 1974

9. Even in these days of mass production it is generally recognised that some kinds of timber are better suited for some particular jobs than others.
Name three different kinds of timber you know. Sketch examples of work for which they are particularly suited and state reasons for their preference.
(SREB) CSE 1974

10. Assume that the trunk of a large oak tree which has already been cut into planks has been given to your school. Make sketches to show how and where you would stack this new timber to dry and describe one method of seasoning it.
(SREB) CSE 1974

TOOLS

11. For the purposes of working on it with shaping tools, a block of wood, irregular in shape, has to be secured to a bench top. Draw and describe a suitable holding device. Point out the features of its design which enable the tool to perform adequately.
(WJEC) GCE 1973

*12. Complete the drawing of the blade of this bevelled-edge chisel which is used in the making of dovetails.

Fig. 10

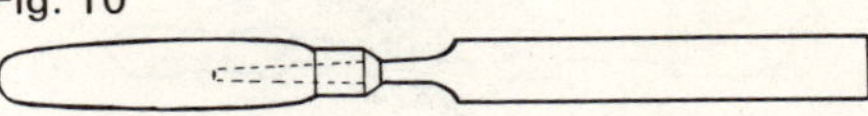

(EMREB) CSE 1973

13. Name the saw shown in Figure 11 and state a use.

Fig. 11

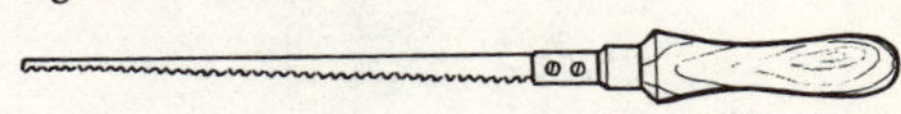

(SREB) CSE 1974

*14. Figure 12 shows the shape of a table top, the edge of which is to be smoothed. Indicate with arrows on the drawing the directions in which you would work with a spokeshave. What difference would there be between the tool used at "A" and the tool used at "B"?

Fig. 12

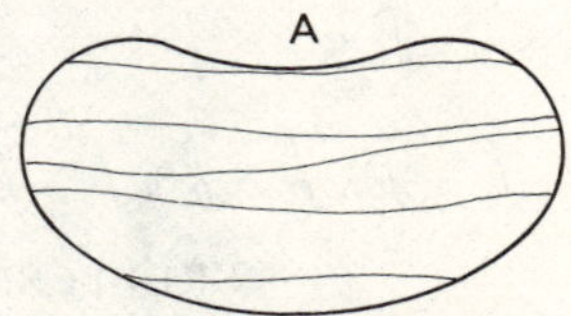

(SREB) CSE 1974

15. Name the tool used to get the housing shown in Figure 13 to an even depth.

Fig. 13

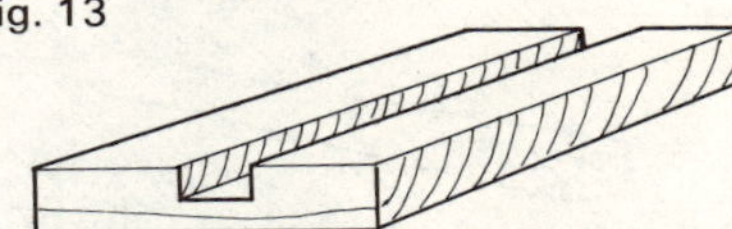

(EMREB) CSE 1973

16. Name the hand tool you would use to form the pen-holding depression in the part of a desk top shown in Figure 14.

Fig. 14

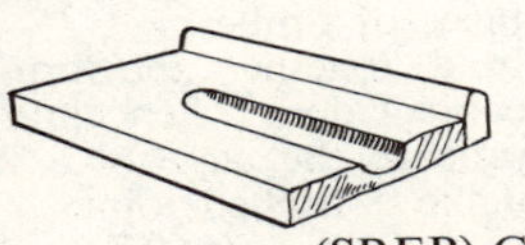

(SREB) CSE 1974

121

17. Name these tools. (The drawings are not to scale.)

Fig. 15

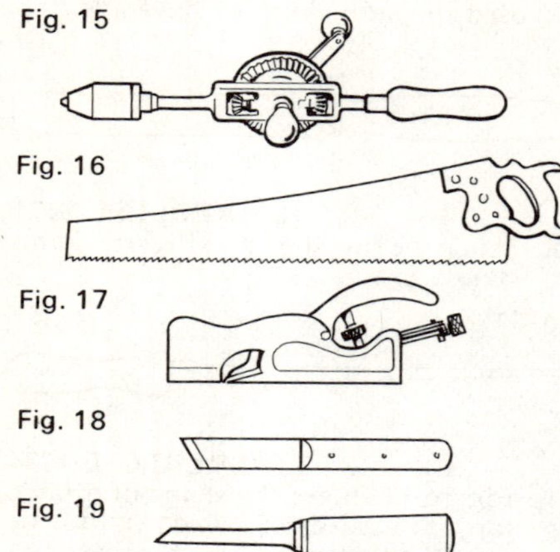

Fig. 16

Fig. 17

Fig. 18

Fig. 19

(MREB) CSE 1973

18. Two sets of saw teeth are shown in Figure 20. Why are they sharpened differently?

Fig. 20

(SREB) CSE 1974

19. The end of the screwdriver in Figure 21 has become badly worn through misuse. Make a similar sketch showing the shape to which it should be reground.

Fig. 21

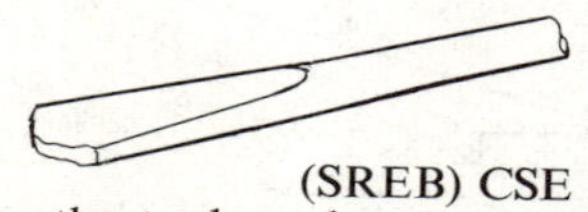

(SREB) CSE 1974

20. Name the tool used to:
  (*a*) bore an 18 mm hole in the end grain of a piece of timber;
  (*b*) clean up a concave curve on a back rail of a chair;
  (*c*) gauge a line across the grain of a piece of timber;
  (*d*) hold together the frame of a cabinet door when gluing up;
  (*e*) prepare the edge of a board to make a rubbed joint.

(MREB) CSE 1973

21. Describe, with the aid of drawings, any four of the following small tools.
  1. A centre-bit.
  2. A bradawl.
  3. A screwdriver (particularly the edge which does the work).
  4. A cabinet scraper (show how it cuts).
  5. A slide bevel (mention timber used in the stock).
  6. A cutting gauge.

(OCSEB) GCE 1973

*22. Insert in the drawing the sizes, in degrees, of the grinding angle and sharpening angle of a smoothing-plane blade.

Fig. 22

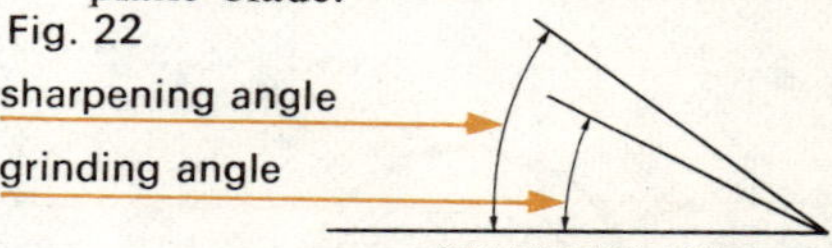

(EMREB) CSE 1973

23. Name the tool shown in Figure 23 and state for what purpose it is used.

Fig. 23

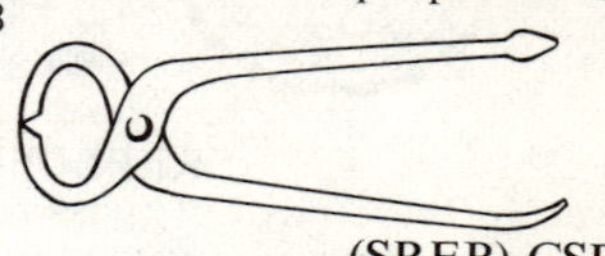

(SREB) CSE 1974

24. Name two patterns of the tool shown in Figure 24.

Fig. 24

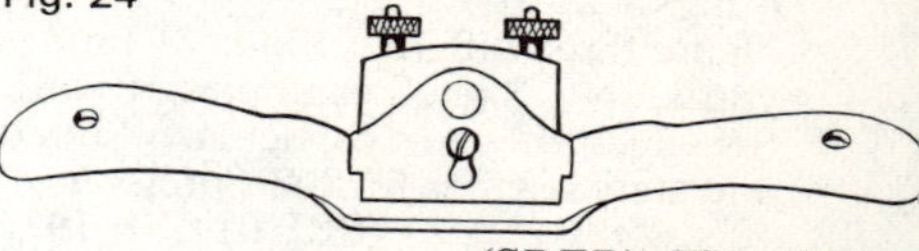

(SREB) CSE 1974

*25. Complete this drawing of a mortise gauge.

Fig. 25

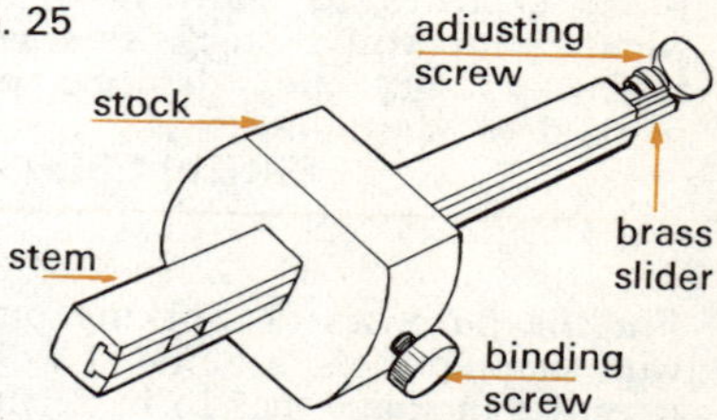

(EMREB) CSE 1973

*26. Add the missing word in each sentence.
  (*a*) The slot made by a saw cutting into wood is called a ———.

(b) If the saw binds in the slot, the teeth may have lost their————
————.

(c) The type of handsaw used to cut across the grain of a plank is called a ————.

(d) The type of handsaw used to cut down the grain of a plank is called a ————.

(e) Complete Figure 26 by adding the details of the bottom part of the slot cut by a tenon-saw.

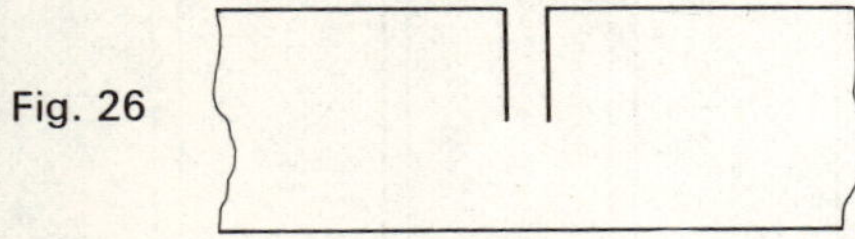

Fig. 26

(MREB) CSE 1973

*27. On Figure 27 make the marks indicating Face Side and Face Edge. There are four stages to planing a piece of wood to size. The first two are given below. Add the other two in correct order.
Face Side.   Face Edge.
Name a jig which would help you to plane end grain square.

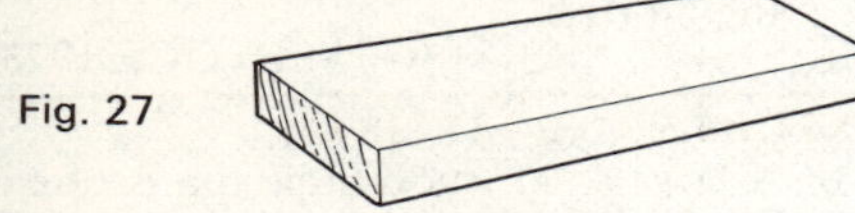

Fig. 27

(MREB) CSE 1973

28. When a tenon-saw was used to saw a piece of wood across the grain, it was found to cut very slowly, and instead of cutting vertically down the blade tended to veer to the right. Assuming the faults lay with the saw, suggest the causes of these faults and then explain in detail how you would put the saw in good order.
(WJEC) GCE 1972

29. Make sketches of:
(a) a bevelled-edge chisel, and
(b) a mortise chisel.
What are the important points in the construction of each chisel?
(SREB) CSE 1974

JOINTS

30. Sketch and name the joint normally used at the corner of a picture frame.
(SREB) CSE 1974

31. Name each of the following joints.

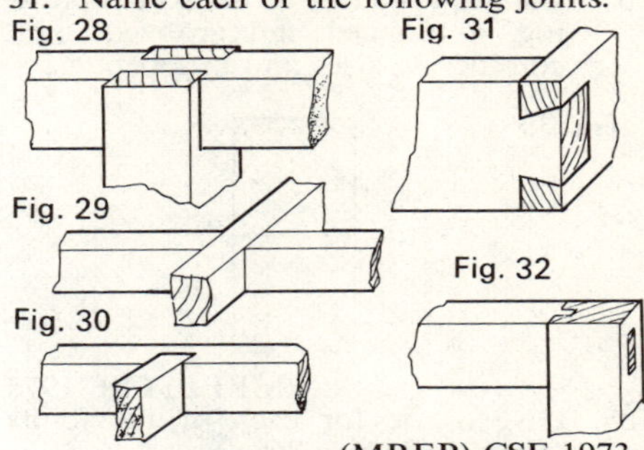

Fig. 28   Fig. 31

Fig. 29

Fig. 30   Fig. 32

(MREB) CSE 1973

*32. The joint used at the back corner of a drawer is called a ———— dovetail joint.
(EMREB) CSE 1973

33. Make freehand drawings of the following joints.
(a) A bridle joint.
(b) A dovetail housing.
(c) A lap dovetail.
Draw a piece of woodwork or part of a piece to illustrate a correct use of one of these joints.
(OCSEB) GCE 1972

*34. Complete the sketch of a haunched tenon below.

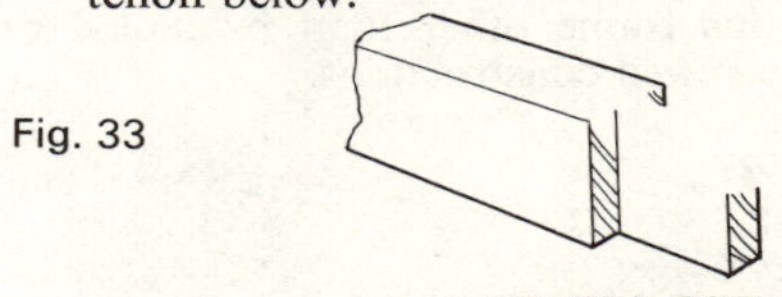

Fig. 33

(SREB) CSE 1974

35. Sketch clearly any kind of halving joint used in a framework construction.
(EMREB) CSE 1973

*36. The pieces A and B are to be joined by a through dovetail joint. Sketch in the joint, showing carefully the position of the pins, knowing there is a load on piece A.

Fig. 34

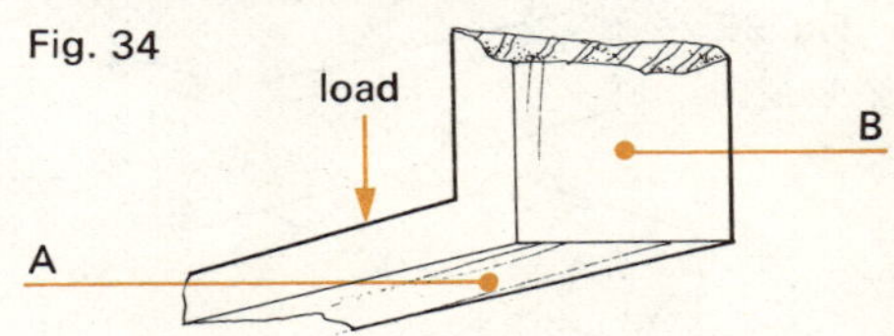

(EMREB) CSE 1973

*37. Carefully sketch, in the scaled drawing, a tongued and grooved joint, considering sizes and proportions.

Fig. 35

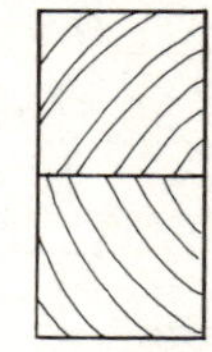

(EMREB) CSE 1973

38. Give a use for each of the joints shown in Figure 36.

Fig. 36

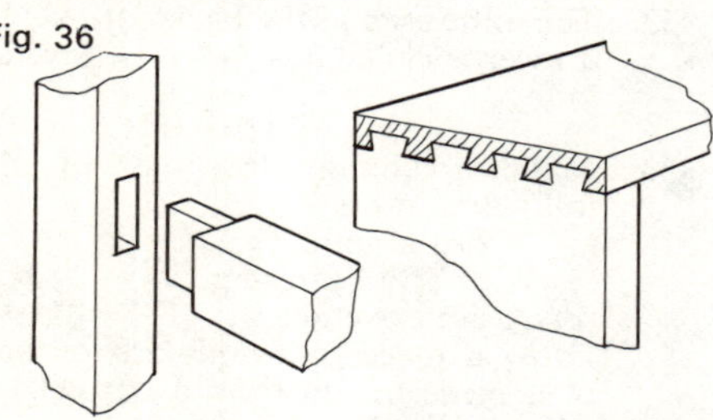

(SREB) CSE 1974

39. Name the joint you would use to join these rails together to make this frame other than by nailed or screwed constructions.

Fig. 37

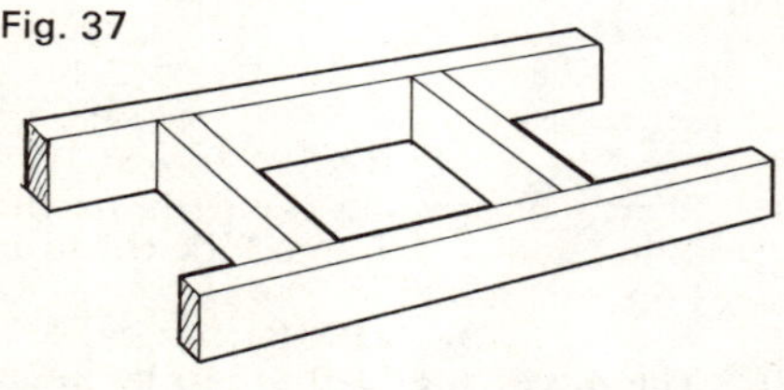

(EMREB) CSE 1973

*40. Complete the exploded sketch of a cross halving joint shown in Figure 38.

Fig. 38

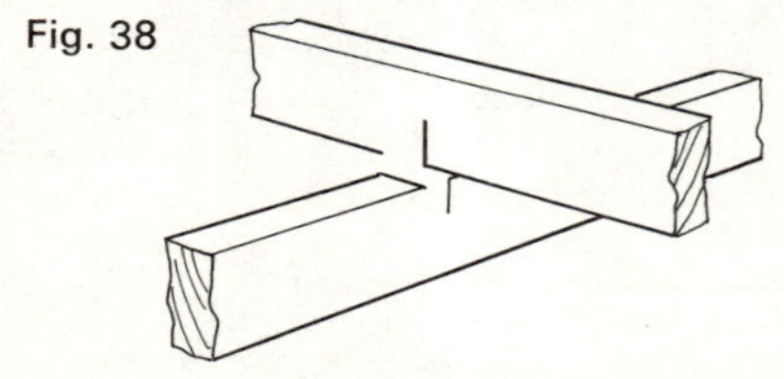

(SREB) CSE 1974

*41. In Figure 39 the outlines numbered 1–4 represent the end of a piece of wood. Show on the outlines the method of sawing down a tenon. Use broken lines to show how far the saw cuts.

Fig. 39

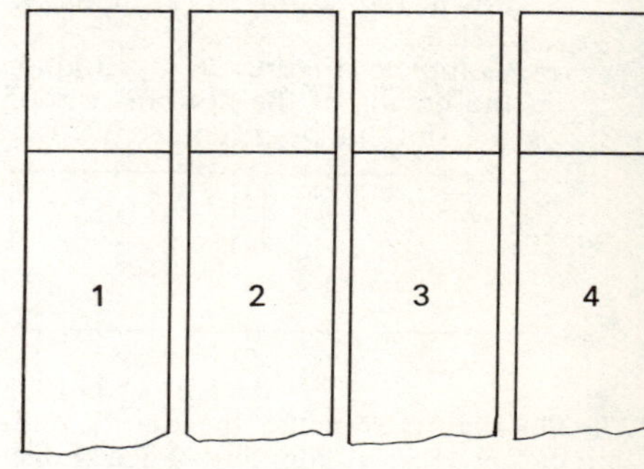

(MREB) CSE 1973

42. Make a freehand drawing of a haunched mortise and tenon joint, and describe how you would cut the recess for the haunch at the end of the mortise.

(OCSEB) GCE 1973

FIXTURES AND FITTINGS

43. A large solid wood table top is often fixed to the framework by means of "buttons". Make sketches to illustrate what these are like and how they are used. State why this form of fastening is necessary.

(SREB) CSE 1974

44. Sketch:
   (a) a hinge suitable for use on the door of a small cabinet
   (b) a hinge suitable for use on a garden shed door made of tongued and grooved boards.

(SREB) CSE 1974

45. Sketch the following hinges:
   (a) back-flap
   (b) butt
   (c) tee.
   Give a typical use for each one, indicating why its main features make the hinge suitable for that particular purpose.

(WJEC) GCE 1972

46. The method of fixing a table top to its supporting frame has to allow for certain difficulties which arise when solid timber is used. State what these difficulties are and show, by the use of sketches, how the use of buttons is an effective way of overcoming them. Make an enlarged sketch of the section through a button when in position, showing clearly the leverage principle involved.

(WJEC) GCE 1972

47. Name the fittings shown in Figure 40.

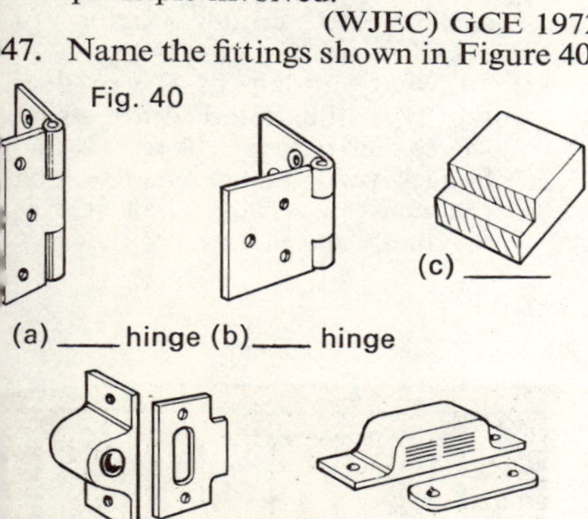

(a) ____ hinge (b)____ hinge

(d) ____ catch   (e) ___. catch

(MREB) CSE 1973

48. Tabulate stage by stage:
   (a) how you would fit a countersunk wood-screw, and
   (b) how you would fit a butt hinge to a small cabinet door.

(OCSEB) GCE 1973

WOOD TURNING

49. Name a tool you would use in wood turning to turn the outside surface of a wooden cylinder.

(EMREB) CSE 1973

50. A bowl is to be turned on a wood-turning lathe.
   Make three freehand sectional drawings to suggest alternative designs. Describe stage by stage how you would make one of these bowls. In your answer be quite specific about the tools which you would use at each stage and their cutting or scraping action.

(OCSEB) GCE 1974

*51. The figure shows a lathe. Name the parts labelled (a) to (e) in the spaces provided.

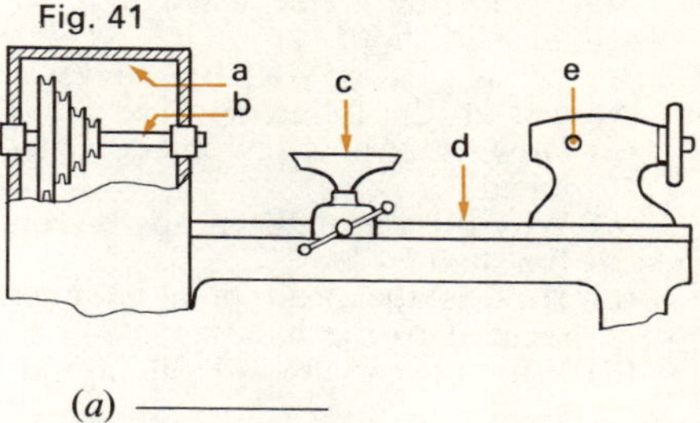

(a) ____________
(b) ____________
(c) ____________
(d) ____________
(e) ____________

(MREB) CSE 1973

52. Describe how you would set up a piece of wood between centres on a wood-turning lathe and turn it parallel using a gouge. Be quite specific about how you would make the gouge cut rather than scrape. Also draw diagrams to show the cutting angles of a wood-turning gouge and a wood-turning skew chisel.

(OCSEB) GCE 1971

MISCELLANEOUS

53. (a) Name three types of oilstone and say if they are natural or manufactured.
   (b) How would you true up a worn oilstone?
   (c) Tabulate in brief notes all the important points about the care of oilstones.

(OCSEB) GCE 1972

54. What glue would you recommend for a job which comes into contact with water?

(EMREB) CSE 1973

55. A new parcel of Scotch glue has just been opened. Describe, with notes and sketches, all that you would do to prepare this glue so that it is completely ready for use.
   What are the advantages and disadvantages of Scotch glue?

(MREB) CSE 1973

56. Why is glass-paper often wrapped around a block when glass-papering a piece of wood?

(SREB) CSE 1974

57. State one safety rule listed in your school workshop.

(EMREB) CSE 1973

58. Answer all the following:
    (*a*) How is a bow-saw blade tensioned?
    (*b*) Why does a mallet head stay on the shaft?
    (*c*) How is the head of a hammer secured to the handle?
    (*d*) Why do we use oil on an oilstone?
    (*e*) What are winding sticks?
    (*f*) In what is beeswax dissolved to make wax polish?

(OCSEB) GCE 1973

59. Make fairly large sketches of three different kinds of nails, showing clearly the shape of the head and the cross-section. Give an example of the use of each type. Sketch the tool that you would use to set the nails below the surface of the wood. Make a simple sketch to show how you would use a pair of pincers to remove a bent nail.

(SREB) CSE 1972

60. What is the name of the material shown in Figure 42? How would you treat the edge if using it to make a table top?

Fig. 42

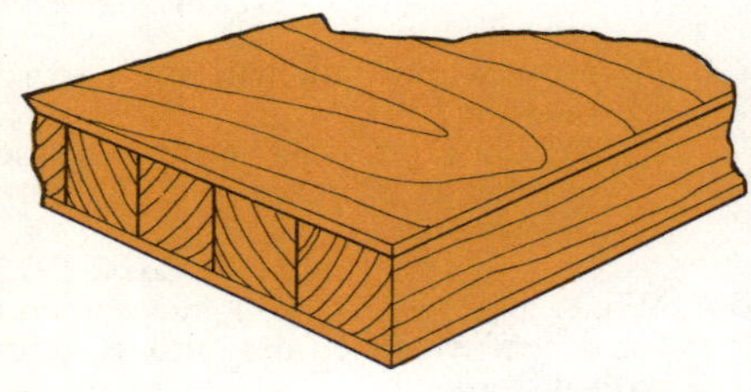

(SREB) CSE 1972

HISTORY OF ENGLISH FURNITURE DESIGN

61. Look carefully at the drawing shown in Figure 43 and then answer the following:
    (*a*) Give an approximate date for the chest.
    (*b*) State the name of the period in which it was made.
    (*c*) What type of wood was used?
    (*d*) What type of joint has been used for the front frame?
    (*e*) In what way are the joints strengthened?
    (*f*) What is the name given to the type of carved panel used?
    (*g*) Suggest why it was so called.
    (*h*) What was the name given to earlier and cruder forms of chest?
    (*j*) In what fundamental way does the type illustrated differ from the earlier types?
    (*k*) Suggest two possible uses to which the chest was put when it was originally made.

Fig. 43.

(JMB) GCE 1973

62. What are the characteristics of furniture produced in England in the 1650s? Give reasons for your answer and sketch a typical piece of the period.

(JMB) GCE 1973

63. Either
    (*a*) With the aid of sketches, write explanatory notes on two of the following techniques introduced into furniture making during the nineteenth century:
    bentwood; cast iron; papier mâché.
    Or
    (*b*) Make a sketch of a piece of furniture you are familiar with at home. Comment on its construction, appearance and fitness for purpose. Suggest possible improvements to the design.

(JMB) GCE 1973

INDEX